HEALTH PSYCHOLOGY FOR EVERYDAY LIFE

A bio-psycho-social thinking approach

Dr. Cheryl A. MacDonald, Psy'D.

Health Psychology Center Bo
Oceanside California

D1614812

HEALTH PSYCHOLOGY FOR EVERYDAY LIFE
A bio-psycho-social thinking approach

Health Psychology Center P.C. Book
2181 El Camino Real Ste. 204
Oceanside, Ca. 92054

1st edition 2015

Visit the Web site: www.healthpsychology.org

Library of Congress Control Number: 2015902195

Printed in the United States of America

ISBN Paperback: 978-0-9861600-0-4
ISBN Kindle: 978-0-9861600-1-1

Cover art based on: Violin and Candlestick, Georges Braque,
1910. (Image in the public domain in the United States because it was first published outside the United States prior to
January 1, 1923.)

Design, Layout, and Typesetting by Alexander Becker
www.alexanderbecker.net

Acknowledgements

I would not have been able to take on this project without acknowledging the support of my mentor, coach and friend Anna Walden, Ph'D.

I Thank You!

Chapters

Preface
Health Psychology and the
Bio-Psycho-Social Model

A Health Psychology position is with promoting knowledge of how biological, sociological, environmental and cultural circumstances link to physical and mental health. Investigations are beginning to demonstrate that negative emotions such as rage, anger, jealousy, envy, anxiety, and depression, have a relationship to one's physical fitness. One common pattern of the mind-body association is when people feel anxiety or stress the heart rate increases. Overall wellness depends on a healthy mind and body.

In the area of physical fitness and emotional well-being, health psychology concentrates on examining physiological, psychological, sociological, societal, and environmental parts of life and in what way each of these influences physical health. There are a few who include the spiritual or religious features to this design, however, traditionally the standard incorporates biological, psychological, and social elements. While it may be accepted knowledge among some groups to appreciate about the negative impacts that a person's emotional mindset can have on health, there remains to be a remarkable amount of rejection about the functions of their interactivity. Physical health can be directly influenced by the circumstances in which we live and the principal approach studied within health psychology is the bio-psycho-social design. The British Health Society (2011) emphasizes that health and sickness are the results of the blending of biological, psychological and social factors. Biological determinants consist of genetic conditions, the outcomes of a physical condition and inherited personality characteristics. Psychological factors are anxiety and depression levels, personality styles and lifestyle. Social determinants consist of cultural beliefs, family bonds and support systems. Health psychology's motives have the belief that everyone merits conventional medical and psychological attention even when everyday practices, career, or family life stressors add to a reduction in physical fitness and/or emotional health. The bio-psycho-social model views health, wellness and illness as being a result of many different inter-related sections affecting a person's life from biological components, to behavioral and social situations (Belloc & Breslow, 1972).

Emotional factors related to physical health have been a general focal point since the beginning of the 20th century. The results emphasize that people who eat proper meals, sustain a healthy weight, do not smoke, drink limited alcohol, get sufficient sleep and exercise routinely are in better shape, therefore, live longer. Psychologists at this time were also finding connections between psychological and physiological processes. These incorporate the physical consequence of stress on the cardiovascular and immune systems and consequently seeing that the functioning of these systems could improve with training. There was also a rising recognition of the value of having sound communication skills during physician appointments. The American Psychological Associations division 38 is health psychology which concentrates on interpreting the relationship between health, illness, emotions and lifestyle. This division focuses on investigating the psychological determinants that impact health and contributes data to the health care management system. The three domains pertaining to health psychology are:

<u>Clinical Work:</u> In medical and clinical settings, health psychologists customarily conduct behavioral evaluations, engage in clinical discussions and administer personality tests. They often cooperate in training interventions with individuals or groups relating to educating people about anxiety reduction techniques, offer addiction cessation information and guide people on how to avoid unhealthy lifestyles. Physical Health can be influenced by the things people do, by the way they process knowledge, career choice, family dynamics, perceive life struggles and the conditions in which they live. For example, someone living in a damp, mold infested home has a real possibility of contracting respiratory or sinus difficulties and may produce illnesses.

<u>Public Policy Work:</u> Health psychologists may operate in private or government settings and have a position in shaping public policy on health related affairs. Their concern might point to recommending executive groups on health care reform, address inequalities in health care, or lobby government bureaus.

<u>Research:</u> Health psychologists manage investigations on a variety of health-related matters. For instance, researchers may focus on examining effective preventative actions, search for health promotion methods, study the elements of health dilemmas, develop ways to stimulate people into seeking treatment, and how to help people cope with a disease or emotional distress.

Genetics and Physical Health

Researchers have identified that people whose parents experience specific conditions, such as addictions, hypertension, diabetes, and some cancers are predisposed to receiving these diseases. Biology unquestionably plays a fundamental role in the fitness and health of everyone. Nevertheless, emotional, environmental and social circumstances are also pivotal areas that associate to any ailment (Marks, Murray, Evans & Estacio, 2011). For illustration, when a mother is diagnosed with breast cancer then nearly all medical specialists would urge her daughter to receive screening regularly once she approaches a specific age. It would not matter, if the daughter did not smoke or kept away from the damaging rays of the sun, she is a cancer risk on account of the genetic predilection for the illness that appears in the family history. However, there is no guarantee that children of mothers that have breast cancer will experience the same, this only indicates that the DNA (the genetic matter that people share with their family) may hold a marker that leaves her more responsive to the disease than someone else who does not have this marker. Some people born from alcoholic parents manage to have more addictive temperaments than those whose parents were not alcoholic. A few emotional and mental ailments directly relate to the abuse they suffered in childhood others tend to be more genetic in quality. Though, psychological, social and environmental factors all present key notable positions in regulating illnesses along with this genetic tendency.

At times when people feel ill, weak, or overrun, or when they catch certain conditions, it is not only in response to a virus or bacteria infiltrating the central nervous and immune systems, but a reply to what is occurring within the body, brain and unconscious mind. Getting a cold is just one example. Take heart, these teachings clearly do not leave out the biological element, indicating the virus that overwhelmed the exhausted immune system. Heart related conditions, breathing disorders, muscle and joint pain diseases and various physical ailments are prevalent among those coping with the emotional and mental pressures of modern day life. The discharge of the "stress" substances in the body impairs the shields in fighting off an attack. The more people realize the power of the mind, the more they will understand that physical health directly links to thoughts, feelings and behaviors (Cohen, McChargue & Collins, 2003).

One way to explain the basics of health psychology is by examining the smoking habit. Part of the smoking addiction is the physical element of dependence to nicotine as withdrawal manifestations set in once the process of quitting begins. The standard practitioner will order medicines to subdue the physical addiction signs of withdrawal, approaching the smoking addiction as only a physical problem. However, investigations reveal that there is an exceptionally strong likelihood that the individual will just start smoking again. A chain smoker that uses a nicotine product may have trouble stopping if they continue to think that smoking is not harmful, or if smoking helps them to unwind. In these situations, even with the product the smoker may simply return to the practice. The average adviser or physician is only managing the physical withdrawal aspects of smoking. There is a psychological element to the addiction as the smoker stands to achieve compensations no matter how brief from each cigarette. Smoking may stifle the appetite, extend an opportunity to relax and unwind, or produce a temporary diversion to current stresses. There is likewise a behavioral slant to smoking, such as having a cigarette right after dinner, using a cigarette as a stress reliever or, regularly lighting up when getting in the car, instead of exercise.

Every year investigators are finding novel insights into how the brain, body and mind inter-relate and the means in which they connect to each other in harmony. The human brain is one of the most obscure, mysterious, and influential organs of entire creation. Science has been able to conjure up ideas in the mind such as, concepts in mathematics and imagine worlds that at this time do not exist. These thoughts stem from people wanting to explore the unknown aspects of the mind which has a relationship to the brain and the environment in which they live. There is a distinctive respect for what the mind is capable of achieving in relation to the brain, medicine and psychology. Science understands much more than even twenty years ago regarding the interaction between emotions and pain, of the thought processes involving healing and the remarkable healing powers of the human body.

Community and Cultural Factors

Mokdad, Stroup and Gerberding (2004), reveal that fifty percent of all deaths in the United States can be associated to ways of life or other risk determinants that are for the most part preventable. Health psychologists work with individuals in hopes of eliminating these risk factors to decrease failing health and improve overall health. Expectations and gender roles can put a large amount of pressure on someone to behave and act in a distinct fashion. Racism and religious factors often are stressors in people's lives and over time these pressures have an impact on overall health. For example, white, middle-class people tend to have better overall health than inner-city minorities. Health psychology explores the underlying factors that have a direct and indirect impact on quality of life (Cassileth et al., 1984). When assisting people develop a healthier lifestyle, career choice is another area that health psychology explores. There is a direct relationship between choices of work and physical and emotional health, as the more frustrating the project the more risk people are placing themselves into developing an emotional and/or psychological illness. When someone is under stress, the body produces chemicals and hormones that it does not require and some of these substances may be harmful. The difficult conditions and the release of these substances results in a weakening of the immune system. When an immune system is weak people are more susceptible to physical and mental ailments (Ader & Cohen, 1975).

The Bio-Psycho-Social Model as it Applies to Health Psychology

Millions of people all over the world are under tremendous amounts of stress as the economy is suffering and unemployment remains high. People who are employed are working more hours and are taking on more responsibilities for less pay. Those that have lost their jobs worry about paying their bills, feeding their families and holding onto what they have worked so hard to achieve in the past and some are wondering if they are normal. When health psychologists talk about the bio-psycho-social model, behaviors are key ingredients contributing to physical health. Do people smoke? Do they drink alcohol regularly? Do they eat junk food? Have a stressful job? Are finances tough? Do people exercise regularly? How is the family? How is the social life? These are just a few questions that a health psychologist may explore. There are behavioral and social conditions that directly or indirectly relate to the state of overall physical health.

Stress derives from the instinctual nature of the desire to survive and the psychological community labels this concept the 'fight or flight' response. When the mind perceives a warning to the body, whether that threat is real or a product of the imagination the brain responds as if in danger. The brain calls for adrenaline to be pumped throughout the body, which allows it to run faster (away from the problem) or fight with a bit more strength than it naturally possesses (face the problem). The production of adrenaline in association with the flight or fight response is only intended to be for brief periods of time for survival. When people are facing chronic stress at home or work, the physical body is under constant tension adapting to this "fight or flight response." As a result, people tend to feel run down and tired more often, they may experience aching joints, muscle aches, lower back pain, headaches and increases in blood pressure. All of which are the common side effects of repeated stress and increases in adrenaline. While some in the health professions do not tend to think about stress as being abnormal, it does indeed take a heavy toll on a person, both physically and emotionally. One key factor in lowering the stress level is determining how an individual recognizes and responds to stress and how this relates to their quality of life. Health Psychologists work in clinical settings promoting behavioral change that relates to the everyday anxieties of life. They also inform the public, conduct research, teach at universities and work in the field of sports medicine.

While sad or anxious feelings may not directly cause poor physical health, they are certainly contributing factors associated with health and an individual's enjoyment of life. The field of health psychology focuses on promoting health which includes the prevention and treatment of physical diseases. The Health Psychologists focus is on understanding how people react, cope and recover from illness, along with improving the quality of lives of people with chronic and terminal illnesses. When there is little hope of recovery, it is a health psychologist who can improve the quality of existence by helping those involved work with loss and recover at least some sense of emotional well-being. One other interest is with identifying the best ways for providing therapeutic services for the bereaved in coping with the loss of a loved one (Lander & Graham-Pole, 2008).

Clinical Health Psychology strives to produce answers to the following topics:

1. How should a particular disease be treated?
2. What is the connection between the body, mind and environment?
3. What role does psychology play in the relationship to health and disease?

4. What is the relationship between emotional health, physical wellness and disease?

The world of health psychology is changing lives one day at a time and with some expert guidance and support people can experience the healthy, vibrant life that they desire, and all it takes is unlocking the secrets of the brain, the body, the mind, and behavior. The simple fact of life is that human beings are extraordinarily complex and an illness can be the result of a myriad of factors (Frieden & Mostashari, 2008). These factors emerge from biological, psychological and environmental facets of daily life. Most often medications alone will not provide the positive results necessary for people to achieve maximum health. Just because, medicines do not fully aid in recovery or reduce the pain, does not mean that all options for improvement have been exhausted. Health psychology principles clearly have not been fully utilized or recognized at this point in time, by conventional western medicine.

Chronic Pain and Illness

Physical ailments are real, people will say, "they are not in my head." Some patients and physicians view health psychology concepts as being a personal affront to the gaining knowledge and do not believe that pain relates to overall emotional well-being. Others fear that people working in the health psychology fields will judge them or their pain as being "abnormal." A few medical professionals try to discredit patient complaints of pain and intimidate people into attempting to make them think that the problem simply does not exist, and that the pain is all a figment of the imagination. Science is evolving and the problem may simply not be medically understood, or the location of the pain cannot be found in the body at the time. There is a relationship between the brain, the mind and pain (Siegel & Hurn, 2013).

Health psychologists attempt to assist in the manner of communication between doctors and patients during medical consultations. There are many difficulties in this process, with patients showing a significant lack of comprehension of many medical terms (Boyle, 1970). One central area of investigation relates to "doctor-centered" consultations, which are directive and involves the one seeking help answer questions and performing less of a part in decision-making. Many people object to the sense of authority or disregard that this spurs and in favor of patient-centered consultations which focus on the patient's needs. Patient centered consultations involve listening to the patient completely before reaching a decision and the person seeking help plays an active role in the process of choosing treatment (Dowsett et. al., 2000).

Health psychology strives to find strategies to decrease and do away with pain, as well as have knowledge of pain peculiarities such as analgesia, causalgia, neuralgia, and phantom limb pain. Despite the fact that measuring and reporting pain are questionable, the McGill Pain Questionnaire has helped make improvements (Melzack, 1975). Treatments for pain are patient-administered analgesia, acupuncture, biofeedback, and cognitive behavior therapy. Do not be tricked into believing that an illness is a figment of imagination as this belief may cause psychological problems and increase physical symptoms. The above thoughts are generalized examples of what it means when people say healing comes, in part, from the underlying psychological aspects of the mind (thoughts and emotions), behaviors and the brain. Clinical health psychologists identify this way of thinking as being a bio-psycho-social model. The standard encourages a positive shift in the way people think about health, illness, and healing.

Imagine by changing the way people think and cope about a problem in life that can move clients in a direction towards pain-free living or assist in decreasing blood pressure. People can achieve this by learning a few techniques, and applying and believing in this theory will increase the quality of life.

While healing with "health psychology" is certainly much more complicated than just changing a thought or behavior, most people do not believe in this concept and until recently it has been overlooked by those in the medical community. A difficult task for health psychologists is motivating people to adhere to medical direction and follow the treatment plan. This lack of adherence is possibly due to treatment side effects or life circumstances and some ignore taking medicines or consciously stop. Compliance measures are hard to quantify, however, studies explain that this could improve by tailoring medication schedules to an individual's daily life (Cohen, McChargue, & Collins, 2003). These specialists have advanced training in a variety of research designs, which allows them to conduct investigations, provide expert consultation or collaborate on research (Miller, Chen, & Cole, 2009).

Health psychologists conduct research to clarify puzzling questions such as:

1. How is stress connected to heart disease?
2. What are the impacts or influences on healthy eating?
3. What are the emotional consequences of genetic testing?
4. In what ways can therapists help people reach their goals and change health habits to improve health?
5. How an illness affects a person's emotional happiness. Stressors can lead to depression, reduced self-esteem and anxiety.

This field also concerns itself with improving the lives of those with terminal illness. When there is little hope of recovery, these therapists can improve the quality of life by helping recover thoughts and feelings associated with psychological well-being. These therapists also identify the best ways to provide therapeutic services for the bereaved (O'Brien, Forrest, & Austin, 2002).

Health Psychology is a relatively new sub-category of psychology and is not well known to many people. These clinical psychologists take a more effective approach by exploring the physical, psychological, and behavioral aspects considering the problem in a holistic fashion. The practice of using health psychology principles significantly improves the likelihood of successfully quitting any addiction. Specialists can help people become more physically fit, assist with decreasing chronic pain, improve the quality of life with those diagnosed with a terminal illness, prevent further complications of any serious physical ailment and assist in learning new ways to cope with the tensions and transitions that govern everyday life. Health psychology principles' and cognitive behavioral therapies continue to be overlooked by the general population and the medical professions, as these methods require the physician to be aware of other successful treatment modalities (Marks, Murray, Evans & Estacio, 2011).

Health Psychology principles requires individuals to make a commitment to take responsibility for their own physical and emotional health. Until these principles are accepted by the medical community and until the client begins to follow these principles, the emotional and physical conditions will continue to ravage society. Once people are in touch with their emotions, they then need to determine how they are going to manage or control the feeling. Sometimes feelings are not true or based on facts, and people can perceive situations incorrectly, as they are of the imagination. If the feeling is not based on facts, then attempt to undo this misperception, as people are only hurting themselves. Try not to get caught up with feelings of shame and guilt as these emotions are a waste of valuable time and for most of us are by products of the imagination. However, for short periods of time if the imagination or dreaming makes people happy, it is acceptable to enjoy the feeling. Just remember that this is wishful thinking and that people are tricking themselves into feeling pleasure. To learn new ways to cope with feelings associated with physical health, start with a small baby step. For example, if there is a problem with anger, attempt to be aware of the feeling, and take a few deep breaths before reacting.

Tips for Taking Care of Emotional and Physical Health

1. <u>Take care of yourself physically.</u> Many people do not understand the fact that when they take care of themselves physically, they take care of themselves emotionally. There is a relationship between neglecting the body and the development of emotional and physical problems. This neglect creates a toxic cycle. To end this cycle, strengthen the body with enough rest, food, and liquids. Make sure that there is enough air, nutritious food and exercise in your life. Warm and refresh yourself when needed. Become aware of what you are consuming, a healthy, proper diet is beneficial for the body and mind. Research has proven that exercise improves mood and has numerous benefits for physical and emotional health. I am aware that this is limited information; however, many people do not understand these basic facts. People do not have to be perfect and try not to to let physical care become an obsession, which may then become another problem. Consider the fact that when people ignore the physical needs of their body this abandonment will create an emotional and physical problem, which in turn creates a toxic life cycle. Therefore, people feel physically and emotionally unstable.

2. <u>Pay attention to body signals.</u> When the body is in need of something, people experience feelings that correspond to what their body is lacking. One example of ignoring a signal is when people do not pay attention to hunger when trying to lose weight and they begin to starve themselves. This starvation, in turn, slows down the metabolism and will in the long run prevent weight loss. The body sends messages when to eat, sleep, relax, calm down, play and

comfort ourselves. Go to bed on time. Lack of sleep strains the heart, may increase weight, and undeniably sparks up the crankiness meter. Do not ignore the protective bodily signals and listen to what it is saying.

3. <u>Be socially active.</u> The bottom line is that love and attention are almost as valuable as the air that we breathe. Most will crave it unless they receive it, so seek it out, for emotional health. Take the time out for relaxation and socializing as this is useful for emotional and physical health. Give and receive love and attention to both others and yourself. As quoted, from C.J. Lewis, "Affection is responsible for nine-tenths of whatever solid and durable happiness there is in our lives." People are social beings from birth to death.

4. <u>Take care of yourself with relaxation.</u> People should be spending a third of their time on leisure and/or play. Relaxation is another form of nurturing mental health as the mind needs the opportunity to re-charge. People also need time to process or understand thoughts and emotions. If someone stays busy all of the time, then they are not giving themselves enough time to process and strengthen the mind and body. If a third of the time is too much to ask for, then at least set aside an hour or two a day. Set aside some time to relax and have fun.

5. <u>When you fail</u> at something have the courage to try again. Everyone makes mistakes in life. Try to work at forgiving yourself for making those mistakes. Trying again improves self-esteem and creates an overall sense of feeling empowered, which in turn increases endorphins, thereby lifting mood.

6. <u>Visit the appropriate doctor,</u> the one that is the perfect match for the condition. Going to the appropriate doctor can make all the difference in overall health, especially if there is a complex illness that requires a specialist. Try to be open to seeing a mental health professional, if feelings and emotions are getting in the way of recovery.

In conclusion, unhealthy behaviors, from smoking cigarettes and poor diet, to living a sedentary lifestyle and having poor coping skills, are all significant factors leading to disability and death. Take the time to care for both the mind and body because everyone has the ability to make positive, healthy changes in their life by choosing to develop and enhance specific ways to live a physically and emotionally healthy life, thereby prevent disease.

Chapter 1
Fitness of your Immune and Central Nervous Systems

The immune system defends the body like the Gladiators of Rome defended their turf. On call twenty-four hours a day standing guard to resist any foreign substance that may pose a threat to physical health. When someone encounters an event that is physically or emotionally threatening the body will respond biologically. This physical response guarantees the body has whatever it requires to maintain balance. If people learn how the immune system operates they can then discover ways to keep their emotions and body healthy, consequently warding off some of the physical and emotional triggers. The prevention of disease is at least to some extent in our control and that is the health psychology connection.

The immune system includes several organs which have billions of immune functioning cells including the thymus gland and bone marrow that develop and mature the cells. The peripheral immune system includes the blood, lymph nodes and the spleen. The endocrine system provides hormones that aid the central nervous system by delivering the appropriate types enabling us to survive (Sompayrac, 2012). The true gladiators are the white blood cells that continuously wander, rummaging for foreign invaders in the blood and tissues. The white cells purpose is to activate the immune response against the daily attacks from viruses, germs and bacteria. Indirect invasions on physical health are environmental agents associating with anxiety, poor diet, pollution, smoking and alcohol intake. Direct invasions on physical health are engagements with contagious environmental substances, such as viruses. (Medzhitov, 2007).

A Brief History of the Immune System

The science that explores the organization and role of the immune system is Immunology which stems from modern medicine even though primitive researchers also studied the causes of illness. Two hundred years ago Greek experts thought diseases were produced by poisonous vapours or "miasmas", meaning pollution from decaying organic material. The earliest known reporting on immunity was written in 430 B.C., during the plague of Athens while fighting in first years of the Peloponnesian War. The capital was under attack by Sparta and the residents had been relocated to live within the city walls creating overcrowding. The poor water supply, inadequate sewer system and humid temperatures explain how viruses could spread conditions very swiftly (Littman, 2009). One report of the disease was from Thucydides who recovered from plague symptoms, observed other sufferers and proceeded onto document a precise accurate account. Thucydides wrote that people who had rallied from a prior bout of the illness were able to care for the sick without contracting the disease a second time.

In the late 1700s, British scientist Edward Jenner had heard stories of dairymaids who contracted the disease cowpox who were by some means protected against a much more lethal illness, smallpox. Jenner studied the likelihood of transporting this protection person to person. In 1796, he extracted pus from a dairymaid's sore applying it to the wounds of a healthy 8-year-old boy who then fell ill. After the boy recovered Jenner spread this time the fatal smallpox virus onto a cut consequently discovering that the boy was immune. In

1802, Jenner was publicly mocked for this experiment as one cartoon image portrays people who were immunized sprouting cows from different parts their bodies. However, smallpox disease is the only infectious disease that has been eradicated in this fashion, and the name given to this procedure is vaccine, from the Latin word vacca signifying cow (Silverstein, 2009).

For centuries mankind invented multiple mysterious beliefs about the nature of disease, and in the 18th century Maupertuis started trials with scorpion venom observing that some dogs were resistant to the poison. Louis Pasteur thought that if a vaccine could be attained for smallpox then it should be likely to eradicate different conditions by producing a vaccine. In the 1880s, Pasteur successfully confirmed that by injecting chickens with a diluted form of the cholera bacteria stopped the animal from dying of the disease. Pasteur was in frank opposition to the miasma theory and capitalized on his view of acquired immunity in perfecting a vaccination, thereby introducing a germ theory of illness. A range of pioneering research from the mid-1800s onwards discovered by Louis Pasteur and later by Robert Koch, explained that diseases were produced by the presence of microorganisms that penetrate and then reproduce within the body. Germ Theory' proposed that investigators should search for microorganisms aided by following the collection of rules designed by Koch. The Latin word immunitas refers to the unique status of security or exclusion from taxes awarded to soldiers by Roman Emperors and this protection from disease today refers to this status, having the name immunity. Jenner's, Pasteur's and Koch's discoveries gave medicine the hope of preventing, healing and treating diseases. Despite these incredible improvements no one understood the mechanism of triggering or in what way and for what reason immunity occurred (Pancer & Cooper, 2006).

Ilya Mechnikov a Russian zoologist was a difficult, inconsistent, volatile man although a profoundly energetic, talented researcher capable of producing different brilliant insights. In the 1880s while vacationing on the coast of Italy, Mechnikov was intrigued by the way simple marine animals digest and absorb nutrients. As he looked at a group of moving starfish larvae under a microscope, Mechnikov came up with the notion that these roaming cells were guarding against invaders. By taking a piece of a rose thorn and forcing it into the larvae, Mechnikov observed a mob of mobile cells encircling the thorn, like flies flowing around and landing on meat these cells seemed to devour and eliminate the intruding rose thorn. Mechnikov called these cells phagocytes originating from the Greek phrase "phagein" meaning to swallow and the biology suffix 'cyte' signifying cell. He proposed that phagocytes were the organism's primary line of defense and that their responsibility was to engulf and break down any foreign material. Most people have had a cut and have seen the purulent drainage that forms around the tissue, the dead white blood cells and other cellular rubble left behind after the phagocytes have completed their work. Koch's assistant, Paul Ehrlich was a critic of Mechnikov who developed techniques for staining bacteria and tissues with chemical dyes had the idea to create drugs that specifically recognize and destroy the invading microorganisms. In 1897, he introduced a theory explaining how cells react to a variety of different threats. Ehrlich stated that cells manufacture side chains, which ultimately splinter off, travel in the blood stream fastening to toxic materials released by the bacteria. These side chains connect to the target in a very precise fashion, like keys match a lock, barricading the toxins from reaching their destination into the organism. Antibodies are today what Ehrlich creatively termed side chains (Pancer & Cooper 2006). Convinced that only one or the other option could be right scientists largely ignored Mechnikov's cell-based theory.

As time marched on, the two theories were found to be accurate because there are two branches forming the immune system. Mechnikov's phagocyte cells do produce a first order of defense that describes innate immunity as cells devour enemies and clean up the trash from the immune-systems battles. Ehrlich's side chain, or antibody theory, is known as acquired immunity, a segment of the immune systems response that learns and masters how to sufficiently attack an invader. Ehrlich's view that antibodies produced a key that can identify the "locks" of various pathogens encouraged generations of investigators in the field, however, the fallout from this debate meant that decades passed before the broad scope of the immune system was uncovered. Ehrlich's view that side-chain molecules are formed by all cells is false because antibodies are produced by a unique type of white blood cell.

In 1890, Emil von Behring injected small, weakened doses of the bacteria that produce diphtheria or tetanus into animals discovering that they manufactured chemicals in their blood that neutralize the disease-causing poison. He also discovered that transfusing the blood carrying the antitoxins to other animals awarded them immunity from the illness. Active' immunity is the defense produced by the immune system. Passive immunity is obtaining certain antitoxins from other sources (CDC, 2013). Von Behring revealed that children inoculated with the antitoxin-containing serum were cured of their diphtheria symptoms. This was a significant finding as the vaccines invented by Jenner and Pasteur prevented illnesses, but von Behring's discoveries explained how a disease could be treated and cured. In 1901, the evidence to support Ehrlich's theory of antibodies won the first-ever Nobel Prize in Medicine. The accomplishments of von Behring, Metchnikov and Ehrlich, opened the gateway to creating a new area of science called immunology and this portal attempts to investigate the hidden performances of the body's internal defense mechanisms. Once the anti-toxin theory had provided credible experimental evidence for Ehrlich's explanation investigators raced to examine these toxin-neutralizing molecules.

Nearly 200 years after Jenner presented his pioneering detections with smallpox, and 100 years since the famous cells-versus-blood debate between Metchnikov and Ehrlich, Doherty and Zinkernagel finally earned the Nobel Prize for Physiology in Medicine in 1996. These researchers explained the mysteries of what immunologists presently describe as being the "cell-mediated immune defense system". Cell-mediated immunity is an immune response that does not include antibodies, but is the activation of phagocytes, antigen-specific cytotoxic T-lymphocytes and the deliverance of different cytokines in reaction to an antigen.

Anaphylactic Shock

The immune system provides a complex security system, but, every so often this defense mechanism can act against people, creating a health crisis. Anaphylaxis, or anaphylactic shock, is the term assigned to an immediate, at times, deadly allergic response affecting the whole body to seemingly safe foods, like peanuts, and often associates with bee stings. The Charles Richets study in 1900 on anaphylaxis had an unusual beginning because he was inspired while vacationing on a sea voyage while experimenting with the toxins of sea anemones. He found that dogs that were unharmed by an initial dose of poison always went into shock, and died soon after experiencing a much lower dose a few days following. He was surprised to discover that the initial dose did not increase immunity to this poison instead making the animals highly sensitized. Charles Richet found the biological laws pertaining to anaphylaxis relating to the Greek terms "ana", indicating against and "phylaxis", indicating "protection". This research promoted the initiation of medical alert systems that recognize and identify people who are susceptible to a deadly hypersensitivity. Richets' interpretation of how the immune system over reacts in such a damaging way awarded him the Nobel Prize in Medicine in 1913 (Parham, 2009).

Autoimmune Diseases

The concept adopted to explain autoimmunity was coined over a century ago by Paul Ehrlich, who originally gave the emotionally disturbing label "horror autotoxicus", meaning the horror of self-toxicity. No one understands precisely what causes autoimmune conditions and the causes are likely to include a combination of factors, investigators hope to identify techniques to subdue the overactive portions of the immune system by having a greater understanding of the biological, psychological and sociological triggers of autoimmune disorders. In a few circumstances the body turns on itself wrongfully producing antibodies that strike its own tissues, and this mistaken production points to developing an autoimmune disease. For example, in the pancreas T lymphocytes cells destroy insulin-producing cells causing Type 1 diabetes and other assaults on the body's cells lead to severe joint soreness felt by those suffering from rheumatoid arthritis. Baruj Benacerraf's exploration of the immune response genes reveals that the major histocompatibility complex (MHC) performs a vital function. A large proportion of autoimmune disease sufferers have a distinct genetic variant of this histocompatibility antigen. For example, scientists understand that many sufferers of rheumatoid arthritis have a distinct "self" antigen named HLA-DR4 (Silverstein, 2009).

The Future of Immunology

The Nobel Prize in Medicine experienced an astonishing growth period for longer than a century during which several mysteries of the immune system functions were uncovered. The impact of this research has been extensive and most distinctly known for the production of vaccines to prevent many conditions that protect billions of people worldwide. Today, scientists have a high-level of understanding of the biological ways the body senses intrusion which then triggers the innate immune reaction, thus establishing antigen specific adaptive immunity. This awareness provides priceless insight into exploring allergies, autoimmune diseases, infectious diseases, and the risk-rejection that associates with organ transplantation. However, there is much that needs to be done as effective vaccines are required to tackle drug-resistant classes of pathogens that cause ailments like tuberculosis, and malaria along with preventing further threats. Scientists are exploring methods that allow patients to undergo transplanted organs and tissues without the need for the risky continuous treatment of immune-suppression drugs. Investigators are also examining the ways in which the immune system is confused or defeated by cancers and viruses (Gladwell, 2014). The century ahead professes to be another hopeful one for exposing more information about the defense mechanisms that shape the immune system, and uncovering the answers to these riddles will require further discoveries.

The Central Nervous Systems Role

The brain and spinal column form the Central Nervous System, and all thoughts that flow through the mind, every action and emotion people experience in this world passes through the CNS. The Central Nervous System can be compared to acting like a computer's motherboard, which without it the machine would not exist. We activate a computer by the push of a button that signals the motherboard to turn on the hard drive stimulating the operating system which transmits signals to start programs. When triggered, the central nervous system initiates a system of physical responses that interprets and communicates experiences, thoughts, feelings and actions to the rest of the body, via a network of cells, neurons and organs.

When the stimulation stops the body needs to be restored to its primary functioning in order to remain in healthy balance. Norepinephrine and epinephrine links to breathing, calms the sensations and strives to restore the muscles into a relaxing state, and allows other bodily duties, such as thirst, appetite, and elimination to resume. Without these security maneuvers the human body could not preserve itself from burning out, or dying like a hamster that continues to race around on its wheel. When the stressful state passes more than a few people will feel exhausted do to the extra glucose administration and this stress response typically leaves people a low measure of blood sugar, feeling as if they have not had anything to eat. The answer to combating acute stress is to advance to a state of balance, or homeostasis. The blood sugar and blood pressure will return to its customary status, as will heart activity and alertness reverts to calm. For optimal survival the human body does its utmost to maintain this sense of balance implying that the goal is to remain at a uniform level of functioning. The CNS is accountable for overseeing the functions that allow us to survive and directs the best reply to stressful situations by launching epinephrine or cortisol to help adjust to the threat. The Central Nervous System also regulates the production of serotonin regulating daily living functions like hunger, sleep and the desire for sex.

Neurons, the Wiring of the Brain and Psychology

The average brain contains approximately 86 billion neurons that receive communications and nerve impulses at speeds of 1/5000 of a second, and these substances that transmit the messages are neurotransmitters. It is the speed of communication on this neurological platform that empowers people to react promptly to various environmental conditions. Serotonin is commonly known as being the happiness hormone, even though it is not a hormone, but, a neurotransmitter contained in the spaces between the neurons (synapses) of the brain. Serotonin's role in a healthy functioning central nervous system is to regulate essential functions such as sleep, sex drive, mood and appetite. The synapses are the areas of the brain that may be interrupted when suffering from symptoms of depression.

Cortisol is also present in the bloodstream and the brain's hypothalamus governs the available quantities. A healthy hypothalamus will ensure that cortisol is present in proper amounts and that it secretes at appropriate times to maintain homeostasis. The highest levels of this hormone are usually found between 8 AM and 4 PM. Laboratory studies conducted on those who experience symptoms of depression exhibit an unusual amount of cortisol either having it peak at odd times or levels being consistently high. A raised cortisol level over time may lead to problems associated with the metabolic, immune and cardiovascular systems. Excess or fluctuating levels of cortisol also affect the rate at which the body produces serotonin, a mood enhancing neurotransmitter. When people report positive mood states there is less cortisol production compared to times when feeling gloomy. Neurotransmitters like serotonin, epinephrine, norepinephrine, endorphins and dopamine affect mood, and consequently, the way people think, feel and behave in the world.

On an emotional level there is a segment depressed individuals who have demonstrated low levels of serotonin, and some researchers believe that these lowered levels directly link to clinical depression. Scientists are striving to determine precisely how this occurs, but low serotonin levels establish the foundation of why the medical profession prescribes most modern anti-depressants. Studies reveal that almost half of depressed patients tested had unusual cortisol levels in their bloodstream. While it is inevitable that prolonged stress can give rise to bouts of depression these conclusions suggest that there could be a physiological relationship between serotonin, cortisol levels and depression (Katon, 2011).

Approximately 19 million Americans experience depression and this ailment affects between 10 and 25% of women and 5 and 12% of men in a lifetime. In this fast paced modern society, symptoms of depression are as frequent as the common cold and the research is beginning to explain how personality traits and conditions can transform nature's biology, at times having hazardous effects.

Health Psychology and the Bio-Psycho-Social Approach

The Central Nervous System and the Immune System work remarkably hard attempting to destroy and eliminate stress reactions. The adrenal glands produce the hormone cortisol which discharges during moments of tension in efforts to diminish the fear. Centuries ago while hunting for food humans were subjected to the dangers of being low on the food chain as the animals hunted were often wild and fierce. It was the Central Nervous Systems physical response mechanism that helped to ensure survival. Primitive people would respond to a confrontation from a dangerous animal by fighting if prepared, or running away in flight. In modern times the stress that people experience tends to be lifestyle orientated resulting in stress that is a chronic condition and is critically damaging to physical health. Anxiety is a silent killer causing severe health problems directly related to heart disease, obesity, diabetes and addiction.

The Two Types of Stress

1. <u>Acute Stress</u> is an immediate physical response to something in the world which can be negative or positive in nature (surgery, accidents, arguments, marriage, birth of a baby, a job promotion).

2. <u>Chronic Stress</u> is a persistent physical response to something consistent in life and may be related to work, financ-

es, family problems, abuse, disease, physical pain, diet, or substance abuse.

The autonomic nervous system (ANS) is a section of the central nervous system containing a widespread labyrinth of nerves spreading out from the spinal cord, directly influencing all organs. It has two divisions, the sympathetic and the parasympathetic, which have opposite impacts. The sympathetic ANS helps people cope with stressful states by launching a "fight or flight" response. After the threat has passed, the parasympathetic ANS takes over, relaxing blood vessels and reduces the heart rate. The sympathetic nervous system is responsible for triggering the response directed towards the anxiety in which initiates the reaction. This means that the body decides whether it will surrender (give in to infection) or manage (fight it off) the threat. The parasympathetic nervous system is responsible for relaxing the body once the stress has been removed from the situation. When anxiety levels remain constant the relaxation time cannot occur and people become more vulnerable to becoming ill. In healthy people, the two divisions of the ANS maintain balance, resulting in an action accompanied by relaxation. If stressors are continually present, and people believe they are under relentless assault, the fight-or-flight response remains activated. The subsequent overexposure to epinephrine, cortisol and other stress hormones can upset nearly all the body's functions, including immune system functions. If anxiety provoking situations become chronic, a variety of stress-related signs and disorders can develop.

How Acute and Chronic Stress affects the body

Acute stress is an instant response to anxiety provoking situations. This could imply a physical or emotional threat, such as evading a bullet, getting into a dispute with your partner or the birth of a baby. If people are suddenly in a stressful situation a series of reactions take place. The hypothalamus in the brain activates. Its' position is above the brain stem, and the hypothalamus is responsible for connecting the nervous system (the communicator) to the endocrine system (a collection of organs that discharge hormones) via the pituitary gland. This set of reactions proceeds along the sympathetic nervous system relaying the message to get moving. This part of the nervous system manages the fight-or-flight response and is the body's method of maintaining balance when under acute stress. When someone is shouting, people will either fight back or escape into a safe place. The physical consequences of acute stress vary from an increased heartbeat to shallow breathing and enhanced awareness because of the higher stream of oxygen flowing into the brain and body. These reactions occur because of a discharge of adrenaline which is the chief stress hormone, and there is also a release of cortisol, another stress hormone delivered by the adrenal gland that increases blood pressure and blood sugar. The liver also starts to manufacture glucose and provides extra energy. Scientists are stating that being better prepared points to being less distressed and that being less distressed will generate less production of daily cortisol. The healthy psychology relationship is that people can discover ways to become more organized, which leads to a reduction in anxiety and lower production of the physically damaging cortisol (Gladwell, 2014).

Inflammation is the primary cause of all chronic degenerative diseases such as; arthritis, allergies, asthma, diabetes, lupus, heart disease, chronic fatigue, fibromyalgia, and a host of others. Inflammation causes a strong response from the immune system to pathogens that cause injury and physical illness. When the stress response does not turn off or relax, the immune system is overloaded and is in a weakened, compromised state causing people to become susceptible to contracting a physical illness.

Causes of Chronic Inflammation

1. Toxins (Pollution, Pesticides, Food poisoning)
2. High levels of insulin in blood (Diabetes)
3. Infection (Skin Conditions, Poor Healing)
4. Oxygen free radicals (Cell death, Aging)
5. Allergens (Pollen)
6. Lack of Exercise
7. Chronic stress
8. Medication
9. Insomnia
10. Diet

The Cortisol Connection

As introduced, both cortisol and adrenaline are hormones that are manufactured by the adrenal glands in the kidneys. When people come in contact with an acute stress situation, the adrenal glands will respond by producing adrenaline. If people are exposed to prolonged stress the body will respond by producing a different hormone called cortisol, which is regulated by the hypothalamus in the brain. This physical reaction comes about because of the desire to maintain a sense of balance. When exposed to chronic stress, the physical body will react by releasing cortisol in preparation for the fight or flight situation. Cortisol effectively mobilizes the body on every functioning level to ensure it has sufficient incentive to survive the danger (Parham, 2009).

When someone has chronic stress, cortisol's' role is to improve the ability to maintain balance by releasing this hormone in hopes of achieving: 1. Immediate energy and strength to endure, 2. A Reduction or a desensitization to pain, 3. Improvement in memory function. These chemical processes and the release of hormones for survival are normal. However, high levels for long periods of time are dangerous to psychological and physical health. Therefore, these protective responses can be extremely hazardous. When stress hormones circulate in the bloodstream for prolonged periods of time they can cause physical conditions including blood clots, angina and heart disease. In response to chronic stress, the increase in cortisol produces the following physical effects.

1. Slows down digestion, which relates to weight loss and weight gain.

2. Increases the blood sugar level, which is a direct link to Diabetes.

3. Metabolizes protein, fats and carbohydrates by converting them into glucose and increasing the probability of becoming diabetic.

4. Reduces the inflammatory response, and may increase susceptibility to physical irritations and infections.

5. Depresses the immune system by deactivating white blood cells decreasing the ability to fight off infections, viruses and bacteria.

6. Increases blood pressure causing a strain on the heart.

Common Conditions linked to the immune system that may be reversed

Anxiety

The brain, the mind, and the body are inseparable, and communication between them can create physical changes. The brain notices a stressor, and then a physical response triggers emotional effects that can produce mental and physical harm. A few problems such as muscle tension and headaches are oftentimes directly induced by the physical responses that follow anxiety.

Pain

Stress complicates underlying painful ailments such as fibromyalgia, lupus, herniated discs, chronic pain syndromes and repetitive strain injury (RSI). Migraine patients say that stress contributes to headaches, which can last for days. Neck, shoulder and back aches are remarkably widespread due to poor posture and inactive lifestyles. Continued stimulation of nerve tissue through prolonged stress can point to muscular spasm such as backache.

Type 2 Diabetes

There is some indication that persistent stress may affect diabetes especially in people who have the genetic predisposition. The National Academies Press (2001) states, that it is possible that stress provokes the immune system to suppress insulin-producing cells.

Infertility

People who are attempting to become pregnant are more likely to conceive during celebrations or when facing little stress, and fertility therapy is more successful during these times. There is the general association that anxiety interferes with pregnancy and that psychosocial worry contributes to the causes of some types of infertility (Wasser, Sewall & Soules, 1993).

High Blood Pressure

Identified as hypertension, this is a somewhat common chronic condition which ordinarily has no noticeable signs. Nevertheless, hypertension increases someone's chance of acquiring heart disease, kidney failure and stroke. Anxiety elevates blood pressure, and chronic stress may contribute to an enduringly inflated blood pressure. If there is a family recorded history of hypertension and heart problems, people should have routine checkups with their physician, and follow the advice.

Dermatology Problems

Stress can intensify skin conditions such as eczema, psoriasis and acne, and likewise has a relationship to unexplained itchy skin diseases. These dermatology difficulties are themselves profoundly anxiety provoking.

Vulnerability to Infection

When people are under stress, the immune system is suppressed making them more vulnerable to infection. Allergies and autoimmune diseases including fibromyalgia, arthritis, lupus and multiple sclerosis may be intensified by anxiety. Emotional tension also slows the pace at which people recuperate from any ailment. Stress can be partly balanced by social support from family and friends.

Chronic conditions that are linked to a weakened immune system

1. Arthritis
2. Allergies
3. Insomnia
4. Infections
5. Depression
6. Inflammation
7. Persistent Pain

8. Digestive disorders

9. Poor wound healing

10. Chronic Fatigue and Fibromyalgia

11. Asthma and other respiratory disorders

12. Two or more colds/flu's a year with slow recovery

13. Chronic fever, diarrhea, and swollen lymph glands

How to Achieve Health and Prevent Illness

All living organisms strive to maintain balance, or homeostasis, which is routinely challenged by internal or external triggers. Stressors' are triggers which are physically harmful and these triggers are emotional, physical or environmental. Stress threatens stability or homeostasis and the ability to re-establish balance which can be accomplished through behavioral and physiological responses that attack the intruders. (Viruses, bacteria) The magnitude and chronicity of the stressor is crucial in understanding because when any trigger exceeds a certain severity it activates the Central Nervous System's adaptive response (Shomon, 2002). In other words, a little anxiety in life that is short lived (forgetting where you placed the car keys) is much less physically and emotionally damaging than facing a housing foreclosure. The challenge is learning techniques or ways to cope with life's problems thereby decreasing the biological response, as listed below:

Anxiety Reduction: Stress produces a bio-chemical reaction and the overproduction of cortisol and adrenaline lowers the immune system's ability to fight off physical illness (Reiche, Nunes, & Morimoto, 2004). This process explains why the common cold virus may take hold during difficult times, as the weakened immune system simply does not have the strength to fight off infections. Find ways to reduce stress. Listen to music, go for a walk, practice relaxation techniques, or find someone to talk to about the anxiety to discover a personal way to reduce stress.

Learn to Become More Organized: Studies show that being organized decreases anxiety levels and reduces high cortisol levels that decrease the immune system's ability to fight off infection. Take the time to plan the day.

Physical Exercise: Regular gentle exercise, like walking helps protect the immune system by encouraging the organic killer cells eliminates bacteria and viruses in their tracks. People become less physically active with age, therefore, those over the age of 55 may benefit the most from physical exercise. A walk refreshes the immune system by reducing anxiety and encourages or assists the antioxidants that protect us from disease (Strickland, 2001).

Get Adequate Sleep: The body needs rest to return to balance. Sometimes sleep is the best medicine especially when trying to fight off a cold or the flu. Learn a relaxation method. Develop a routine to prepare yourself to calm down which produces a restful night's sleep. This "wind down" time should be at least one hour (Majde & Krueger, 2005) (Bryant, Trinder & Curtis, 2004).

Hand Washing: A powerful and basic behavior that fights germs. Use soap and water and wash vigorously for 15 to 20 seconds. During flu season avoid hugs and physical contact with associates, friends and co-workers to prevent the spread of germs.

Maintain a Healthy Diet: Foods that are eaten have a direct influence on the immune system because deficiencies can impair the ability to fight off infection (Langley-Evans & Carrington, 2006). All fats weaken the immune system because they confuse white blood cells and impair recognition of foreign foes. Tissues and organs decay through oxidation, thereby, causing common diseases and the antioxidants strengthen the organ cells assisting with stability by slowing down the oxidation process. The solution is straightforward; eat more fruits, vegetables, oats, grains, legumes, nuts, berries and mushrooms. Buy some organic produce to reduce pesticide consumption. The micro-nutrients are higher and pesticide levels are less in Organic foods (Hunter et. Al., 2011) (Acharya, Muralidhar, & Krishi, 2003). If fast food is a must, choose healthy fast food menu items and pay attention to calorie intake along with consuming less sugar, salt and fat.

Everyone can consciously choose to live a less stressful life and this is the good news because people are in charge of understanding that there are choices and make these decisions. Changes in habits and routines can be accomplished whenever there is a genuine desire to live a healthy productive life. The goal is to build on that healthy lifestyle from one day, to many days, then to months and ultimately to your lifetime.

Chapter 2
Burdens of the Heart

All over the earth people identify love with hearts and if love is gone there is impairment of the relationship. When the mechanical heart is not pumping oxygen adequately there is damage to cells or no growth, the heart is a token of life. There is a relationship between the physical well-being of the heart and psychology. The heart has numerous indispensable duties, and it seems reasonable for all to promote distinct methods to maintain its vitality. People need to discover ways in which to take responsibility for and care of their heart.

Theories about the connection between the heart and mind are in the medical documents throughout antiquity. Some civilizations as in ancient Egypt believed that the heart was the foundation and root of emotions. As Western medicine steadily disclosed this absence of association thoughts about the bonds between the heart and mind went by the wayside. Behavioral cardiology is a novel field that is attempting to join them together again, this time with reliable scientific bonds and this theory is presenting new approaches to the treatment and prevention of heart disease. Heart conditions include the entire cardiovascular system and are the leading causes of death in the United States and throughout the globe. The Centers for Disease Control and Prevention (CDC) declare that roughly 61 million people in America have heart disease and the World Health Organization (WHO), states that 29 percent of all deaths worldwide are due to these diseases. The

American Heart Association (AHA) continues onto explaining that nearly 870,000 people died from heart disease in the United States accounting for more deaths in females per year than the next six causes combined. To prevent heart disease, recent guidelines emphasize lifestyle modifications.

A Brief History of Heart Disease

To answer precisely when society originally became knowledgeable of heart disease is challenging. Heart scans of Egyptian mummies 3,500 years old present evidence of atherosclerosis, or thickening of the arteries, that most contemporary investigators thought was a condition induced by modern day lifestyles. In ancient times there was heart disease although it was not as widespread, not recognized or diagnosed.

Nevertheless, it is clear that Leonardo da Vinci (1452–1519) studied coronary arteries and professionals continue to give credit to William Harvey (1578–1657), a physician to King Charles for identifying how the blood circulates through the heart. Nearly twenty five years later, Friedrich Hoffmann (1660–1742), a leading educator of cardiology at the University of Halle, speculated that coronary heart disease sprang from the "reduced passage of the blood within the coronary arteries." In the 18th and 19th centuries Angina, which is tightness in the chest that is oftentimes a sign of heart disease bewildered countless practitioners. Originally defined in 1768, Angina was thought to be related to blood flowing through the coronary arteries even though many believed that it was a harmless ailment. William Osler (1849–1919), a cardiologist investigated Angina extensively and was one of the principal forerunners in indicating that these were symptoms rather than a disease. The cardiologist James B. Herrick, (1861-1954) reasoned that the slow, progressive narrowing of the coronary arteries could be the basis for angina pain, also coining the phrase "heart attack" (Savona & Grech, 1999).

The 1900s record a time of heightened attention, research, and understanding. In New York City (1915), a gathering of physicians and social workers created the original "Association for the Prevention and Relief of Heart Disease" that became the American Heart Association in 1924. These physicians were affected by the disease on account of understanding little about its cause and effect and could advise their patients little promise for a treatment. A pediatric cardiologist, at The Cleveland Clinic, Mason Sones (1918–1985), improved methods for delivering high-quality diagnostic pictures of the coronary arteries. This unique test produced an objective diagnosis of coronary artery disease for the first time in history. A few years following physicians began the practice of examining the coronary arteries with catheters that would later develop into cardiac catheterization or coronary angiogram. In modern times, these methods are regularly applied to assess or verify the appearance of heart disease confirming the necessity for additional treatment.

In 1950, John Gofman (1918-2007) a University of California researcher and his colleagues classified two familiar cholesterol types: low-density lipoprotein (LDL) and high-density lipoprotein (HDL). They found that males diagnosed with atherosclerosis had raised levels of LDL and low levels of HDL. Also during this time, Ancel Keys (1904–2004) was a scientist who discovered while travelling that heart disease was unusual in some Mediterranean cultures where people ate a low fat diet. He remarked that the Japanese also had low-fat diets and low rates of heart disease influencing him to speculate that fat caused heart disease. These decisions along with the Framingham study directed the medical professions first efforts towards encouraging Americans to modify their dietary regimen to maintain a healthy heart (Bhupathiraju & Tucker, 2011) (Walker & Reamy, 2009).

In the 1960s and '70s procedures like bypass surgery and angioplasty were primary practiced in treating heart disease. Later in the 1980s, the use of stents became popular to open a narrowed artery and as a result of these approaches heart conditions were no longer deemed a death sentence. Although diagnostic standards have evolved, heart disease was not unknown before 1900; nevertheless, it is accurate to say that there has been a mysterious increase in the number of cases recorded in the US since 1918. Great advancements in understanding, diagnosing and managing heart disease have been established since the 1900's and prior to this time there was no heart disease as professionals recognize it to-day. Heart disease in the year 2014 has evolved into being the number one condition that kills in the United States (Centers for Disease Control and Prevention, 2014).

The time of technology has caused life for people to be less physically active and this inactivity makes people predis-posed to developing heart disease. Before the Industrial Rev olution almost everyone earned their living and survived by performing a manual activity. With the advent of motoriza-tion, life grew less physically demanding and manual work was replaced or assisted by machines. Cars, dishwashers, washing machines, elevators, conveyors, and vacuum clean-ers became common and modern amenities made physical activity unnecessary. Along with the shift in lifestyle people began to alter their diet because of machines being invented to process cheese, make ice cream, churn butter and homoge-nized milk. Before the Industrial Revolution and automation such high-fat foods had to be produced manually, and now in modern times hamburgers, fried foods, candy and sugary cakes are the staple foods.

The blending of an inactive lifestyle and diet points to the escalation of clogged blood vessels, heart attacks and strokes creating these diseases of the heart to be commonplace. However, an obvious rise in recorded deaths related to heart disease was the addition of the diagnosis "arteriosclerosis" to the International Classification of Diseases, in 1949. The incidence of heart disease rose so clearly between the 1940 and 1967 that the World Health Organization declared it the

planet's most dangerous disease. In 1948, a thirty-year inquiry began in Framingham, Massachusetts, recognized as the
Framingham Study. This study included 5127 people aged 30
to 62 who exhibited no manifestations of heart disease and
every two years, the participants underwent a comprehensive physical examination which lasted thirty years, and contributed valuable data for predicting heart conditions (Oppenheimer, 2005).

In 2011, a U.S.-Egyptian investigation team involving a University of California professor and cardiologist Dr. Gregory
Thomas M.D. examined CT scans of mummies discovering
that nearly fifty percent displayed evidence of coronary atherosclerosis in one or more of the arteries furnishing blood to
the heart and brain. The research was presented to the American Heart Association and formulated by Dr. Gregory Thomas after he learned about Pharoah Merenptah at the Egyptian
National Museum of Antiquities. This Egyptian mummy
died at age 60, in the year 1203 BC, and had atherosclerosis.
Dr. Thomas thought that some indications of atherosclerosis might still be present in other mummies and formed a
team of cardiologists and Egyptologists to scan a group of 20
in the museum. All of the mummies held high social standing. Among the findings were 16 of them in which arteries
or hearts could be recognized, nine had calcification plain-
ly observed in the arteries or in the trail where the arteries
should have existed. The disease certainly was age-related,
and males and females were affected proportionately. Seven
of the eight mummies who were older than 45 had calcification, compared with only two of eight that were younger. One
of the oldest troubled with atherosclerosis was Lady Rai, who
was a nursemaid to Queen Ahmose Nefertiti and died around
the age of 40 in 1530 BC, 200 years before King Tut and 300
years prior to the time of Moses. These upper class Egyptians
fed on a diet high in fat from ducks, cattle, geese, and salt that
was used to preserve food, both of which are contributing
factors related to heart disease. Despite some similarities, the
investigation's conclusions indicate that researchers need to

examine beyond current risk factors to completely explain the causes of heart disease (Thomas, 2013).

The Functions of the Heart

The heart is around the size of your fist and weighs 300 to 350 grams (11 to 12 oz.) in males and nearly 250 to 300 grams (9 to 11 oz.) in females. This organ quickens up or slows down in response to nerve signals from the brain describing degrees of physical exertion. The heart contracts and relaxes between 70 and 80 times per minute, beats around 80,000 to 100,000 times per day and pumps approximately 2,000 gallons of oxygenated blood throughout the system. This task is without conscious awareness because this organ is a specialized muscle (involuntary) that continually beats. There are four chambers of the heart, 2 chambers on each side. The upper chambers are the atrium, and the lower ones are the ventricles. The heart functions as two pumps for the circulatory system. The right atrium of the heart receives blood which is non-oxygenated then carries blood to the right ventricle into the lungs in which the blood absorbs oxygen. Without oxygen, all cells die and the heart supplies the body with a fresh supply of oxygen and nutrients that assist in removing hazardous waste material. The left atrium accepts oxygenated blood from the lungs to provide all organs and cells of the body with oxygen. This blood also distributes hormones from the glands and nutrients from the digestive system. The cells in the immune system travel throughout the bloodstream seeking out infection, and forwards waste material to the kidneys and liver to be filtered and excreted.

The hearts four chambers contract or beat in an orderly manner is due to having an electrical stimulus because the chamber contracts when an electrical surge moves across a particular path. This stimulus begins in a small collection of unique cells in the right atrium, called the sinus node (SA node). A detonation from these vital "pacemaker" cells causes the heart to contract as they generate electrical impulses. The electrical stimuli produced by the cells in the SA node travel through the right and left atrium, causing the cells of the muscle to contract and then the electrical stimuli proceeds down the specialized cell passageway through the ventricles. The signal's arrival causes the ventricles to contract simultaneously squeezing and pumping the blood forward along the path. The hearts physiology determines the route of this electrical stimulation which brings about a coordinated ordered contraction of the four chambers known as the heartbeat. These electrical movements flow through the tissue threads by personal communication from cell to cell via channels, named gap junctions that synchronize the contraction. If the pacemaker misses, the cells do not get their move along commands, and the heartbeat slows down or becomes erratic. Emotional reactions can alter the heart rate pertaining to this electrical discharge and this is one physical connection that relates to psychology. People can learn to regulate emotional reactions, therefore, reduce the stress that it places on the heart and at times reduce heart rates, when there is no major physical damage. One example is that the rate of the heartbeat can be regulated and influenced by physical exercise.

New research hopes to transform ordinary cardiac cells to pacemaker cells by expressing a master regulator gene to replenish those lost by disease or injury. In the absence of an electrical impulse, the heart is relaxed, with the threads held apart by a protector protein termed troponin C. The mysterious ion that produces the contraction is calcium. Every electrical surge discharges calcium that connects to troponin C, and pushes it out of the way to trigger a contraction. However, the calcium is promptly captured and moved back into stores, so the heart relaxes, before the process begins again. The EKG measures this electrical heart rhythm when people have this diagnostic examination and physicians are evaluating the hearts electronic path for manifestations of injury (Cedars-Sinai, 2012).

How the Heart relates to Blood Pressure

- First Stage (Systole) is when the ventricles of the heart are squeezing or contracting which results in blood being pumped out to the lungs and onward pushing through the rest of the body. This is the top number of the blood pressure.

- Second Stage (Diastole) the ventricles of the heart are relaxing and the atriums of the heart are filling with blood. This is the bottom number of the blood pressure.

The Physical Illnesses related to the Heart

Cardiovascular disease includes many disorders. These conditions alter the blood vessels which are veins and arteries leading to and from the heart or the heart muscle. Women who have cardiovascular disease tend to exhibit forms that affect blood vessels while men develop conditions that impact the muscle. Conditions such as diabetes mellitus, hypertension, and hypercholesterolemia are causes of cardiovascular disease (Kvan, Pettersen, Sandvik & Reikvam, 2007).

1. Angina Pectoris is a heart disease that causes severe mid chest pain or discomfort on the left side the chest along with pain in the jaw, throat, stomach, and between the shoulder blades. The thickening of the arteries supplying blood to the heart causes this discomfort.

2. Aortic Aneurysm is a bulge or out pouching of the main artery, the aorta. These bulges can occur in the abdomen below the kidneys or the chest cavity. The aneurysm occurs when the lining of the aorta becomes weakened and thin by the buildup of plaque. Aneurysms are dangerous because of the possibility of rupturing, thereby causing massive bleeding.

3. Atherosclerosis is the disease process caused by plaque buildup (cholesterol, fatty substances) in the inner lining of an artery. Over time, the plaque ruptures the lining that in turn produces blood clots. These blood clots inhibit blood flow to the cells causing them to die. Complications of a blocked artery can lead to the development of gangrene, heart attacks and strokes.

4. Cardiomyopathy in the strict sense means "heart muscle disease" (cardio = heart, myo = muscle, pathy = disease). Cardiomyopathy is the breakdown in functioning and health of the heart muscle. Those diagnosed are at risk of developing arrhythmias (irregular heart rhythms) that precipitate unexpected cardiac death. There are two types:

   • Dilated Cardiomyopathy is more common and relates to the heart cavity having inflammation. Progression of the disease includes the development of arrhythmias and congestive heart failure.

   • Hypertrophic Cardiomyopathy is the growth or thickening of the wall between the ventricles creating a blockage in blood flow. Physical symptoms include chest pain, shortness of breath, fainting and dizziness.

5. Congenital Heart Disease is an error that takes place during the development of the heart during gestation. The blood vessels near the heart or the heart muscle develop improperly. Researchers and physicians often do not understand the basis of these defects, but some attribute the mistakes in development to viral infections, poisons or drug and alcohol abuse during pregnancy (Klatsky, 2009).

6. Congestive Heart Failure is a chronic disease that tends to deteriorate over time. CHF is characterized by the hearts inability to adjust to the amount of blood flow in the four chambers. The disease process usually begins with left-sided heart failure and impairs the functioning of the left ventricle. At times, heart failure occurs on the right-side and can at times affect the complete heart muscle.

7. Coronary Artery Disease is when the arteries around the heart become hardened and narrow because of plaque buildup (atherosclerosis). This gradual buildup of plaque can lead to chest pain, heart arrhythmias, heart failure and heart attacks.

8. Coronary Heart Disease refers to the hearts inability to provide sufficient circulation to surrounding tissues and the cardiac muscle. It often co-occurs with coronary artery disease. However, coronary heart disease can have other causes, such as spasm. Conditions provoked by CHD are myocardial infarction (heart attack) and angina pectoris (chest pain).

9. Endocarditis is a well-known disease describing inflammation of the inner lining of the heart (endocardium). Inflammatory heart disease is inflammation of the tissues surrounding the heart or heart muscle. The most common structures affected are the heart valves.

10. Heart Murmurs are faulty heart valves, which lead to regurgitation of blood or constrict passage of blood through the valves opening. A systolic murmur is detected when the heart muscle contracts. The diastolic murmurs occur when the heart muscle relaxes in between beats. Heart murmurs can sound remarkably soft to exceptionally loud and the different qualities are identified and heard using a stethoscope. During pregnancy, fevers and toxins can produce heart murmurs.

11. Hypertensive Heart Diseases are induced by high blood pressure. Ailments include congestive heart failure, coronary heart disease, cardiac arrhythmias, left ventricular hypertrophy and hypertensive cardiomyopathy.

12. Peripheral Vascular Disease is of two types. Organic peripheral vascular diseases are abnormal blood vessels surrounding the heart and brain. This ailment can cause narrowing of the blood vessels that supply oxygen and nutrients to the kidneys, stomach, arms and legs. Functional peripheral vascular diseases do not reveal anomalies in

blood vessels' and are produced by spasms. Manifestations include numbness, a cramping pain, and may involve skin discoloration.

13. Valvular Heart Disease is the process that alters one or more heart valves. There are four primary heart valves which may be influenced by this illness, the aortic and mitral valves on the left side of the heart, and the aortic and tricuspid valves on the right side of the heart.

The Psychological Factors related to Heart Disease

The National Institutes of Mental Health (NIMH, 2013) states that up to 65 percent of coronary heart disease sufferers who have a history of having a heart attack experience some form of depression. Although these symptoms are not unusual, they should be treated as soon as possible because Major depression can hamper the recovery process and worsen the disease. Prolonged depression associated with cardiovascular disease contributes to subsequent strokes and heart attacks.

Many people may believe heart disease correlates solely with physical actions (a lack of exercise, poor diets, smoking, excessive drinking), however, attitudes, emotions, and thoughts are equally significant. Thought processes can accelerate the onset of heart disease and hinder taking concrete strides to promote health and prevent disease. Some heart patients may sense a loss of control over their life with taking medication, making time for exercise and giving up favorite foods. Making modifications in everyday life is not easy because it takes training to instill these new practices and develop habits. To sneak a cigarette or cheat on a diet may satisfy an immediate desire, but will hinder the long-term goal of improving health. Cultivating a healthy lifestyle can diminish the risk of heart disease or manage the condition, even if a higher risk is due to uncontrollable determinants such as sex, family history or age.

Psychological determinants influence health directly (such as stress causing the release of the hormone cortisol) and indirectly (via behavioral decisions) that harm or preserve health. Health psychologists use a biological, psychological and sociological guide in recognizing health practices. This method centers on understanding wellness to be the result not only of biological processes (physical, hormonal and endocrine functioning) but also of mental processes such as approaches toward health and how people cope with stress in their lives. These clinical psychologists then look at factors that relate to socioeconomic status, culture and ethnicity to formulate treatment plans, interventions and prognoses. Research confirms that while roughly 20 percent of the US population endures an episode of depression in their life, the number soars to 50 percent among those with heart disease. Long-term investigations report that men and women diagnosed with clinical depression are more than twice as likely to acquire coronary artery disease or experience a heart attack (American Psychological Association, 2013).

Heart disease has several brain, mind, body associations. Prolonged stress due to difficulties at home or work can contribute to circulation problems that link to high blood pressure and other heart conditions. As with many conditions, anxiety effects vary from person to person. Some manage stress to motivate while others may lose their temper and become frustrated. How people manage tension, influences cardiovascular responses. Studies have shown that when stress consistently makes someone irritable or angry that person is more likely to develop heart disease (Kivimäki, 2012). In fact, how people respond to stressful situations may be a greater risk factor contributing to the development of future heart related ailments than high cholesterol or smoking. Clinically depressed people are at substantially higher risk of suffering a heart attack or stroke and they are twice as likely to suffer heart related conditions. Depression can also hamper recovering from a stroke, recuperation from heart surgeries and heart attacks. The tension is associated with immediate shock of coming so close to death along with the added fear of possibly having a long recuperation, as well as the worry that another, potentially more dangerous event could occur without warning (American Heart Association, 2013).

Krantz and McCeney (2002) found that the pervasiveness of heart disease in sufferers of depression is high, making the connections between heart disease and depression obvious in investigations of community representations and those with depression. They also illustrate the ties between heart disease and psychological determinants involving Type A behavioral patterns, anger and hostility and fatigue. Understanding and harnessing psychological factors, can improve health by working directly with individual patients, indirectly in large-scale public health programs, or by training healthcare professionals. Health Psychology can be associated with the similar field of clinical psychology, with divisions within health psychology, which, include public and occupational health. The relationship between psychosocial determinants and heart disease is so clear that cardiologists should begin the conversation by questioning patients about stress, energy, mood and support systems (Kelly, Bridget & Fuster, 2010). Most conventional cardiologists do not, at least at this point in time.

Psychosocial Factors related to Heart Disease

Psychosocial factors have been associated with increases in tumor necrosis factor, interleukins and C-reactive protein. All of which are signs of increased inflammation, which represents significant parts in developing the artery-clogging atherosclerosis. Psychosocial determinants could impact heart disease via a secondary physiologic route, through practices that point toward heart disease or away from it. For example, isolation or depression can hinder people from taking the heart medications they need while a positive viewpoint or active social network can assist people watch their weight or stop smoking. There are plenty of theories of how social conditions, behaviors and emotions affect heart disease, however, studies related to stress hormones top the list. Stress hormones speed up the heartbeat, constrict blood vessels and cause them to be exceptionally sensitive or reactive to further stress. Psychosocial determinants affect heart disease in two fundamental directions. Some factors attach to atherosclerosis, the gradual, destructive means that weaken artery walls placing people at risk for a stroke or heart attack. Other circumstances add to direct attacks that trigger a heart assault or stroke (Steptoe & Kivimäki, 2012).

Many investigators discuss a comprehensive international study affirming that the psychosocial contributions to heart attacks are on a level with obesity, high cholesterol, smoking and high blood pressure. There conclusions did not just relate to the wild paced world of the West but in China, the Middle East, Hong Kong, Africa and Latin America. Below is a summary of the results (Lancet, 2004).

1. Anxiety. Intense fear, the kind associated with heights, crowds, enclosed places, snakes and the like, can at times produce a sudden cardiac arrest. These often-fatal heart attacks occur when the heartbeat abruptly becomes fast and irregular.

2. Anger/hostility. In the Harvard-based Determinants of Myocardial Infarction Onset Study, 1 in every 40 heart attack patients reports an incident of agitation in the two hours before the heart symptoms development, anger can trigger heart attacks. Atherosclerosis appears to progress faster in people who score high on hostility or anger ranges.

3. Depression. People who display the symptoms of depression after a heart attack, stroke, heart surgery, or the onset of heart failure do not manage as well as those who are not exhibiting signs. Indications of depression, as well as full-blown major depression, contribute to heart disease.

4. Unexpected emotional stress. Sudden emotional disturbance can set off a critical, but reversible heart failure named broken heart syndrome. Researchers at Johns Hopkins have documented its occurrence in people after a loss in the family, a surprise party, a burglary, a car collision, and even fear of talking in public (Krishnan, 2003).

5. Chronic stress. Persistent stress that associates with a shaky marriage, financial difficulties, work related problems, taking care of a parent or spouse, or residing in an unsafe community correlates highly with the appearance of heart disease. People that have chronic stress also have challenges with rehabilitation following diagnosis.

6. Social support. Social isolation is nearly as significant as high cholesterol, high blood pressure, and smoking at prophesying long-term survival, among heart attack victims.

Heart Disease Risk Factors

Genetics' or a positive family history of chronic heart disease is known to increase the risk.

Hypertension or elevated blood pressure accelerates the atherosclerosis process especially if hyperlipidemia or high triglycerides are present. This combination plays a significant role in development of heart attacks. However, heart attacks can be prevented and managed if people are diagnosed early and if they understand the recommended dietary treatment plan and follow instructions.

Diabetes Mellitus. The risk of developing a severe heart disease is two to three times more among diabetics. Type 2 Diabetes in most cases in a highly preventable disease.

High Cholesterol (Normal <200 mg/dl). Cholesterol has two components, the low density lipoprotein (LDL) and high density lipoprotein (HDL). LDL is the most directly associated with Coronary Heart Disease. However, High density lipoprotein (HDL) cholesterol is considered to be protective against development of Coronary Heart Disease. (It should be more than 40 mg/dl).

Oral Contraceptives lead to higher systolic and diastolic blood pressure which in turn increases cardiac risk.

Being Overweight is associated with high rates of cardiovascular deaths and heart failure with different rates among men and women. Obesity affects the blood pressure, increases levels of lipids in the blood, and increases the risk for developing Type 2 Diabetes.

Smoking. The toxins in the cigarettes and the associated inflammation are considered to be one of the main causes of development of atherosclerosis. Atherosclerosis is a thickening of the walls of arteries which result from the accumulation of fatty plaques, scarring and hardening of the walls.

Physical Inactivity is associated with high risk because inactivity increases the lipid levels in the blood. Physical inactivity and diet are considered to be leading causes of obesity, lipid panel abnormalities, elevation of blood pressure and diabetes mellitus.

Alcohol Intake of more than three drinks a day has a harmful effect on the heart muscle. Heavy drinking raises the triglyceride level by supplying excess fats into the body circulation. Over time, heavy drinking can damage the heart and leads to high blood pressure, stroke and congestive heart failure.

Multiple Risk Factor Combinations. Increased body weight is a good example of a risk factor for heart disease that plays a role for development of other risk factors, like increased lipids level in blood (hyperlipidemia), elevation of blood pressure (hypertension) and other diseases like diabetes mellitus.

Multiple risk factors significantly increase one's chances of developing heart disease (McTigue and Hess 2006).

Psychological and Behavioral Tips on how to prevent Heart Disease

1. People are in command. The brain reports to the body and the body reports to the brain. Everyone can learn to manage their mental self-talk to improve health.

2. Take time out each day to relax. Begin to take note of things that cause stress. Try to accept the fact that some situations are not reversible

3. Take responsibility and care for the body. Get enough sleep. Exercise on most days. Eat a healthy diet.

4. Control stress at work. Leave work at lunchtime and take a short walk or relax outside the business environment. Take a 15-minute leisure break to practice a relaxation exercise. Switch from caffeinated to decaffeinated coffee or herbal tea.

5. Get the help. If people have a hard time managing the stress alone or are using habits, such as drugs, alcohol or cigarettes, to diminish the tension, they may require help discovering ways to regulate anxiety. Here are a few of the many possibilities: Individual counseling, Group counseling, Support groups Self-help books, Stress management courses.

6. Take control over the schedule. Prioritize what needs to be done every day.

7. Avoid negative self-talk. Try not to concentrate on situations in which there is no control. Take a moment to give recognition for jobs well performed.

8. Learn Relaxation Techniques and Applications. There are many techniques, mindfulness, yoga, visualization, deep relaxation and focusing to name just a few.

In conclusion, the stopping of the heart-beat always results in death that applies to everyday language associating with love. People identify love with hearts, if there is no love there is destruction of the relationship, and when the heart is not pumping oxygen adequately there is destruction of the heart. It seems reasonable for all to develop new ways to maintain its strength. Health Psychologists enhance the recovery of cardiac patients by providing tools to cope and ways to manage the physical changes associated with this disease. They focus on primary and secondary prevention of by utilizing strategies to address the emotional and behavioral barriers in building lifestyle changes. This is the work of the health psychologist who employs a biological, psychological and sociological approach strategy.

Chapter 3
Traversing Cancer

Discussing this disease is challenging because millions of people have had their lives changed or is secretly informed of someone who has had cancer. When initially diagnosed, it is understandable, justified and logical to want to know the cause of the problem. After all, cancer prevalence, or those living with the disease seems high for everyone affected. Expectations of over one and a half million new cancer diagnoses are the predictions for 2015, and approximately 600,000 Americans die of cancer, nearly 1,600 people a day. Cancer is the second most common cause of mortality in America and accounts for one in every four deaths (American Cancer Society, 2013).

What is Cancer?

All life forms contain many types of cells and in a very controlled manner these cells divide, grow and develop to produce more cells needed to maintain health. Normally when cells become defective they die and the body regenerates healthy cells, however, sometimes there is a disruption in this orderly process. Cancer is many diseases. The 100 different diseases of cancer usually have the name after the cell or organ in which they originate. For example, cancer that begins in the bladder has the name bladder cancer, basal cell carcinoma begins in the basal layer of the skin, and the cells are different in each organ. This system of labeling is true for all classes of cancers and treatment methods are specifically targeting the uniqueness of each organ's cancer cell.

In every life form, the body frequently produces defective cells and the immune system usually eliminates them before they cause any physical harm. Cancer cells start out as expected, healthy body-organ cells, but they become damaged or there is a biological slip made in their regular cell cycle development. The DNA or genetic materials of a cell can become altered or broken which cause mutations that affect normal division and cell proliferation. Cancer is a disease in which defective or irregular cells divide and spread out of control. These cells have the capacity to contaminate other tissues and may penetrate other parts of the body via circulatory and lymphatic networks. The damaged cells continue to divide quickly and begin to accumulate, and change their appearance or mutate. Serving no role in maintaining health, the abnormal cells continue to multiply and grow sometimes evolving into forming a mass of tissue, which medical professionals call a tumor (Weinberg, 2013).

A Brief History of Cancer

Humans and animals have been diagnosed with cancer throughout the ages, and men have spoken of this condition since the beginning of time. In ancient Egypt, the assumption was that the cancer was an infliction caused by the Gods. There is also an indication that the early Egyptians were capable of understanding the distinction between benign and malignant growths. Although the word was not identified, the ancient classification of cancer was found in 1500 B.C in a document written in Egypt in the legendary Edwin Smith Papyrus, an ancient Egyptian textbook on trauma surgery. This papyrus outlines eight representations of ulcers or growths of the breast that were treated by cauterization with a tool called the fire drill. According to writings, exterior growths were surgically removed in a comparable fashion as in recent times. The papyrus states, "there is no treatment." Cancer was found in fossil bones of mummies from Egypt and growths suggestive of bone cancer described as osteosarcoma along with bony skull damage as observed in cancer of the head and neck have been found (Halperin, 2004).

The source of the word cancer is attributed to the Greek physician Hippocrates (460-370 BC), who has the title "Father of Medicine." Throughout the centuries, the belief has been that cancer could take place anywhere in the body. Hippocrates used the phrases "carcinos" and "carcinoma" to characterize non-ulcer patterning and ulcer-forming growths. In Greek, this word represents resembling a crab on account of the finger-like flowing projections from the cancer growth that reminded Hippocrates of the creature. He studied and produced sketches of visible tumors on the skin, nose, and breasts because it was the Greeks religious belief not to perform autopsies or penetrate the body. The treatment approach of this time was based on the humor theory meaning there are four bodily fluids, phlegm, black and yellow bile, and blood. Corresponding to the patient's balance of humor, therapy consisted of blood-letting, laxatives and/or diet. This theory continued to be a common belief until the 19th century that began the identification and classification of cells and microorganisms.

The Roman physician, Celsus (28-50 BC), later altered the Greek term "carcinos" into "cancer" and is a Latin word for crab. Galen (130-200 AD) was another Roman physician, who selected the name "oncos" which is a Greek word for the swelling that describes some tumors. The crab resemblance of Hippocrates and Celsus continues to be an illustration for malignant growths and Galen's word applies to modern day cancer specialists, oncologists. An abundance of black bile in different body localities was thought to produce the disease. The belief in the humor theory of cancer carried on throughout the Roman and Middle ages for over 1300 years, and Galen embraced this theory in his medical teachings. The continued ban of the surgical exploration of the body before and after death, for religious reasons, restricted the advancement of medical information.

Beginning in the 15th century, experts accumulated a greater understanding of the human body and scientists like Galileo and Newton began to apply the scientific method. The German teacher Wilhelm Fabry thought that a milk clot in a mammary duct precipitated breast cancer. The Dutch professor Francois de la Boe Sylvius assumed that all disease was the result of a chemical process and that acidic lymph fluid was linked to the illness. His contemporary, Nicolaes Tulp supported the evidence that the cancer was a toxin that gradually spread and had the ability to transfer from person to person. Human dissections became more acceptable in the 17th and 18th century, as Giovanni Morgagni (1761), performed autopsies to associate the disease process to pathologic understanding, thus, setting the groundwork for experimental oncology. A leading Scottish surgeon John Hunter (1728–1793) inferred that a few cancers might be cured by surgery and claimed that if the tumor had not attacked nearby tissue and was moveable then there was no reason to remove the growth. A hundred years later the discovery of anesthesia permitted surgeries to increase and cancer operations, such as the radical mastectomy became well-known treatments. With the extensive application of the microscope in the 18th century, the idea that the "cancer poison" ultimately spreads from the original tumor through the lymph nodes to other areas in the body became popularly known as "metastasis".

In the 19th century, asepsis enhanced surgical cleanliness and as survival statistics improved, surgical extraction of the tumor became the primary treatment. During the same period, the belief that the body was composed of different tissues that included millions of cells placed rest to the humor theory beliefs about fluid irregularities causing disease. Marie Curie and Pierre Curies' discovery of radiation brought about the earliest most useful non-surgical cancer procedure and also became the starting point of using multi-disciplinary approaches to treatment. The surgeon was no longer functioning in isolation but acted collectively with hospital radiologists. The difficulties related to communication along with the requirement that treatment be in the hospital led to a means of organizing data that established analytical case research.

The genetic evidence relating to cancer was observed in 1902 by Theodor Boveri, professor of zoology in Würzburg Germany, who discovered the physical process of how the body produces cells with many copies. He hypothesized that chromosomes carried separate inheritance factors and that mutations could create a cell with endless growth potential that may be transferred onto descendants. By the midpoint of the 20th century, scientists had the tools they required to operate on the complex puzzles of chemistry and biology. James Watson and Francis Crick earned a Nobel Prize in 1962 for their work on the precise chemical composition of DNA, the fundamental substance in genes. DNA is the foundation of the genetic code that delivers commands to all cells and after discovering how to decipher this code, researchers were able to learn how genes operate and in what way they could be damaged by mutations. The modern techniques of biology and chemistry solved many perplexing mysteries. As the knowledge of genes and DNA accumulated, researchers determined that it was an injury to DNA by radiation, chemicals, or the initiation of new DNA chains by viruses that frequently led to the production of cancer growth. It was then possible to pinpoint the exact place of the damage on a particular gene. Scientists noticed that at times, imperfect genes are inherited, and they are defective at the identical spot in which the chemicals exert their influence. For instance, most of the circumstances that create cancer (carcinogens) produce genetic harm (mutations) that resemble the mutations that were inherited and would result in the same types of cancer (Feinberg & Tycko, 2004). It did not matter how the first mutation (genetic or spontaneous) began, the cells that arose from these mutations led to many copies of abnormal cells called clones. The mutant clones over time have multiplication abilities and the cancer progresses. The significant distinction between normal tissue and cancer is that normal cells with injured DNA die and cancer cells multiply.

Researchers continue to believe that cancers are induced by physical or chemical injuries, radiation, or pathogenic organisms. Medical specialists are identifying the oncogenes that motivate cells to reproduce out of control and the tumor suppressor genes which are healthy genes that reduce cell division. Scientists are also investing how to repair DNA mistakes, and how to command abnormal cells to die. Cancer associated with heredity is lower than 15%, however, it is essential to understand these cancers because the medical profession may be capable of identifying the people at exceptionally high risk. Once scientists identify the impact of the genetic variations they can start to develop targeted treatments or drugs to master the outcomes in tumor suppressor genes and oncogenes (Feinberg & Tycko, 2004).

The American Cancer Society was established in 1913 by physicians and businessmen under the title American Society for the Control of Cancer and the contemporary title was selected in 1945. The federal "war" on cancer originated with the National Cancer Act of 1971, a United States national law. The document was designed to improve the Public Health Service Act to strengthen the National Cancer Institute to more efficiently carry out the public's desire in finding a cure for cancer. Since 1971, America has spent over 200 billion dollars on cancer research and despite this large investment, the nation has observed only a five percent reduction in the cancer death rates between 1950 and 2005. Longer life expectancy may be a relevant factor because cancer and diagnosis rates rise significantly with age and more than three out of five people with this diagnosis are over the age of 65 (Mandel, 2014).

The Cancer Stigma

Historically this disease was profoundly stigmatized from the belief that a behavior or personality style could induce the disease which was considered to be a punishment from God. Even in today's modern times individuals diagnosed with cancer often feel doomed and many believe their illness is a symbol of personal vulnerability. People having these false beliefs often hold back information or delay treatment which further conceals the problem. One of the primary hurdles to diagnosis and treatment continues to be this stigma, or a "what will the neighbors think attitude" that some assign to cancer. Professionals of all health disciplines have lessened the stereotype considerably in the past fifty years, but this concern continues to be a hurdle that can lead to late diagnosis and treatment.

Cancer patients are at high risk for suffering from feelings of guilt and shame, often having ways of coping that involves avoidance and denial. This is understandable because those diagnosed have to expose themselves to the physical and mental judgments and treatments of physicians, caregivers, society, friends and family. The word "malignant" raises alarm in all because the condition in itself is offensive. Complications, as well as treatments, are often disfiguring and obituaries explain about the "battle" in which the patients lose. People who are sick are afraid of the blame from others for developing an illness that associates with how they manage emotions, or because of what they eat, inhale, drink or weigh.

As the reader flips through these pages, concentrate on a few details: Is there a health psychology connection? How do professionals blend detailed medical knowledge with health psychology beliefs that will serve in the prevention and treatment of Cancer? How can society profit from employing health psychology methods that accept a biological, psychological and sociological approach strategy.

Cancers relationship to The Immune System

The immune system is a collection of organs that have specialized cells that produce substances to assist in shielding people from some diseases and infections. These immune substances and the distinct cells travel through the body defending it from the pathogens that produce illnesses. Viruses, bacteria, and parasites are unfriendly alien troops that are not usually located in the body and they strive to attack to carry out their individual desires, which injure people in the process. Physicians frequently apply the term foreign to portray invading pathogens not usually detected and the immune system is the body's defense team. It aids in keeping invading bacteria away, or helps eliminate them if they do penetrate the boundary. Pathogens such as viruses, bacteria and pathogens, have substances on their exterior surfaces, such as proteins that are not usually detected. The immune system views these alien substances as being antigens which are substances that cause an immune system attack. The National Cancer Institute states that, in some ways, the immune system helps shield from cancer because these cells are different from healthy cells, often having unusual substances on their external surfaces which can behave like antigens. The immune system acts by maintaining a record of all substances in the body and every new substance that it cannot identify will send forth a warning, prompting the system to engage. This response begins the process of extinction of anything carrying the antigen, such as bacteria or cancer cells.

The cells and organs that makeup the body's immune system form a defense shield against foreign invaders like bacteria, viruses, and receiving something as common as a snagging a splinter from a piece of wood. These distinct cells guard and protect the body equal to the gladiators of Rome, and they may respond to invaders by calling for backup from other cells to attack and kill. The immune system has the capacity to understand the difference between one of the body's own cells and cells from a foreign invader, and the mission is to defend against attacks. A healthy immune system can easily and efficiently locate a foreign body. When it pertains to cancer, a cell that is dividing abnormally and showing other unusual signs should be identified just like any other foreign cell. In theory, a healthy immune system should destroy cancerous cells before they divide, multiply and overwhelm the organ because everyone has cancer cells swirling about in the body at times, and yet not everyone develops cancer. When cells do not divide into a tumor, it is because they are spreading in a clumsy, inefficient fashion making them easily defeated by a strong, organized, well nourished, and rested army of immune cells. At other times, the cancer cells are stronger and more organized than the immune systems' response cells and they avoid being destroyed.

The immune system identifies cancer in several different forms. Immune cells, called natural killer cells have a unique skill in finding cells that might be contaminated with a virus, bacteria and are pre-cancerous because they look unhealthy. The body's natural killer cells are the Macrophages, Dendritic cells, T cells, and Lymphocytes which are the specialized cells of the immune system protecting from foreign invasion. The natural killer cells then proceed onto euthanizing foreign invaders. Another approach is one in which the immune system identifies a cancerous cell by scanning for proteins that would not be normally located on the surface of a healthy cell. Try imagining someone with a cut on their arm that is bleeding, most people would agree that something is wrong because blood is not usually found on the outside of a person and something is amiss. It is in this fashion that the lymphocytes operate as they assess the cells, and when they detect a protein that should not be on the surface, they recognize that something is wrong and advance to attack. The immune systems killer cells then either transmit chemical instructions to different immune cells to remove the cancerous cell or they destroy all attackers.

However, the problem is that the immune system does not always recognize cancer cells as being foreign invaders. Therefore, cancer as with other diseases may arise when the immune system breaks down and does not function properly in the presence of foreign invaders. As cancerous cells divide, they can acquire features that hide or defend themselves from the immune system's identification. Cancer cells can mix up the signals between immune cells and they send out their own messages just to confuse, preventing the immune system from responding effectively. In other words, cancer cells are very intelligent. The immune system is more reliable at identifying and striking germs because they are vastly different from regular human cells and are quickly recognized as foreign, but cancer cells and healthy cells have fewer distinct discrepancies. On this account, the immune system may not regularly distinguish cancer cells as being foreign because cancer cells are less like the fighters of invading troops and more like spies within the human cell community.

At one time, experts thought Cancer was simply an immune deficiency disease, explaining further that, for someone to develop cancer the immune system had to be ineffective which in turn enables the cells to evolve, mature, divide and spread. Scientists now understand that the progression of cancer is not merely the effect of a weakened immune system because the natural ability to resist cancer has limits, but, countless people with healthy immune systems still develop cancer. The immune system may not identify the cancer cells as being different on account of the cancer cells (and their antigens) not being different enough from those of healthy cells (Dzivenu, Phil, & O'Donnell-Tormey, 2003). At other times, this system identifies the abnormal cells, but the reply may not be robust enough to destroy the cancer. The cancer cells may send off substances that keep the immune system in balance and to overcome the process scientists are attempting to create ways to support the immune system's ability to recognize abnormal cells, hoping to stimulate a response that will eliminate the cancer.

69

Stress and the Immune system

Psychologists have undertaken the examination of the emotional and behavioral features of those diagnosed with cancer. Health psychology has also played a fundamental role in discussing prevention, diagnosis, treatment, rehabilitation, recurrence, along with focusing on the impacts of death and dying. More than a few suggest that these interventions directly improve the psychological status of cancer patients which may at times have some effect on disease outcome. Future investigations will likely question the generalizability of data in setting down common principles of people being able to adjust to the diagnosis and treatment. Many scientists are investigating the role stress has in inducing carcinoma and there are many differing views stirring up controversy. Most people recognize that they are more prone to getting sick if experiencing anxiety, one common example is a student who catches a cold during final exams. These researchers believe that the stress reduces the body's immune system abilities. Anxiety inducing chemicals like adrenaline and cortisol have effects on the functioning of the nervous, endocrine and immune systems. Multiple researchers think that adrenaline and cortisol stifle the natural killer cells ability to assess for abnormal cells. This suppression allows people to become more receptive to viral infections and immune system dysfunction (Reiche, Nunes & Morimoto, 2004).

The release of cortisol and adrenaline in response to physical and emotional stress seems to reduce immune cell function, which may impact the growth of tumors. Noradrenaline is also delivered in response to stress and investigations have shown that noradrenaline influences cancerous cell growth in some animal models. However, research has yet to associate this conclusion in humans to parts of the immune and central nervous system that regulate anxiety, and this area certainly warrants additional investigation. Psychological stress has not been proven to provoke cancer, but emotional strain that persists for a long time will affect overall health and one's ability to cope with the diagnosis. People who are better at managing anxiety have a happier, healthier quality of life while they are enduring treatment for cancer, however, this does not necessarily correlate with surviving longer. A few investigations have shown a connection between multiple psychological factors and a heightened chance of acquiring and surviving cancer, but others have not shown any connection. Possible links between emotional tension and cancer could begin in many ways and be multifactorial. People experiencing stress may have habits, such as sun bathing, drinking alcohol, or smoking, which increase the risk for developing cancer. Someone who has a relative with cancer may have a greater risk, because of acquired inheritability, not because of anxiety related life stressors.

Overall, the research on the linkage between the biological response to stress and tumor growth reveals a questionable picture and there is an obvious call for additional research to further assess this relationship. One study considered the incidence of cancer in women and measured stress levels for five years prior to diagnosis and found no correlation between stress level and cancer, therefore, stress may not directly influence an increased risk of developing cancer. However, once there is a confirmation of cancer there are several studies confirming that a lower stress level will at least improve the patients' ability to problem solve, decrease anxiety, decrease depression and improves the quality of life for all concerned (Strickland, 2001).

Ways to improve or maintain a healthy immune system

1. <u>Get plenty of rest:</u> Sleep aids the body to reboot hormone levels, decreases blood pressure, and allows the body time to recover and restore any damage. Restful sleep promotes

the various immune cells guard against foreign invaders. (American Society for Cell Biology, 2013)

2. <u>Wear sunscreen:</u> UV radiation caused by the sun can cause breaks in the DNA of the body's cells and these breaks lead to mistakes in cell cycle production that can result in manufacturing precancerous cells. Therefore, it is a good idea to make sunscreen a part of the daily routine (Farmer & Naylor, 1996).

3. <u>Maintain a healthy diet:</u> The food's people consume have remarkably potent impacts on physical health. Foods including antioxidants are skillful at eliminating free radicals, which can occur from substances like UV radiation. If left unaided, free radicals can produce DNA injury. This DNA damage can begin an error in cell cycle development and raise precancerous cells. Discovering the distinctions between what to eat and what not to eat is crucial for sustaining health (National Cancer Institute).

4. <u>Vaccinations:</u> When the body encounters a new germ, it might take two to four weeks to launch a strong immune response. However, when the immune system identifies the germs features, it starts mounting a defense in less than two days hoping that people will experience symptoms for a shorter period of time. Vaccines improve the immune systems functioning by giving the body a sneak preview or representation of the pathogen such as the measles or polio virus.

5. <u>No tobacco or toxic inhalants:</u> The lungs are the primary line of protection against airborne pathogens. This mucosal immunity involves a system of cells and antibodies which clear away inhaled bacteria. Smoke and some inhalants suppress the role of the immune system causing people to be more susceptible to inflammation, infection and injury.

Emotional Stress and Cancer Recovery

Countless patients, family members and friends have over-heard or observed a sick person given the advice "What will help is that you remain positive". This general recommendation is currently under serious scientific scrutiny. The discussion about the degree to which mental processes can directly affect physical health has undergone significant recognition.

There is an intricate relationship between how people view their life events, stress levels and disease. Emotional experiences, stress levels and outlooks on living have some foundation in brain chemistry and life science, and it appears that stressful thoughts or perceptions may then have at least some impact on physical health. A clear example is when people feel anxious, they experience muscle tension, increased heart rate, increased sweating and at times this leads to an increase in blood pressure. Although much more research is necessary, there continues to appear to be a clear association between the body, mind and the brain in terms of maintaining physical health.

People who have cancer will find the emotional, physical, and social influences of the illness to be stressful. Those who manage this anxiety with risky practices such as smoking, drinking alcohol, or becoming sedentary most likely will have a reduced quality of life during and after cancer treatment. In opposition, people who are able to use tactics to cope with tension, such as relaxation, yoga and meditation exercises have lower levels of sadness, fear, and symptoms associated to the diagnosis and cancer treatments. Even though there is no firm indication that a stress directly influences cancer outcomes, some data does imply that people can acquire a sense of helplessness and hopelessness when tension becomes overpowering. This hopelessness, helplessness feeling has an association with higher incidences of death, although the mechanism for understanding this is unclear. It may be that people who feel hopeless or helpless do not search for treatment when they notice symptoms, give up too early, fail to adhere to potentially effective treatment, employ risky practices such as drug use, or do not have a healthy lifestyle, ending in untimely death.

Today, the strength of the relationship between thoughts and developing diseases such as cancer cannot yet be determined and correlation is not is this case causation. Psychological interventions to reduce negative thinking and decrease anxiety levels are useful for mental health, improving quality of life and reduce symptoms of anxiety and depression (Zimmermann, Riechelmann , Krzyzanowska, Rodin & Tannock, 2008).

How cancer patients can cope with emotional stress

Many experts advise that all cancer sufferers be evaluated for distress early in the sequence of treatment. A number also recommend re-screening at critical times along the progression of care. Health care providers can utilize a variety of screening instruments, such as a distress measure or questionnaire, to evaluate whether cancer patients need support to manage emotions or with other practical matters. People who exhibit moderate to severe discomfort are then referred to a clinical health psychologist, social worker, chaplain, or psychiatrist. Emotional and social support can assist in discovering new ways to cope with emotional tension. Such assistance can reduce levels of sadness, anxiety, and disease treatment-related symptoms. Suggestions include:

1. Exercise

2. Educational cancer lectures

3. Social support in a group setting

4. Medications for anxiety or depression

5. Psychotherapy, counseling or talk therapy
6. Training in stress management, meditation or relaxation

Conclusion

The human body creates millions of cells every day and occasionally for no purpose at all a mistake is made that gives rise to the production of a precancerous cell. There are many mental health topics that bubble up to the surface when cancer has been diagnosed and fortunately, scientists and medical doctors are making progress in the area of oncology and cancer research every day. The more people read about cancer, the immune system response and how thoughts and emotions affect physical health the less mysterious and scary the cancer diagnosis will become. This is the health psychology relationship. It is possible to combine accurate medical information with health psychology techniques to assist in the prevention and treatment of those afflicted. In conclusion, loved ones and our entire society can benefit from utilizing health psychology principles by applying a biological, psychological and sociological approach strategy.

Chapter 4
The Epidemic of Diabetes Type 2

Historically, this serious chronic disease concerned people of low-income groups and professionals thought the causes were due to poor environmental conditions in association with food consumption. Experts recognize that poor nutrition and a sedentary lifestyle are primary causes of obesity and Type 2 Diabetes; however, the rise in statistics is no longer associated with a lower income bracket, representing a cultural shift in terms of how society psychologically views healthy eating habits. The danger is that few people are aware of the reality that diabetes is a condition that cannot be managed by prescriptions alone, because lifestyle changes are a requirement to prevent complications. The typical causes of Type 2 Diabetes involve obesity due to inactivity and/or toxic diets. The appearance of this medical condition significantly alters a person's life and this epidemic cries for regular exercise, maintaining a healthy body weight, proper nutrition, and avoiding smoking to reduce or stop the spread.

According to the World Health Organization (WHO) one in ten adults has diabetes. The American Diabetes Association declare that there are over 25 million people who have this diagnosis in the US, and almost a third are not aware of the fact that they may have had the ailment for several years. Diabetes is the seventh most common cause of death and the leading cause of blindness in the United States. In 2004, more than 3.4 million people died in the world from complications with the expectation that this figure will double before 2030. The prevailing form of diabetes experienced by over 85 percent of the population is Type 2, a condition in which the body has to cope with resistance to, or insufficiency of, insulin.

History of Diabetes

Sushruta was a chief Indian surgeon living during 600 B.C. who composed The Sushruta Samhita, a Sanskrit document on surgery that includes the history of the 3rd and 4th centuries. Sushruta was an Indian healer who identified diabetes, labeling the disease "Madhumeha," signifying honey indicating sweet urine. The disease was one of the first conditions written in this Egyptian document listing symptoms relating to "too great emptying of the urine," and these early Indians tested for diabetes by watching to see if ants were drawn to a sufferer's urine. This manuscript is one of three foundational documents of Ayurveda or Indian traditional medicines including 184 chapters, classification of 1120 ailments, 700 healing plants, 64 mixtures from mineral origins and 57 helpful treatment compounds from animal sources. The first detailed cases describe Type 1 Diabetes, although Type 2 was categorized as a separate ailment, distinguishing Type 1 with youth and Type 2 with being overweight. The ancient Chinese, Korean, and Japanese terms for diabetes have their basis on equivalent characteristics indicating "sugar urine disease" (Tattersall, 2009).

Apollonius Memphites was a physician, born in Egypt, lived around the 3rd century BC, and wrote a book on the names of the parts of the human body in which the authorities gave him credit for coining the term diabetes. The name "diabetes" implies "to pass through" or "siphon" was first described in 230 by this Greek, Appollonius of Memphis. Aretaeus is another well-known Classical Greek physician, whose life few people can identify many details. There is conjecture considering his country and age, but it appears likely that Aretaeus practiced in the 1st century. He wrote in Classical Greek a comprehensive book on physical conditions, and this valuable publication exhibits high precision in the specification of symptoms to understand the distinguishing characteristics of the disease. Aretaeus supported the rules of Hippocrates, though gave less regard to "the physical actions" of the material body and, counter to the work of Hippocrates, he did not hesitate to attempt to offset them, when symptoms appeared to be serious. Aretaeus freely prescribed laxatives and purges, did not oppose narcotics and had fewer objections to practicing bleeding techniques. Hippocrates, the Father of Medicine, gives no report of the illness, which may symbolize that he may have thought the disease was hopeless since Diabetes Mellitus was a death decree in classical times. Aretaeus did strive to control symptoms, yet could not offer a favorable prognosis mentioning "life is short, disgusting and painful." Diabetes must have occurred rarely during the time of the Roman Empire as the physician Galen notes only recognizing two occurrences in his career.

Avicenna (980-1037) was a Persian, who died in Iran, lived as a Muslim physician and was a prominent philosopher-scientist of the Islamic world. He is recognized for his advancements in the areas of Aristotelian medicine and philosophy. Avicenna composed the Book of the Cure, a comprehensive philosophical and scientific encyclopedia and The Canon of Medicine, which is among the several influential works entered in the annals of medicine. Avicenna was the first to report Diabetes Insipidus very precisely and like Aretaeus before him distinguished Type 1 and Type 2 Diabetes. He explained the presence of sufferers having an unusual appetite, deterioration of sexual abilities along with the presence of producing sweet smelling urine and additionally described diabetic gangrene. Aretaeus treatment for diabetes was prescribing a blend of lupine, trigonella and zedoary seed which generated a notable decrease in the removal of sugar (Tattersall, 2009).

In the year 1425, the Diabetes diagnosis was first recorded in an English medical text and is the shortened description of the full version Diabetes Mellitus (Type 1). The thoughts and idea's descends from the Greek word diabetes, which indicates to pass through, or siphon and the Latin word mellitus meaning sweet or sugary that is a consequence from excess sugar noted in serum as well as in patients' urine. Thomas Willis in 1625 added the name "'mellitus'" in the late 1600s to isolate the disease from Diabetes Insipidus (Type II), included the symptom of frequent urination.

Discovery of the role of the pancreas

Sushruta, Arataeus, and Thomas Willis were the ancient explorers of the treatment of diabetes. Greek practitioners dictated exercise to relieve excess urination and a few unusual types of treatment included drinking wine, eating to counterbalance for loss of fluid weight and starvation diets. The medical practitioners' of the 1700's listed Diabetes as denoting "the pissing evil." In 1776, Matthew Dobson verified that the sweet taste of urine was caused by excess sugar in the urine and blood. In 1889, Joseph von Mering and Oskar Minkowski identified the role of the pancreas, and noted that dogs whose pancreas was removed had all the signs of diabetes and died quickly. Even though diabetes has been recognized since ancient times, and remedies of different effectiveness have been understood in many countries since the Middle Ages, the physical mechanisms of what develops into diabetes has only been known since the early 1900's. In 1910, Sir Edward Albert Sharpey-Schafer discovered that diabetes results from a deficiency of insulin. He termed the substance regulating blood sugar insulin from the Latin "insula," meaning island and connected this to the insulin-producing islets of Langerhans in the pancreas.

Discovery of insulin

In 1921 Sir Frederick Banting and Charles Best replicated Von Mering and Minkowski, and, proceeded to prove that they could reverse provoked diabetes in dogs, by providing them a concentrate from the pancreatic Islets of Langerhans taken from healthy dogs. In 1922, at the University of Toronto, Banting, Best, and their chemist associate Collip refined the hormone insulin from pancreases of cows which began an effective treatment and made the patent available free of charge so all diabetics worldwide could benefit from the medicine. In 1922, Leonard Thompson age 14 was a charity case who became the first person to receive an injection of insulin to manage his diabetes, and survived 13 years before dying of pneumonia at the age 27.

In 1980, the U.S. biotech corporation Genentech formulated biosynthetic human insulin. The insulin was isolated from genetically modified bacteria, which contain the human gene for manufacturing synthetic human insulin which could produce large quantities. Originally this discovery was not judged by the medical profession as being a clinically significant development. Nevertheless, by 1996, the origins of insulin equivalents had enhanced absorption, distribution, metabolism, and excretion properties of Diabetics that were based on this new biotechnology and were indeed clinically meaningful (Tibaldi, 2012).

Diagnosis of US Diabetic Statistics from 1980 through 2011

1. 0–44 yrs. Percentage of people with diagnosis increased 167% (from 0.6% to 1.6%)

2. 45–64 yrs. Percentage of people with diagnosis increased 118% (from 5.5% to 12.0%)

3. 65–74 yrs. Percentage of people with diagnosis increased 140% (from 9.1% to 21.8%)

4. Above 75 yrs. Percentage of people with diagnosis increased 125% (from 8.9% to 20.0%)

In 2011, the percentage of diagnosed diabetics among people aged 65–74 was more than 13 times that of people younger than 45 years of age. Throughout this time period, the percentage of people with diagnosed diabetes increased drastically among all age groups (Centers for Disease Control and Prevention, 2012).

The Two Types of Diabetes

Type 1. The National Institute of Diabetes and Digestive and Kidney Diseases states that this type is an autoimmune disease in which the immune system damages beta cells in the pancreas that produce insulin. Insulin is a hormone that is vital for transferring sugar and several other nutrients from the blood to other body cells. All cells require sugars and other nutrients to allow the body to function properly. Type 1 Diabetes ordinarily affects young people, but can take place at any time in life. Along with genetic factors, experts now conclude that a virus or toxin may cause the immune system to begin destroying these insulin-making cells.

Type 2 is by far more prevalent than Type 1 and approximately 90 percent of Diabetic sufferers today are of this kind. Symptoms and indications occur later in life, and the causes are due to the pancreas not manufacturing enough insulin, or the body does not use insulin efficiently (insulin resistance). The physiological outcomes are the same as with Type 1 Diabetes because sugar and other nutrients accumulate in the blood instead of being transported into the cells. The accumulation of glucose (sugar) in the blood affects the entire body causing long-term severe consequences. An increase in urination may lead to dehydration and pressure on the kidneys, and severe dehydration is a precursor to someone going into a diabetic Coma. Persistent high levels of blood sugar can affect the eyes, heart, small blood vessels and kidneys: All of which makes the sufferer vulnerable to infections, strokes and heart disease.

In order to cope and avoid complications, the diabetic must avoid prolonged periods of high blood glucose levels (hyperglycemia) and also periods of low blood glucose levels (hypoglycemia). To balance these two extremes, a diabetic needs to monitor and manage their blood sugar levels on a routine basis or confront a multitude of side effects and unpleasant complications if glucose levels are not under satisfactory control. There are two ways to maintain a physically fit body and two ways to prevent diabetes, introducing an exercise program along with following a healthy dietary regimen (Diabetes Prevention Program Research Group, 2012).

Type 2 Diabetes and Obesity

Approximately 90 per cent of people diagnosed with Type II Diabetes are also overweight. This excess weight influences the ability to manage blood glucose levels that can cause the body to become resistant to insulin. On account of this insulin resistance overweight people who do not have diabetes are at extremely high risk. The Cell Metabolism journal published in the July 2009 issue findings from Matthew Watt, Associate Professor from the Monash University discuss a new protein that ultimately explores the relationship between obesity and diabetes. According to this study, fat cells release a protein, which desensitizes muscles and the liver to insulin causing the pancreas to produce more insulin to counteract this effect. The overworked pancreas eventually slows the production of insulin, causing Type 2 Diabetes. Professor Watt explains his excitement about the potentials for counteracting this effect with new medications, but the writers for the medical journal believe that treating Diabetes Type 2 with drugs is the wrong approach. In their June 2010 issue, Lancet writers call the epidemics of Obesity and Type 2 diabetes "a public health humiliation." They call this chronic illness a "mostly preventable disease," which requires changes in lifestyle and nutrition, claiming that by treating diabetes with medications, "the medicine might be winning the battle of glucose control, but it is losing the war against diabetes."

The New England Journal of Medicine diabetes prevention program research group (2002) discovered that as little as a 7% weight loss can cause a 58% reduction in the risk of developing diabetes. They are asserting that lowering weight in the pre-diabetic stage, by only 7% can diminish the possibilities of acquiring Type 2 Diabetes by over fifty percent. For example, a 200 pound overweight person will reduce their chances of getting Diabetes Type 2 if they lose fourteen pounds. Changing the ways in which people cope and how to manage an illness is the health psychology relationship.

Detecting the early onset of Type 2 Diabetes can be difficult because signs are so mild that many people do not notice them, and some may not even be aware of the fact that they have an illness. Mild symptoms, such as increased thirst, hunger, blurred vision, frequent urination, weight gain, tingling in feet, are often easy to ignore, but prolonged accumulation of sugar in the blood can ultimately be life-threatening.

Complications of Diabetes

1. Eye Damage is often the first problem. Damage to the small blood vessels of the retina can lead to an increased risk of developing cataracts, glaucoma, and blindness.

2. Nerve Damage: Accumulation of sugar in the blood can damage the walls of the small blood vessels that feed nerves, particularly in the legs. The first symptoms are tingling, numbness and pain at the tips of the toes or fingers.

If untreated, this can cause loss of awareness of feeling in the limbs.

3. Foot Infections due to poor blood circulation in the feet increases the risk of various complications because simple cuts can become seriously infected, and if left untreated, may require amputation.

4. Cardiovascular Problems: Diabetes increases the risk of heart attack, coronary artery disease, stroke, atherosclerosis and high blood pressure.

5. Kidney Damage: Pressure from frequent urination due to dehydration and damage to the small blood vessels in kidneys can lead to kidney failure or kidney disease, treatable only with dialysis or a kidney transplant.

6. Osteoporosis, Alzheimer's' disease, skin problems and many other health issues can be affected by diabetes, if left untreated.

Psychology, Psychopathology and Diabetes

The value of psychology increases because it is essential for a diabetic to make fast and radical modifications to their lifestyle. Virtually overnight a diabetic may move from a sedentary lifestyle of consuming junk food and watching TV, to having to consume regular healthy meals, exercise routinely as well as monitor blood sugar levels. This rapid change in lifestyle can generate many problems for diabetics. Mood and stress disturbances are most prevalent and occur often in patients with diabetes than in the overall U.S. population (Lustman, Clouse, Alrakawi, Rubin & Gelenberg, 1997). Roughly one-third of sufferers have psychological difficulties at some period during their life. These disturbances can affect inadequate glycemic control through changes in neurotransmitter and neuro-hormonal functioning and cause disruption in self-care. Major depression affects approximately one out of every five patients with diabetes and critically reduces the quality of life and influences all phases of daily functioning.

Depression has significance because of its association with treatment noncompliance, inadequate glycemic control and increases the chance for micro – and macro-vascular illness disease. Depression continues to be unrecognized and untreated in the majority of cases despite its connection to diabetes. Greater levels of depression correlate with many health practices and beliefs, in particular less physical activity and a belief that people do not have the ability to change dietary practices. Depressive signs also relate to clinical risk factors, such as having a higher BMI and higher fasting insulin levels (Lustman, Griffith & Clouse, 1997).

One in every four diabetic patients suffers from reappearing difficulties with anxiety, and some may have an eating disorder. These ailments respond favorably to psychological treatment, and in countless instances, relief of suffering correlates with enhanced glycemic control. A separate field of concern is the rising amount of documented eating disturbances among people with diabetes (Harris & Lustman, 1998). Whether these problems are more common in diabetics compared to the general population continues to be under investigation. Despite these findings eating disorders are clinically relevant because of the connection with inadequate glycemic control and an increased risk for complications. Eating disorders can be adequately managed with psychotherapy; unfortunately, both eating disorders and depression tend to be repetitive requiring repeated treatment.

Shifting social views and implementing a lifestyle modification is a challenging goal for many nations and a relentless worldwide crusade advocating the importance of maintaining a healthy lifestyle should be executed. This campaign will entail viewing obesity as a manifestation of a problem that does not just associate with physical appearance. Therapy should be incorporated into the treatment of diabetics because this is one condition that can be avoided by shifting cultural views and implementing healthy lifestyle decisions. The majority of diabetic treatment is self-care, and there can be severe problems if a person does not have the motivation, as the habits needed to control blood sugar levels to curb the progression can be very complicated. Physical health can degenerate resulting in blindness or the amputation of limbs, and it is crucial for doctors to employ health psychologists to help the patient recognize the seriousness of the disease.

While there are several dietary regimes advertised that promote being "diabetes-fighting," to prevent the assault of Type 2 Diabetes experts recommend following a healthy food plan. This schedule should incorporate a diet abundant in vegetables, fruits, grains and fiber, coupled with consistent exercise. People who already have the illness might require a more individualized food program depending on other difficulties they have as a result of the ailment. For a generic guideline, nutritionists promote a diet that is low in calories, high in different complex carbohydrates (beans, vegetables, fruits and whole grains), low in saturated fats (stay away from cheese, butter and fatty meat) and high in monounsaturated and polyunsaturated fat (use olive oil.). This is no great wonder as this is the identical diet suggested for sustaining a healthy weight.

The Role of the Psychologist in Diabetes Care

Seven of the ten leading causes of death in the United States link with practices of overeating, using tobacco, and extreme alcohol consumption. Emotional difficulties (stress, depression) also have unfavorable impacts on many physical conditions via a variety of physiological and behavioral pathways. The importance of the mental health professional in the management of medically unhealthy individuals has expanded with the collection of data associating health and behavior. Health psychologists intervene to promote healthy behaviors, eliminate unhealthful habits and to alleviate emotional suffering in patients with obvious psychopathology. The psychologist furnishes personal services to the diabetic via assisting in the development of health behaviors and therapy for emotional difficulties, and further gives consultation to the medical team in what ways to combine psychological principles into the patient's treatment plan to improve clinical results.

Despite the widespread opinion, that the life of a diabetic is not all that challenging only those who have the ailment understand the everyday problems associated with the regular monitoring of their food intake and fitness levels. The world of a diabetic requires following a daily system of monitoring insulin levels and consuming medicine along with following a diet and exercise. That demands fortitude and motivation on the part of the sufferer. So a complex plan of self-care management needs to be reinforced rigorously, and psychologists can support diabetics in adhering to the regimen. Common everyday difficulties, adverse life situations and the added strains of coping with diabetes cause tension. Stress may have primary influences on fitness via high blood glucose values and incidental impacts on health via interruption in behavioral patterns and habits (sleeping and eating). The psychologist can be a helpful source in recognizing maladaptive responses to stress including encouraging sufferers to acquire more beneficial and efficient techniques related to coping. Treating diabetic patients with counseling has not been an accepted approach by the medical specialists administering care, although this position has been shifting as physicians begin to recognize that the everyday world of a diabetic improves with therapy.

Psychologists can perform a vital role in assisting people learning ways of managing the diabetes and help them become more comfortable with the prescribed precautions. Studies confirm that cognitive behavior therapies along with behavioral interventions are effective methods in increasing the ability of diabetics to regulate stress. Diminishing anxiety and depression are crucial to ensure a desirable quality of life while living with diabetes. Psychological intervention encourages diabetics to keep motivated to preserve emotional and physical health. Diabetes treatment co-existing with counseling should be considered complementary treatments because with the aid of therapy the life of a diabetic can be drastically improved thereby preventing complications.

The Health Psychologists role in treating Diabetes

1. Promote adherence to the diabetes treatment process (blood sugar monitoring)

2. Support pro-diabetic coping behaviors (exercise and diet).

3. If required refer to a psychiatrist for medication assessment.

4. Provide assistance to any emotional discomfort associated with the illness.

5. Increase family education, communication and problem solving abilities.

6. Stifle high-risk health behaviors (high fat intake, alcohol consumption, smoking)

7. Assess and manage psychopathology, especially associated with anxiety, eating disorders and depression.

Health psychologists are a suitable addition to the treatment team for the assessment, diagnosis and treatment of emotional health difficulties associated with the illness. Clinicians with expertise in motivational approaches, cognitive learning theories, and behavior change principles are extremely beneficial given the value of having these abilities will promote wellness practices. While not all psychologists are aware of how to treat diabetes, it is the recommendation that clinical psychologists working with diabetic patients have training in health psychology.

Diabetes Prevention

Millions of Americans are at high risk for diabetes, a severe and expensive condition that has attained epidemic dimensions. The positive message is that diabetes Type 2 can be prevented and managed successfully in one's life. Most of the food people consume changes into glucose, or sugar for the body to use for energy. The pancreatic cells produce insulin to assist glucose to move into the cells of the body, and with diabetes, the body does not create adequate insulin or cannot utilize insulin efficiently which causes glucose to increase in the bloodstream. Diabetes can be dangerous, but living a more active life and making proper food selections can significantly inhibit or even prevent this disease from developing. Prevention is as plain as increasing physical activity, dropping the excess weight and consuming healthy food. Developing a few modest health practices and making adjustments in lifestyle will avoid the grim health difficulties associated with this condition, and it is not ever too late to begin. Here are a few recommendations from The American Diabetes Association.

Diabetic Prevention Tips

1. Eat Healthy: Eat extra fresh vegetables, fruits, and whole grains. Purchase leaner meats (chicken, turkey, lean cuts of pork or beef) and lower fat dairy products (low-fat, skim milk and yogurt). Buy whole grain breads and cereals. Reduce soda, sweets and chips.

2. Boost Physical Activity: Helps maintain and keep blood glucose, blood pressure, HDL cholesterol and triglycerides on target. Activity lowers the risk for pre-diabetes, type

2 diabetes, heart disease and stroke along with reducing stress.

3. <u>If Overweight Lose those Extra pounds:</u> Being overweight increases your risk for Type 2 diabetes, heart disease and stroke. Being overweight can create other physical illnesses, like high blood pressure, unhealthy cholesterol, and high blood glucose (sugar). Losing weight can help prevent and manage these problems and people do not have to lose much weight as 10-15 pounds can make a significant difference.

4. <u>Family History:</u> Anyone can develop diabetes; however, a physician can determine hereditary factors that place people at risk. Those at high risk are Latinos, African Americans, Asian Americans, Native Americans, Pacific Islanders and older adults.

Thousands of people from all over the planet are struggling to regulate, and maintain their blood sugar to prevent diabetes from creating severe harm to their bodies. In the meantime, remarkably little is being done to reduce the chief culprit inducing the disease: A harmful lifestyle with little or no exercise and poor nutrition. Children who are modeling their parents' lifestyle are becoming obese and increasingly manifesting the onset of Type 2 Diabetes in early adolescence. The fundamental message is to realize is that there is a choice concerning Diabetes Type 2, because maintaining physical health is in our hands, and it is possible for everyone to reach their goal of living a healthier lifestyle. With the estimate of those diagnosed with diabetes to increase to 300 million in the next 20 years, it is essential that doctors begin to recognize the undeniable benefits of psychology and incorporate health psychologists into the treatment program.

Chapter 5
The Chemistry of Emotions

Although, the psychological treatment methods of emotion research continue to be ongoing, various prevailing points are emerging which manage to promote a viewpoint that many psychologists have long supported. This is not unexpected because the field is continuously discovering how feelings affect perception, reasoning, problem solving abilities and the ways people adapt to life circumstances. What investigations present are the biological justifications for the health psychology position in human emotions being biological, psychological and sociological in nature. This introduction will provide a basic foundation of the role the emotional system has in learning, memory, adjusting and coping, and the following chapters will provide potential treatment applications of this research.

Earlier historical reports of emotions have been inconsiderate and avoidant. Contemporary neuroscience affirms that those earlier assumptions were wrong, and in these modern times believe that emotions are not trivial indulgences or invaders that interfere with logical thinking, but are the prime organizing methods where awareness, understanding, and memory are established. If the message people sense in a situation fails to evoke an emotional reaction, it will also fail to be regarded as important and will have little probability of being selected into long-term memory. Investigations are also confirming that for someone to learn new ways of adapting they must possess a fascination about what they are trying to learn. Love, joy, happiness, curiosity, surprise, greed, anger, sadness and pride are not ephemeral or baffling states but are motivators that nudge people to travel in ways that assist with thriving and surviving.

Emotions were perceived as elements of man that contribute to people being unreasonable and confused, or they were immoral self-indulgences from which they must purify themselves if they did not want to be driven into performing sinful deeds. The notion that emotion was a sin that needed to be purged through absolution and confession has its roots in the teachings of Plato, and the theory was supported 600 years later for the church by St. Augustine. Farther along in time, Rene Descartes is known as being the founding father of modern philosophy and in the 17th century declared "I think, therefore, I am." His published book "Discourse on Method of Thought" was so compelling that it has impacted every philosopher since, and drafted the case that human sensations and emotions interrupted the practice of creating rational, orderly thinking. Moving forward into the 20th century, the judgment of the behaviorist school of psychology in its attempts to regulate human behavior through punishment and reward thought the drab realm of emotions were insignificant in the training process. By not realizing that emotions are valuable to psychological adaptations, some have turned psychiatric practices into shallow, mechanical districts lacking the very emotional care required to create the kinds of reasoning and coping skills the profession so desperately wants to improve. Additionally, the mental health professions have not fully addressed the important relationship between stimulating an emotionally positive experience and how this experience inter-relates to overall emotional and physical health.

Today, neuro-scientific research points to the outcome that, without emotion there is no long-term memory development. The information tracked by the brain that has emotional significance is what survives so people can focus, organize, and retain the information. Study after study verifies that the greater emotional expression an experience stimulates, the easier it is to remember. Joseph LeDoux (1998), the pioneering leader in defining emotional circuitry, states, "Emotions, in short, amplify memory." Without the importance of recognizing feelings and incoming information, the world would be a colorless, dull, and unmemorable place. The significant theories of emotions can be classified into three central fields: neurological, physiological, and cognitive. Physiological principles suggest that responses within the body have a direct link to emotions. Neurological doctrines assert that activities within the brain direct emotional responses. Lastly, cognitive theories maintain the belief that ideas and other thinking processes perform vital functions in the production of feeling states.

Three Theories of Emotions

1. Schachter-Singer Theory: Identified as the two-factor theory of emotion, this is an example of one cognitive theory of emotional response. This approach suggests that the physiological arousal occurs first, and then the individual must recognize the reason behind the arousal to identify the emotion.

2. The James-Lange Theory: The James-Lange approach is a well-known example of a physiological theory of emotion. Introduced by physiologist Carl Lange and psychologist William James, the James-Lange theory implies that emotions happen as an outcome of physiological responses to events and circumstances. According to this theory, people perceive an external stimulus which in turn creates a physiological reaction. The emotional response depends upon how people perceive the physical effects. For example, imagine someone is driving through in the woods when all of a sudden he or she notices a deer in their headlights. They begin to shake, muscles tense and the heart

begins to race. The James-Lange theory states that this person will understand their physical responses and decide that they are afraid ("I am shaking, and my heart is racing, therefore, I am afraid").

3. <u>The Cannon-Bard Theory:</u> The Cannon-Bard theory of emotion declares that people feel sensations and undergo physiological responses such as sweating, shaking and muscle tension all at the same time. This physiological theory suggests that emotions occur when the thalamus forwards the information to the brain in answer to a stimulus, causing a physiological response.

In the science of mind, emotion is a combined sense of perceiving that ends in mental and physical transformations that impact thinking and performance. Emotionality has a bond with a variety of psychological phenomena covering motivation, mood, temperament, and personality. The author David G. Meyers (2011) writes personal emotion includes "... physiological arousal, expressive behaviors, and conscious experience." Emotions are a combined set of interactions including personal and external factors, mediated by hormonal and neurological processes that generate a feeling and thinking state, leading to the evaluation of the experience. Emotions point to biological changes to the circumstances that spurred the reaction, and frequently to coping styles relating to an individual's mood and behavior.

The Biological Regulators of Emotions

The immune and endocrine systems aid in processing emotions, two integral brain systems share in the regulating duty (Edelman, 2001).

- The cerebral cortex governs higher functions and manages communications with the outside world.

- The brain stem which is located at the base of the brain plus the limbic system formations encompassing it directs people internally, focusing on the emotional, nurturing and survival needs. The brain stem also monitors spontaneous activity, such as heart rate.

The Cerebral Cortex

The cerebral cortex fills 85 percent of the brain's size and is a large covering of neural tissue that is deeply enveloped around the limbic system. It is arranged into countless amounts of profoundly interconnected and outwardly directed neural interfaces that react in milliseconds to different space-time demands. This system stimulates behavioral replies, offers rational decisions along with collecting, classifying and deciphering sensory data. When observed from the top, the cortex separates into right and left hemispheres along a path that proceeds straight backward from the nose. An abridged representation of duties of the two hemispheres implies that they concentrate on various viewpoints of an object or experience. The right hemisphere integrates the background data (the jungle) and the left hemisphere analyzes the foreground data (a tree in the jungle).

While investigations are not precise on the roles the hemispheres play in emotion, a few common patterns are obvious (Corballis, 1991). The right hemisphere appears to represent processing the emotional content of gestures, faces, speech intonation and volume associated with how something is communicated, while the left hemisphere processes the actual content of language or what is spoken. The right hemisphere also processes information that point to withdrawal reactions, for instance, fear and revulsion whereas the left hemisphere processes the aspects of emotion that point to advancing reactions like laughter and joy. Tomasi1 and Dardo (2011) have implied that the average male brain seems to follow a left design of hemisphere specialization; however, the average female brain may disperse more emotional processing across the two hemispheres. If accurate, these organizational variations may serve to clarify regularly seen gender discrepancies.

The cortex is divided into sensory and frontal lobes by a path traced on the head from ear to ear. Frontal lobes concentrate on critical thought and problem-solving abilities related to the present, with the forward section of the lobes in command of planning and practice exercises related to the future. These lobes perform an essential role in balancing emotional states and beliefs. The frontal lobe's management of critical reasoning and problem solving allows it to stop the execution of impulsive behaviors and inhibits someone from committing destructive illegal or immoral acts.

The Limbic System and Brain Stem

The limbic system and brain stem react slower, from seconds to months as it governs fundamental body functions, cycles, and defenses that broadly connect to organs and systems. The reticular formation at the tip of the brain stem integrates the volume, and kind of incoming sensory data into a general level of awareness. The limbic system is formed from many small interconnected networks and is the brain's primary manager of emotion that plays a significant role in processing memory. This system may reveal why emotion is a significant element in memory formation as it is strong enough to reverse both rational thinking and innate brain stem reply patterns, meaning people tend to follow their emotions (Rolls, 2013).

The limbic systems structures that process memory and emotion are the amygdala, the hippocampus, the thalamus and the hypothalamus. The amygdala is the key limbic system structure implicated in processing the emotional content of memory and behavior. It is composed of two little almond-shaped structures that link the sensory-motor systems and autonomic nervous system, which governs survival faculties such as breathing and heart rate. The amygdala also communicates with nearly all other brain regions. Its primary responsibility is to refine and translate advanced incoming sensory data in connection with survival and emotional demands, and then assists in launching relevant actions. Consequently, the amygdala affects both early sensory processing and higher levels of cognition (Schacter, 2002). For instance, on a cold day the amygdala may disregard the feel of a warm coat, but reacts to one that does not have a zipper.

The brain's amygdala and connecting hippocampus can temper the subjective and objective intensity of the memory. This structure processes the personal feelings people associate with the experience, and the hippocampus processes the objective conditions such as area, time, environment and activities that described the experience. The hippocampus joins the amygdala that converts significant short-term events into long-term declarative recollections that are then saved in the cortex. Memories created during a particular emotional state have a tendency to be effortlessly remembered during a related emotional state, at a later date in time (Thayer, 1989; Schimmack & Reisenzein, 2002). For example, during a dispute, people can quickly recall comparable earlier arguments that happened many years ago. This explains why simulations and role-playing exercises heighten learning since they attach memories to emotional connections that will associate and be utilized at a later date. The limbic system affects the collection and organization of events that the brain stores in two classes of long-term memory: Procedural memories are unconsciously processed skills, such as talking and walking, and declarative memories which are the conscious recall of facts, such as dates and locations.

The walnut-size thalamus and joining pea-size hypothalamus are two other major limbic system structures that further regulate emotional and physical safety. The thalamus is the brain's first relay station for incoming sensory data and it notifies the rest of the brain about what is transpiring in someone's environment. The thalamus has primary bonds to the amygdala and authorizes it to broadcast an immediate, but factually restricted statement of a possible threat. This response can trigger a fast, emotionally packed, but possibly also life-saving response before people thoroughly understand what is occurring. It is this system of parts that often carries many volatile emotional outbursts during a typical day. The hypothalamus watches the internal regulatory systems, telling the brain what is occurring inside the body. When the brain has no resolution to a dangerous condition, the hypothalamus can initiate a fight-flight stress reply through its pituitary gland connections that involve the endocrine system. Kandel and Kandel (1994) infer that this process serves as an explanation for repressed memories related to trauma and abuse. The fearfulness related to a traumatic event can begin the release of substances such as neurotransmitters like noradrenaline that increase the attachments in the brain processing the emotional recollection of the experience. Conversely, the painfulness of the event can lead to the discharge of opiate endorphins that reduce connections processing the conscious recollection of the factual conditions surrounding the incident. Consequently, the sufferer has a tendency to shun anything that triggers the fearful emotion, but often does not consciously know why. Many years following a mixture of internal and external factors, a similar place, the behavior of someone, or a feeling may cause the powerful emotional memory to trigger the recollection of the limited factual memory of the initial abuse (Kandel, 2007; Schwartz & Bennett, 2010)).

Peptides are carriers of feelings states

Throughout antiquity, people have held the belief that there is a disconnection between the mind, body and brain. The brain monitors body functions and the body produces maintenance duties for the brain. Scientists at this time believe that there is a unified mind-body-brain arrangement (Sacks, 2011). The emotional operation that predominantly is in the brain, endocrine and immune systems is a biochemical process that affects all organs. The emotions and thoughts are the cement that unites the body and brain, and peptide particles are the bodily demonstration of this process.

Peptide particles or molecules are the carriers that lead to the emotional operation. Researchers identify a peptide molecule as being a chain of amino acids that is smaller than a protein and there are more than sixty kinds implicated in feeling states. Although it is not understood how these molecules offer the data. Peptide productions within the body or brain are named hormones and neuropeptides, and if similarly fashioned molecules are produced outside the body, they are described as being medications. To temper the broad spectrum of feelings such as pleasure and pain, peptides move throughout the body via neural tracks, the circulatory system, and respiratory passages. They intensely influence the choices people make within the continuum of emotionally loaded advancing and withdrawing behaviors, such as to agree-disagree, and marry-divorce, drink-urinate, fight-run. Consequently the shifts in the body's levels of certain molecules indicate emotional response, what people do, when people do it, and how much determination people employ. At the cellular level, peptides manufactured within one cell fasten to receptors on the surface of another, sparking increased or decreased cellular reactions. If this happens in huge groups of cells, it can influence feeling or emotional states. Cell division and protein synthesis are two such activities which are profoundly implicated in the emotionally charged body alterations that occur during puberty (Moyers, 1992). A peptide's communication can vary in different areas of the body, just as a knife can be used in various ways to cut meat. In this fashion peptides are much the same as medications or drugs. For instance, alcohol can stimulate or sedate, depending on one's emotional state and the quantity of consumption.

The endorphins and cortisol are excellent examples of peptide particles that can in turn affect how people experience their world. Whenever the failure to defend danger triggers a stress reaction, cortisol is delivered by the adrenal gland which in turn stimulates essential body/brain protective replies that fluctuate with the type and severity of the stressor. Perfected ages ago when physical perils threatened the survival of man these stress replies do not distinguish between physical and emotional vulnerabilities. Nearly all modern day stress occurs from emotional disturbances and many responses frequently are maladaptive. For illustration, a young child protests to go to bed. The angry parents' stress system inappropriately reacts by delivering clotting factors into the blood, raising cholesterol levels, lowering the defenses of the immune system, tenses muscles, and increases blood pressure, along with many other effects. This parental response only makes sense if the rebellious child is also advancing with a rifle. People pay a huge cost for constant emotional tension, physically and emotionally. Even though low levels of cortisol create the euphoria that people feel when they are in charge, high levels triggered by the stress reply can produce depression and prolonged stress can point to problems associated with circulatory, endocrine, digestive and immune disorders. Chronic high cortisol levels can also damage hippocampal neurons correlated with learning and memory and short-term stress-related elevation of cortisol in the hippocampus can inhibit the ability to discriminate between details of a memorable experience (Vincent, 1990; Gazzaniga, 1989). Consequently, stressful life conditions decrease ones' capacity to live a physically and emotionally healthy life.

On the positive side, the endorphins are a form of opiate peptide that moderate emotions along the pain-pleasure spectrum as they decrease intense pain and increase euphoria. Endorphin levels can be raised by exercise, by positive social connections, music, meditation and many other activities that cause people to feel good about themselves, and the circumstances in which they live (Levinthal, 1988). A pleasant environment that promotes healthy activities will give birth to internal chemical reactions, which will help people discover how to successfully solve challenges in life, such as chronic pain management.

Research reveals that the emotional system is a complicated, broadly dispersed, and error-prone arrangement that describes a person's fundamental personality early in life that is very resistant to change. There are larger amounts of neural fibers that protrude from the brain's emotional center into the rational center than the reverse, making emotion a more influential determinant of behavior than the brain's rational methods. For instance, buying a lottery ticket is an emotional, not a rational choice, as the chances of winning are extremely low. Logic may not heed emotion although it infrequently changes the true emotions on the issue. Emotions allow people to neglect conscious consideration of the problem, and consequently many react too quickly. This reaction may direct irrational fears and unwise ways. Feelings, like color, exist along a spectrum that has a broad array of measurement in degrees called hues. People can readily recognize common discrete emotions by the usual facial and auditory representations, still the power and significance of the emotion will differ among people and circumstances. Furthermore, emotional meaning, like shade of color, may influence the understanding of the feeling. To understand the regularly changing emotional system and its effect on the ability to learn new ways of coping, people must comprehend this system's components and their functions.

Emotions represent an influential function in the way people think and act. It is critical to recognize the three significant elements of emotion. Feelings have a subjective or personal ingredient meaning how people experience an emotion, a physiological element or how the physical body responds to the emotion, and an expressive part or how people behave in reply to the emotion, which is often ruled by societal norms. These distinctive factors play a role in the implementation and purpose of emotional responses. Emotions can be fleeting, such as a burst of irritation at a peer, or long-lasting, such as lingering grief over the loss of a loved one. Why and for what reason do people have emotions? How do they assist in living a meaningful, healthy life?

1. <u>Emotions enable us to understand:</u> Personal emotions furnish valuable knowledge to others, the emotional displays of those around us provide social information. Social interaction plays a significant piece in daily life and being qualified to evaluate and respond to the emotions of others is vital. The ability to evaluate and respond empowers people to react properly and creates a meaningful bond with friends, family, peers and loved ones. Emotions also allow people to interact productively in a variety of social circumstances, from coping with an angry consumer to managing a tearful partner.

   Charles Darwin was one of the pioneering researchers who carefully studied emotions. He proposed that emotional affectations play a major role that relates to safety and survival. If someone encounters a crouching or growling animal, this would obviously show that the animal was angry and defensive, driving this person to retreat thus avoiding potential danger. In much the same fashion, learning the emotional signals of other people provides clear knowledge about how to respond to specific conditions.

2. <u>Emotions assist people to evade danger, thrive and survive:</u> Charles Darwin thought that emotions were modifications that permit animals and humans to survive and procreate. If people are angry, they are apt to face the cause of their irritation. If people experience fear, they are also likely to want to escape the situation or threat. If people feel love, they might search for a partner and reproduce. Emotions play an adaptive function in life by driving people to respond swiftly and take steps that will maximize the odds for success.

3. Emotions affect choices: Feelings have a significant impact on the decisions people make, from what they choose to wear in the morning to which profession they choose to have in life. Investigators have also observed that people with specific types of brain injury that reduces their capacity to experience emotions, also have a reduced ability to make healthy decisions. Still in circumstances where people think their decisions were led totally by logic and rationality, emotions perform a fundamental role. Emotional intelligence is the ability to handle and understand feelings that play an influential role in problem solving and decision making.

4. Emotions allow others to understand: At any time when someone interacts with another person, it is necessary to provide signals to encourage them to understand what they are thinking and feeling. Those cues might include emotional expression through body language, such as various hand expressions connected with the emotions people are experiencing. In other examples, this might include directly saying how they are feeling. When people tell someone that they are feeling sad, happy, frightened, excited, or angry, they are providing a valuable message so that the listener can utilize that information to guide their actions.

5. Emotions drive people to take action: If confronted with an anxiety provoking situation, some might feel performance anxiety. As a result of these emotional effects, some might be more inclined to prepare themselves. This is encountering a distinct emotion that drives people to possess the motivation to take action and do something positive to improve the possibilities of attaining success. Most people likewise favor certain actions in order to feel positive emotions thereby decreasing the possibility of feeling negative ones. Many explore social pursuits or hobbies that present them with a sense of satisfaction, pleasure, and excitement and avoid circumstances that drive dullness, melancholy, or stress.

Prevention, Physical Health and Health Psychology

The psychiatry/psychology profession stresses the importance of treating the whole person, but treatments tend to concentrate on weighable objective points. The health professionals measure appetite, sleep patterns, hallucinations, speech patterns, not emotional health or how life stressors effect symptom development. If the resources get tight administration cuts mental health services like emotional health assessments, therapy referrals, payment for services, and psychiatric research. We know emotion is important in psychology and psychiatry as it drives awareness, which in turn urges learning, coping and memory. However, because the fields do not fully understand the emotional process, they do not recognize precisely how to regulate it or apply it to clinical work beyond explaining too much or too little emotion as being problematic. Psychiatry has rarely incorporated the effects of emotional experiences people have in life comfortably into their treatments and American society is prime for change.

Advancements in the cognitive and neurosciences are opening the locks to the mysteries of how and where the body and brain process emotions (Schacter, 1997). Emotionology is the study of the beliefs or rules that a society or group has concerning emotions and their proper expression, therefore, associating with human conduct. This unprecedented blending of the biology, psychology and sociology of emotion promises to offer important treatment applications. At this time, contemporary emotion theory and research produce more questions than solutions. However, health professionals should acquire a basic recognition of the bio-psycho-social effects of emotion to assist with treating and evaluating upcoming therapy applications.

Emotions just exist, people cannot change them easily, they are acquired differently than the way people master practical skills and neglecting them can create difficulties in life. People can discover how and when to use logical thought to disregard feeling states or at least postpone expression until a situation is rationally evaluated. Everyone can recall earlier disturbances that anger them because of not being permitted to openly verbalize feelings after receiving a judgment. Health psychologists and other health professionals should attempt to promote practices of self-control among clients that support nonjudgmental, non-disruptive release of emotion that frequently occurs before reason. Here are a few professional tips:

1. Incorporating emotional expression in the therapy session does not have to be a difficult process. Try role playing a difficult situation to decrease tension, for example, after a client has an argument with their significant other. Once the clients combined limbic systems have been expressed, rational cortical methods can resolve the problem. In other words, when seeking to determine and resolve a problem, maintain a conversation with continuous emotional information.

2. Most people are already aware of the complexity of emotions and the ways in which they and others encounter them, though they may not be capable of articulating what they perceive. Professions in the mental health field can concentrate further on utilizing metacognitive exercises that stimulate people to discuss their emotions, listen to what others are saying in relationship to feelings, and speculate on the motives of people who are present in their world. For instance, the mere use of why a question shifts the conversation beyond bare details and toward motivations and emotions. For what reasons did your partner start to cry? This type of questioning is much more emotionally charged than ones like why did your partner start to cry?

3. Exercises that stress social interplay and that interest the entire problem manage to produce the most emotional comfort. Games, discussions, assessments, interactive techniques, cooperative exploration (visualization), education, are just a few examples. Despite the profession being aware for a long time that such exercises intensify client knowledge they can be overlooked at times in therapy sessions.

4. Memories are dependent on the environment and activities that bring out emotions, simulations, role playing, and cooperative projects may provide valuable contextual memory prompts that will assist the clients recall the information during similarly linked experiences in their actual world. This is one reason therapists favor clients practicing communicating a problem without the use of reading their notes on the subject.

5. Emotionally stressful situations are counterproductive since they can diminish anyone's ability to receive information and learn new ways to adapt. Self-respect and a feeling of being command over one's circumstances are crucial in managing stress. Highly evaluative and authoritarian styles may promote institutional productivity and accountability, but also intensify nonproductive stress.

As this chapter suggests emotions perform a wide variety of purposes. Feelings can be sudden, tenacious, persuasive, complicated, and also life-changing. They propel people to act in unusual ways and provide the means and resources required to communicate meaningfully in social life. Emotions wield an astonishingly influential force on human performance. In conclusion, society needs to consider humanity as being more than brain tissue, organs and networks because powerful emotions transform the body and brain into being a complex active life force. By utilizing the bio-psycho-social principles in the health care system health professionals can begin to focus on the treating the whole person which in turn benefits physical, emotional and societal health.

Chapter 6
Depression and the Bio-Psycho-Social Approach

Depression is a common debilitating condition which eventually if not treated provokes sufferers to have a distinctly poor quality of life, physically, mentally and socially. Those suffering from this disease may feel entirely alone when tormented by the onslaught of signs that globally trouble millions. One obstacle, that inhibits a successful approach is that educated powerful people in authority continue to view this illness as being a weakness in temperament and not worthy of examination. Consequently, people proceed to endure, do not obtain therapy, the symptoms continue, and the feelings of despair continue to fester. Most people occasionally feel melancholy or down, and these sensations are fleeting ordinarily passing within a few days; however, depression is a persistent, well-known severe ailment. Suffers afflicted with major depression at times do not search for treatment, however, the majority of victims, even those with the most relentless of symptoms, can choose to feel better. If someone has a major depressive episode the manifestations interfere with all aspects of everyday life causing distress not only for the sufferer, but, also for his or her friends, relatives and colleagues. With treatment and time psychotherapies, medications and other techniques are effective in managing all of the signs and symptoms.

Major depressive disorder is one of the common prevalent mental disorders in the United States. In the year 2008, The National Institute of Mental Health states every year approximately 6.7% of U.S adults encounter a major depressive incident. Females are 70% more likely than men to face this suffering during their lifetime, and 3.3% of 13 to 18 year olds have experienced a harshly debilitating depressive episode. Non-Hispanic blacks are 40% less likely than non-Hispanic whites to experience an occurrence during their lifetime. The most common age of assault is 32 years old.

A History of Depression

No one understood this illness despite the theories, and no one distinguished any treatment approach before the 1960s. Those who felt blah, grouchy, and uninterested in life were told to swallow it up, and keep on going by just picking themselves up by the bootstraps and move along. There was no compassion for the distress because there was no acknowledgment of the pain being a significant problem. Nevertheless, the breakthrough came in the 1970s when it was noticed that expressing the feelings of anger eased some of the suffering. Verbally expressing anger was a unique approach because people felt a sense of relief (Riley, Treiber & Woods, 1989). This theory is successful for some, but, there remains to be many unhappy people roaming the globe, even with possessing the capacity to communicate anger. Let's take a glimpse inside the United States archives to understand what fueled depressive suffering and hopelessness:

- Slavery and Exploitation
- Life inside early century sweatshops.
- Starvation during the great depression.
- Destruction and Death from war in the 1940s.
- Restrictions of family life for females in the 1950s.

- General despair and war during the 1960s and 1970s.

There are not many sweatshops left in the US, prejudice and violence against women and minorities is not nearly as intense today. However, mankind continues to suffer through severe periods of economic hardship and depression is widespread. People have adapted to the loss of life through war that existed before Iraq, and now war is virtually a fixed reality.

Causes of Depression

The research illustrates that there is no singular reason for symptom onset. However, there are three principal factors that consistently point to playing important roles pertaining to depression (Sullivan, Neale, Kendler, 2000). These three factors seemingly overlap during a major depressive episode which is why using treatment strategies based on the biological, psychological and social theories have the most impact.

Biological Causes

Depressive episodes correspond with dysfunctions of the brain. Brain-imaging studies, using magnetic resonance imaging (MRI), report that the pictures of the brains in people who have depression look unique, in comparison to those without symptoms. The portions of the brain implicated in thinking, sleep, appetite, mood, and performance appear different. Nevertheless, these images do not explain why or how the depression occurs. At this time, brain-imaging technology cannot be applied to diagnose depression and investigation in this field continues. Serotonin is crucial because it performs a primary task in managing vital biological roles such as concentration, memory, the quality of sleep, and appetite. If someone becomes extremely depressed the level of serotonin in the brain is out of balance leaving the primary function of serotonin in a compromised position. Genetic factors may be implicated with the way in which the neurotransmitter serotonin, balances in the brain. People may be susceptive to depression related to biological factors and genetics, placing them more at risk, which is the reason why physicians prescribe antidepressants, to raise serotonin levels (Antonuccio, Danton, & DeNelsky, 1995). Some types of depression tend to reoccur in families, yet, the illness can appear in people without family histories. Genetic research confirms that the increased risk for depressive symptoms results from the impact of several genes operating collectively with environmental or other factors (Sullivan, Neale & Kendler, 2000). In other words, loss of a loved one, being in a difficult relationship, trauma, or a stressful circumstance may trigger a depressive event; however, a few episodes may take place without an obvious trigger. Scientists continue to examine the genetic influences that may predispose someone to having a major depressive episode.

Psychological Causes

Signs can occur as a consequence of having too many negative life experiences or prolonged life stress. One extremely common dilemma is working in a stressful profession or atmosphere because many people spend a large amount of time at their job. The work environment can be extremely stressful, due to a negligent supervisor, unsupportive coworkers, heavy workloads, demanding deadlines, and unforgiving customers, amongst other things. Unfortunately, when the stress situation gets too high, it often turns into people being very unhappy, and if this dissatisfaction goes on for an extended period of time, contentment can turn into extreme sadness. Another common culprit for producing symptoms of depression is the experiencing of prolonged mental and physical abuse during childhood. In 2008, Bradley and associates emphasize that children, who were victims of mental and physical abuse, tend to have significantly higher rates of depression, than other children who were loved, and respectfully treated. One successful treatment approach is cognitive behavior therapy, which works by helping people understand their thoughts, feelings and behaviors (Clark, Beck, & Alford, 1999). This knowledge opens the doorway to personal change, and ultimately opens the passage into realizing that people have options, and do not have to assume that they are "stuck."

Social Causes

The third factor relates to someone encountering a major traumatic life situation which can be thought of as "the straw that broke the camel's back" possibly losing a loved one, or being fired work. For many people, it may be hard to realize the reason why these events lead to extreme sadness, but the cause is pretty straight forward. The death of a loved one or being fired from a job have something in common, they both bring about the mixture of feelings associated with grief, anger, guilt, and anxiety. They also involve the sense of missing something. People with depression are not equipped with the knowledge that is needed to cope with the emotionally taxing event that is causing them to become symptomatic. The treatment of choice is humanistic in nature, and that is to associate with people that are kind, supportive and caring to be with them during stressful life circumstances. These people may be family, friends, a community, a church or religious group, or a therapist that has these qualities.

Depression: Signs and symptoms

- Restlessness, Irritability
- Decreased Energy or Fatigue
- Lack of appetite or Overeating
- Pessimism or feelings of hopelessness
- Suicide attempts or considerations of suicide
- Persistent worried, unhappy, or "vacant" feelings

- Perceptions of helplessness, worthlessness or guilt

- Excessive Sleeping, early morning awakening or insomnia

- Difficulty making decisions, difficulty remembering details or concentrating

- Lack of interest in hobbies or activities that were once pleasurable including sex

- Aches, migraines, cramps, or digestive problems that do not lessen with treatment

The various Types of Depressive Illnesses

Minor depression symptoms for 2 weeks or longer that do not satisfy adequate guidelines for major depression. People with minor depression are at increased danger for acquiring a major depressive set back if they do not initiate treatment.

Dysthymia or Dysthymic disorder is identified by long-term (2 years or longer) signs that may not be harsh enough to incapacitate a person yet can hinder feeling well or healthy functioning. People with dysthymia may additionally meet one or more occurrences of major depression during their lives.

Major depression is a blending of traits that interfere with a person's capacity to eat, sleep, work, study, and enjoy pleasurable activities. Thoughts of hopelessness and suicide are common because major depression is disabling and hinders a person from performing normally along with significantly lower the quality of life. A few people may experience only a single event within their lifetime, but more frequently suffers have reoccurring episodes.

Unique patterns of depression are complex, and they may occur under unique circumstances. Not everyone in the field accepts how to classify and define these types of depression. They include:

Seasonal Affective Disorder (SAD) which is distinguished by the starting of depressive symptoms during the wintertime when there is lower natural sunshine and, lifts during spring and summer seasons. SAD at times is adequately managed with light therapy, but approximately fifty percent of those with SAD do not feel better with this approach to treatment. Psychotherapy and antidepressant medication can diminish the signs of SAD, either alone or in combination with light therapy.

Postpartum depression is much more severe than someone having the "baby blues" that many women struggle with after childbirth. Researchers estimate that 10 to 15 percent of women experience postpartum depression. This is when physical and hormonal changes add to the new responsibility of attending to an infant that can be overpowering.

Psychotic depression occurs when someone has a severe depression plus psychotic signs, such as having disturbing inaccurate beliefs or a split with truth (delusions), or seeing or hearing upsetting events that others cannot hear or see (hallucinations).

How children experience depression

It may be challenging to reach an accurate diagnosis in children, because the signs are at times common with mood changes that are typical for the developmental stage. A child with depression may hold fast to a parent, fret that someone dear to them may die, have temper tantrums, resist going to school or profess to be sick. In childhood, boys and girls are evenly prone to exhibit symptoms; however, by age 15, girls are twice as likely as boys to have had a major depressive incident. Adolescents may have severe episodes as they begin adulthood and tend to be negative, grouchy, feel misunderstood, mope or get into disputes at school. Depression in adolescence commonly co-occurs with other troubles such as substance abuse, eating disorders and anxiety. These symptoms can point to increased danger for suicide. Symptoms during the teenage years occur at the same time they are developing an identity separate from their parents, forming independent conclusions, and wrestling with gender concerns along with sexuality.

The Differences in Sexuality and Aging

This illness is more prevalent among females than among men. Biological, life cycle, hormonal, genetics, and psychosocial conditions that women encounter may be associated with this greater measure (Simonds, 2001). Researchers have confirmed that hormones quickly alter the brain chemistry that regulates emotions and mood. A few women may have a difficult type of premenstrual syndrome (PMS) termed Premenstrual Dysphoric Disorder (PMDD) that correlates with the hormonal shifts that typically happen around ovulation and before menstruation. Investigators are examining all of the possible associations about how the rise and fall of estrogen and different hormones influence a woman's brain chemistry. During the passage through menopause, some females encounter a heightened risk and osteoporosis, which is bone loss, may be associated with the increase in symptoms. Many women endure the added stresses of employment and house obligations, attending to children, aging parents, abuse, poverty, and relationship struggles. It remains unclear why only a few women confronted with immense difficulties exhibit signs while others with comparable challenges do not experience an episode.

Men usually experience depression differently than females. Whereas women with depression are more prone to possess feelings of worthlessness, excessive guilt and sadness, men are more prone to feeling irritable, have difficulty sleeping, feel very weak, and lose interest in past pleasurable pursuits (Culbertson, 1997; Real, 1997). During times of experiencing the symptoms, men may be more apt to use alcohol or drugs and become frustrated, pessimistic, annoyed, hostile, and at times insulting. A few thrust themselves into their profession to evade speaking about their symptoms with relatives or friends, and may act carelessly. In the US, while more women attempt suicide, many more men die by suicide (Walsh, Clayton, Liu & Hodges, 2009; National Alliance for Suicide Prevention, 2012).

Depression is not a natural component of aging. Seniors are coping with more aliments and physical obstacles, however, investigations reveal that older adults are content with their lives. Nevertheless, when seniors do experience an episode, it may be undiagnosed because they exhibit mixed, less noticeable signs. Countless people believe that the greatest incidences of suicide are among young people, yet, elderly white males 85 and older have the highest suicide rate in the United States. Several possess a long history of symptoms out of their physicians awareness, yet, many victims have visited their physicians within 1 month of taking their life. These people are less prone to acknowledge or confess to reactions of sorrow or despair, and at times, it can be challenging to differentiate grief reactions from major depression. Bereavement after the loss of a loved one is a natural response to the loss and does not require licensed mental health counseling, unless is complicated and persists for a very long time following the death of a loved one. Ongoing research continues to examine the differences between complicated grief reactions and major depression episodes.

Many seniors have physical conditions such as cancer, diabetes or heart disease, and take medication that have side effects contributing to symptoms. Some elderly also experience what physicians call arteriosclerotic depression (vascular depression), that results when blood vessels harden over time, becoming less flexible and are constricting the flow. This hardening and constriction inhibit blood flow to all organs, including the brain. Those with vascular depression are at higher risk for having heart diseases and strokes. Most elderly adults improve if they receive help with counseling, medication or a combination of both treatment strategies, as the research has shown that medication in combination with psychotherapy is effective. For people that have indications of minor depression, psychotherapy alone can be sufficient in maintaining older adults staying symptom free and psychotherapy is especially suitable for those who do not want to take antidepressant medicine. When anyone is experiencing signs of depression, he or she may feel worthless, helpless, and hopeless making it extremely challenging for them take any action, yet as people begin to identify their symptoms, and start to discover coping abilities, they will notice those low mood shifts passing with greater frequency.

How to Cope with Depression

Exercise increases serotonin levels. Health psychology has evolved and includes the physical well-being of by applying bio-psycho-social methods, as a healthy mind depends on having a healthy body. Research consistently reveals that regular cardiovascular exercise is not only beneficial for physical health, but is also advantageous for emotional and cognitive health, such as memory and problem solving skills. Numerous studies have shown that there is a relationship between mental stability and exercise and exercise assists with emotional balance associating with happiness (De Mello et., al,. 2003). Cardiovascular exercise stimulates and can increase neurons in the brain, serotonin helps people cope better with stressful life events and both enhance memory and problem-solving abilities. Try to fit at least 30 minutes of brisk walking into the daily routine.

Social support assists people in coping with stresses in life, however, people who have depression often want to isolate. It is essential for sufferers to try an allow those who care be a part their life. Many researchers have found that not having a solid foundation of social support can lead to feelings of loneliness, which are precursors to symptom development. Therefore, it is important try to go out and develop those old friendships, make new friends, or spend time with loved ones (O'Connor, 1997).

Be open to the idea of going to counseling. These suggestions are a general guideline, and are by no means to be considered a substitute for a professional diagnosis or treatment. A psychologist using the bio-psycho-social techniques will be able to help those with major depression understand the psychological, biological and social factors in relationship to their unique symptoms, and the cognitive therapies have been clinically proven to successfully treat.

How people can help themselves if feeling depressed

1. Establish practical goals.

2. Continue with self-education about depression.

3. Set priorities and divide up large tasks into smaller units.

4. Spend time with people and talk to a buddy or family member. Attempt not to isolate.

5. Positive thought will substitute negative beliefs as the signs respond to therapy.

6. Try to be active and workout. Go for a walk, a movie, or activity that was once fun.

7. Postpone major decisions. Discuss choices with others who have a more objective picture of the circumstances.

8. Consult a professional as early as possible. There is research confirming the longer one delays the greater the suffering.

9. Anticipate the mood symptoms to adjust gradually, not instantly. Oftentimes during treatment, sleep and appetite will improve before the mood.

Someone who has depression will impact family, friends, co-workers and acquaintances as this illness takes a toll on relationships. The most significant action friends and loved one can take in assisting someone who has symptoms is to help them obtain an evaluation for therapy and perhaps medicine for treatment. A family member or close associate may need to secure an appointment and go with them for the evaluation. Encourage them to continue in treatment and investigate a different treatment if no change in symptoms occurs after 8 to 12 weeks.

How to help a friend, relative or co-worker

- Remain attentive and listen
- Provide aid with transportation to the appointments.
- Point out facts and offer hope without dismissing feelings
- Offer understanding, patience, emotional comfort and reassurance.
- Remind this person that with treatment and time, the symptoms will become less distressful.
- At no time disregard remarks about suicide and communicate them to a therapist or physician.
- Invite them out for activities and keep striving, however, do not push a person to take on too many too quickly.

Treatment of Major Depression is no simple task and takes active participation and practice. Nevertheless, utilizing the bio-psycho-social method is a research supported plan to pull through this stormy time in life. Regrettably, successfully pulling through a severe depressive episode customarily takes approximately six months of hard work, may require medication, and weekly talks with a therapist. The message is that this illness can be treated very successfully. In conclusion, depression is a severe problem which regularly leads to unavoidable pain and suffering in many areas of life. Everyone must view and treat this disease just as earnestly as a physical disease. Medications alone are not as effective as one might speculate, and sometime symptoms are treatable, without the need for mood-enhancing drugs. If someone is experiencing symptoms, it is necessary to get an evaluation by a mental health practitioner, so that once again they can begin to feel in charge of life. There are many triggers in life that can lead to the onset of symptoms, but it is especially important to realize that sufferers did not cause the problem. Major depression is an illness that has its basis on biology and life stressors. Some continue to view these symptoms as being an emotional failing which has roots on historical thoughts of the past. Society needs to treat this condition properly by moving forward to living with the modern principles and treatments of the 21st century.

Chapter 7
Exploring the Swings of Bipolar Disorder

Throughout a lifetime, everyone has regular ups and downs that differ from the symptoms of bipolar disease which often destroy relationships, produce poor work performance, and at times these signs lead to suicide. Bipolar disorder is a neurobiological disorder that severely affects the functioning of almost 5.5 million Americans or 2.6 percent of the population and 51 percent of these people do not receive treatment. At least half of all cases develop the disease before age 25 and symptoms are relentless (NIMH, 2014). This condition is a brain disorder that creates extraordinary changes in someone's' capacity to perform daily tasks because it alters activity levels, energy and causes shifts in mood. Previously, known as manic-depressive illness, people with bipolar disorder can lead a content, productive, full life if treated. Anxiety disorder and drug or alcohol abuses are often also found in those with the condition.

The diagnosis is known for the dramatic mood swings that fall from the crashes of depression to the heights of mania. When depressed, people feel hopeless, sad, guilty, and have no interest, energy, or pleasure. There may be excessive crying, withdrawal behaviors, no eye contact and a focus on the negative parts of life. The Mayo Clinic states that suicide risks for those having the affliction 20 years or more are over

6 percent and self-harm or suicide attempts occur in 30-40 of the population. The depressed mood about-faces and people then feel grandiose, euphoric and full of energy. The pronounced elevation in mood is called mania or hypomania depending on the intensity and severity. Person afflicted may behave unusually happy, energetic, or irritable, and the need for sleep is diminished. During this phase poor choices are often made and there is little attention paid the ramifications or outcomes of these decisions. In some, the symptoms of depression and mania occur at the same time along with shifts in mood which may occur many times per day or only a few times a year.

Despite the fact that mania or hypomania's signs are the defining characteristics in diagnosis, depressive symptoms are more common than manic. People with bipolar disorder consume a considerable amount of time living in misery with sub-clinical depressive symptoms. For example, a 12-year longitudinal research investigation included 146 individuals with bipolar I who were asked to complete weekly mood ratings. They reported depressive symptoms as being three times more common (Judd et al., 2002). The outcome of this study explores the fact that these people spent 32 percent of their time with symptoms of sub-clinical depression throughout the 12-year investigation.

Bipolar disorder is difficult to recognize during the initial stages, and many have symptoms for years before accurate treatment and diagnosis. For patients showing a first episode of depression, it is often not possible to predict those who will have recurrent depression and those who will develop a manic episode, thus making the bipolar diagnosis difficult. Someone with this condition spends more than eight years pursuing treatment before they receive an accurate diagnosis and discuss their symptoms with three to four different physicians. The National Institutes of Health explains that the number one explanation of untimely death among those diagnosed is suicide, with 15 – 17 percent taking their lives as a result of adverse symptoms that come from untreated illness.

The History of Bipolar Disease

The theory concerning the relationship between depression and mania can be traced back to Aretaeus, the Ancient Greek, was a physician and philosopher in the first century AD, during Nero's time. This doctor describes a group of people who, "laugh, play, and dance all night and day" and at other times appear "torpid, dull, and sorrowful". Aretaeus of Cappadocia began his quest into investigating the disease by writing down and detailing symptoms, suggesting that both patterns of behavior were the outcomes of one disorder. His notations on the connections between mania and depression went largely unnoticed for many centuries, and the idea did not gain acceptance until the modern era (Healy, 2011).

Mental health professionals credits the ancient Greeks and Romans in defining the terms "mania" and "melancholia," correlating to the modern day words manic and depression. The Greeks and Romans also detected that using lithium salts in baths hushed the manic patients' emotions and boosted the moods of those that were depressed. Lithium continues to be a common medication prescribed for bipolar patients. Hippocrates concluded that symptoms of depression arose from an excess of black bile and the names used for bipolar depression and mania have their influences from these Ancient Greeks. Depression is a clinical term for melancholy that is much more recent in origin and evolves from the Latin word "deprimere" or humble, to a lower or reduce a position. Hippocrates used the word melancholy to explain depression meaning in Greek, melas (black) and chole (bile), and mania is associated with "mainesthai" meaning to rage or go mad. Aristotle, the Greek philosopher, not just accepted melancholy as a disease, but also gave approval to the illness for bringing inspiration to the famous artists of his time (Campbell, 2009).

The Anatomy of Melancholy, written in the 17th Century by Robert Burton explores treating melancholy using dance and music as a type of therapy and the book is a literary collection of reports of depression explaining the effects of the disease on society. While combining with accurate medical information, the text expanded greatly into the treatments and symptoms clinical depression. Theophilus Bone, later in time, wrote a book entitled Sepuchretum, a text that was based on his experiences from performing 3,000 autopsies. He described mania and melancholy as being a single condition called "manico-melancolicus" providing a useful step forward in diagnosing the disease because depression and mania were considered to be distinct disorders.

The contemporary psychiatric view of bipolar disorder has its roots in the nineteenth century. There were little advancements and discoveries for many centuries until the French psychiatrist Jean-Pierre Falret published a document in 1851 describing "la folie circulaire," meaning circular insanity. Falret proceeds to record the first known case describing someone transforming from being severely depressed to a manic excitement state. He also noticed that the condition re-occurred in families, and accurately theorized that one of the causes was genetic in nature. Jean-Pierre Falret (1794–1870) and Jules Baillarger (1809–1890) in 1854 independently presented characterizations of the illness in Paris to the Académie de Médicine. Baillarger explaining that the illness was a "dual-form insanity" (folie à double), although Falret called the syndrome circular insanity (folie circulaire). Besides the accurate portrayal, Falrets' genetic connection is a characteristic that medical professionals believe to this very day. While the investigations and research of medicine progressed, strict religious dogma continued to think that the mentally disabled were possessed by demons and should be put to death, and those afflicted across the globe were executed.

The concept of bipolar disorder grew out of Emil Kraepelin's classification of manic depressive insanity, which brings us to the end of the 19th century. However, as discussed the descriptions of frenetic activity associated with the manic state can be found in the writings of Hippocrates and as far back as the ancient Egyptians. Emil Kraepelin (1856–1926) a German psychiatrist in the beginning of the 19th century studied the untreated, natural course of the condition and discovered people to have somewhat symptom-free times in their life. On this footing, he coined the term "manic–depressive psychosis" to define the disorder and disconnected it from démence précoce (schizophrenia). Kraepelin emphasized that manic–depressive psychosis had an episodic course and a more benign outcome, in contrast to démence précoce. He did not identify between those who had both depression and manic events from those with just depressive episodes. This was the time of Sigmund Freud's theory which included the idea that the suppression of passions or desires played a significant role in creating a mental illness and Emil Kraepelin disagreed with this assumption. The scientific and historical accounts of bipolar disorder were transformed by Kraepelin, who recognized biological causes of this mental illness and he is the first person to investigate the condition in an empirical manner. In 1921, Kraepelin's Manic-Depressive Insanity and Paranoia book explains in detail the differences between manic-depressive illness and dementia praecox, schizophrenia. This type of classification of mental disorders begins the foundation of psychological descriptions used by mental health professionals today.

In the early 1950s, a German psychiatrist Karl Leonhard and colleagues professionally investigated a classification system for mental disorders, hoping to improve understanding and treatment of the diseases. The present day significance on bipolarity and mood elevation being the defining feature of the illness dates to the 1960s. In 1966 Angst and Perris independently confirmed that unipolar depression and bipolar disorder could be distinctly diagnosed in terms of family history, clinical presentation, development, and treatment response. The phrase "bipolar" signifies the opposites of mania and depression and first arose in the American Psychiatric Association's Diagnostic and Statistical Manual of Mental Disorders (DSM) in the third revision in 1980. The older term "manic–depressive illness" was considered to be stigmatizing, thus, a change in language to "bipolar disorder" or 'bipolar affective disorder." It was in this revision that the term mania was removed to prevent people in society calling those diagnosed with the condition "maniacs." A few psychiatrists and those in the mental health profession continue to prefer the term "manic–depressive illness" because it more accurately matches the description.

The previous diagnosis of manic depression closely associates with psychosis, however, not all patients who struggle with mania and depression become psychotic. Therefore, psychosis was not a requirement for a diagnosis. In our modern time, bipolar disorder is a cyclical mood state that involves periods of severe disruptions to behavior and mood mixed with times of recovery. The decisive characteristic is the experience of hypomania or mania, grandiose beliefs and expansive affect that associates with an increase in drive and a decreased need for sleep, which can cause psychosis, especially if not treated (Andreasen & Black, 2006).

The previous theories endured the test of time, and were included in two classification systems: The International Classification of Disease (ICD), published by the World Health Organization and the Diagnostic and Statistical Manual of Mental Disorders (DSM), published by the American Psychiatric Association. Now in its fifth revision the DSM is considered to be the primary guide for diagnosing adopted by mental health professionals in the United States.

The DSM-V lists four subtypes of bipolar disorder including the diagnostic criteria:

1. Bipolar I Disorder is determined by manic or mixed episodes that are for at minimum seven days, or by manic

signs that are severe enough to require hospital care. Often depressive episodes develop as well, usually persisting for at least two weeks.

2. Bipolar II Disorder is determined by depressive and hypomanic episodes without the person having any full-blown mixed or manic episodes.

3. Bipolar Disorder Not Otherwise Specified is determined when the symptoms of the illness are clearly out of an individual usual range of behavior but do not meet diagnostic conditions for either bipolar I or II.

4. Cyclothymic Disorder, or Cyclothymia is a milder type of bipolar and is diagnosed when people have episodes of hypomania and at times a mild depression for at least two years. The characteristics do not meet the diagnostic criteria for any other form of bipolar disorder.

A severe form of the disease is Rapid-cycling Bipolar Disorder and occurs when someone has four or more events of major depression, mania, hypomania, or mixed states, all in one year. It affects women more than men and can be intermittent throughout one's life. One study found that those with rapid cycling had their first event approximately four years earlier (mid to late teen years). This form of bipolar seems to be more common in those who have their first episode at a younger age.

The Causes of Bipolar Illness

Genetic Pre-Disposition

Bipolar is more common in those who have a relative with the disease and scientists are attempting to locate genes that may involve provoking an episode. Approximately fifty percent have a family member with depression which is also, considered a mood disorder. Someone who has one parent with the disease has a twenty-five percent chance of developing the condition. Investigations into adopted twins have inspired researchers to learn more about the genetics (Serretti & Mandelli, 2008). The sibling of a non-identical twin who has the disorder has a twenty-five percent chance of developing the disease, which is the same risk as if both parents had bipolar disorder. An identical twin, meaning someone who has exactly the same genetic make-up has an even greater risk of receiving a diagnosis, an eightfold greater chance than a non-identical twin.

Physiological Conditions

Bipolar disorder is fundamentally a biological illness that materializes in a precise area of the brain. As an organic disease, the onset may hibernate only to be activated or triggered by life events such as psychological or social stress. The importance of treatment techniques using a biological, psychological and sociological approach strategy is important in maintaining stability.

Neurotransmitters are brain chemicals that are nerve conduction messengers seem to play a significant role that also associate with other mood disorders. An imbalance or dysfunction in these messengers, such as, norepinephrine, serotonin and specific hormones may relate to causing or triggering events. Those with the diagnosis appear to have physical changes in the brain. The full value of these unusual differences continues to be under investigation and may at some point in the near future assist in pinpointing one cause (Lahera, Freund & Sáiz-Ruiz, 2013).

Environmental Conditions

A life experience may trigger a mood episode in someone who has a genetic pre-disposition to develop the disease. Physical and emotional health practices, even without a genetic family history or documented hormonal problem can trigger an episode. A significant loss, abuse, stress, or other traumatic life events play an important role in diagnosis and treatment. Although substance use is not considered to be a direct cause, use of alcohol or tranquilizers may induce a more severe depression. The use of amphetamines can worsen a hypomanic phase, interfere with obtaining an accurate diagnosis, create problems with the ability to perform and hamper the recovery. The diagnosis of Bipolar disorder seems to be increasing both in adults and children. This uptick may be due to improvements of the professions ability to assess for the illness or the outcome of changing social and environmental conditions (Schmitt et., al., 2014).

Medication

A few antidepressants are known to cause or trigger a manic state, particularly in those who are susceptible. The importance of this is that people who are experiencing a depressive episode must be managed flawlessly in those who have had previous manic episode. Do to the fact that a depressive episode may shift quickly into a manic episode when an antidepressant medication is ordered, an anti-manic drug may also be recommended. This addition creates a "ceiling," to protect from antidepressant-induced mania.

Other prescription drugs can produce a euphoria that resembles mania. Appetite suppressants and thyroid medications may induce a diminished need for sleep, and an increase in talkativeness and energy, however, after discontinuation of the drug, their mood will return to normal.

Substances that can produce a manic-like episode include:

1. Excessive caffeine
2. Illegal drugs such as Cocaine, Ecstasy, Amphetamines.
3. Excessive amounts of over the counter medications such as cold remedies, allergy preparations and appetite suppressants.

4. Prescribed medications, such as thyroid drugs, corticosteroids like prednisone and some anti-depressants.

Treatment and Risk factors for Developing Bipolar

1. Young Adulthood, being in your twenties
2. Substance Abuse or Medication misuse
3. Genetic pre-disposition (parent or sibling with the disorder)
4. Psychological Stress (major life changes, death of a loved one, trauma, abuse)
5. Social or Environmental Stress (financial problems, lack of employment)

Those with undiagnosed bipolar disorder will at times self-medicate using alcohol or drugs in efforts to relieve their depressed or manic mood states. However, such band-aides rarely provide the kind of long-term aid most people desire. Mood stabilizers are always a part of the approved treatment plan. Despite the fact that bipolar disorder is considered to be a persistent, often chronic condition, there are indeed various effective treatments (Sagman & Tohen, 2009). Those with the illness often seek out therapy according to the depressive or manic cycle in which they are experiencing. When in a manic or hypomanic phase, people may think that there is no longer a need for treatment and discontinue. In a depressive phase, the symptoms are too uncomfortable to bear, and they often return for help.

Treatment for bipolar disorder is, often, divided into three main sections. In the acute or crisis stage, treatment concentrates on reducing symptoms and this focus will continue until remission which occurs when symptoms have subsided for a considerable time-period. Continuation therapy prevents a relapse of symptoms from the current depressive or manic event. Maintenance treatment prevents future recurrences of symptoms that assist in learning long-term coping styles to control mood fluctuations. The draw-backs of long-term medication use are then examined and weighed against the risks of relapse. Unfortunately, those with untreated bipolar disorder have symptoms which tend to deteriorate because the crisis events will increase in frequency and severity. On the positive side, there are various coping skills and practices that people can develop to manage the symptoms.

The recommendation is for people to consult a psychologist or psychiatrist, for the initial diagnosis, although, a wide range of mental health professionals assist in treating the condition. Medications should be monitored and ordered by a psychiatrist who has an extensive background and experience in prescribing these drugs. Psychotherapy, preferably, one that specializes in clinical health psychology will assist in monitoring and managing possible side effects. Health Psychologists will educate in understanding the importance of taking medications to both the client and family members. They will also communicate with physicians, explore and develop coping methods to manage symptoms and work with unlearning patterns of thinking and behaviors that may hinder recovery.

Prognosis for Bipolar Disorder

Approximately, ten to twenty percent of those diagnosed with bipolar will have persistent, unresolved mood symptoms despite treatment. The average person diagnosed is free of symptoms for around five years between the first and second flare-up of the illness, and as time moves along, the interval between events may shorten. This shortened interval is especially true in cases in which the client discontinues treatment (medication and therapy). Researchers estimate that someone who has bipolar disorder will have approximately eight to nine dramatic mood experiences during his or her lifetime (NIH, 2014).

However, the future outlook for someone with bipolar disorder is favorable with proper ongoing treatment and the majority of those diagnosed respond well to the medication and or combination of drugs. Investigations report that approximately fifty percent will respond to lithium alone, and twenty to thirty percent will obtain relief to another drug or combination.

Coping Tips for those with Bipolar Disorder

Become alcohol and drug-free

Substance abuse is an enormous problem that interferes with achieving a positive treatment outcome because the usage affects one's cognitive functioning and mood. Many people believe that illicit drugs help them cope with symptoms when they are in fact, contributing to mood and sleep disorders. Approximately fifty percent of those diagnosed with bipolar illness have problems with substance abuse, many in attempts to self-medicate.

Take medications on schedule and as prescribed

Medications can help people function and lesson mood swings, however, sticking to a schedule may not be always an easy task. Some of these medications require maintaining a blood level and laboratory testing to check for accuracy. Higher levels can be toxic and produce physiological symptoms, and skipping doses can precipitate a relapse.

Learn about medication and side effects

The ideal approach in managing side effects is to educate yourself as much as possible about the medication and monitor for possible complications. Ask your physician, pharmacist or any health care provider to provide you with material to read about the drug.

Monitor Weight

Varying from person to person the side effects of medications prescribed to treat this illness, including Depakote, Lithium and many antipsychotics can trigger weight gain and eventually cause a metabolic disorder. There are various diets and fitness programs that help prevent weight gain from becoming another problem.

Attend weekly sessions with a therapist

Once the mood is stabilized psychiatry visits usually decrease to once a month. Regular therapy, typically cognitive-behavioral or interpersonal therapy can help people develop a daily routine, learn ways to cope with feelings, understand thoughts and assist in maintaining stable relationships. Health psychologists will also communicate with the psychiatrist and provide ways to manage medication side effects. Therapy is crucial for a successful treatment outcome.

Be Aware of Stressors and Triggers

Sleep disturbances, withdrawal, stress, social isolation, and any irregularity from the usual routine can lead to growing signs of depression or mania. Life alterations such as, getting a divorce, a change in job, buying a house, having a baby, being newly married, or going to college, may disrupt the mood. Anytime people feel that they are not in sync with the world can be a trigger and practicing mindfulness techniques will help develop stability and awareness.

Socialize

Overstimulation can be anxiety provoking and trigger symptoms, but so can isolation or under stimulation and this is why it is critical to cultivate balance. Moving thoughts away from problems and focusing the mind onto an activity can be very beneficial, such as an outdoor sport, hobby or volunteer work.

Develop a Support Network

Try to accept friends or family that are supportive and attempt to share your life and they might be able to assist in avoiding stress or help recognize the signs of depression or mania. There is also the opportunity to become active in organizations such as, The National Alliance on Mental Illness (NAMI) or The Depression and Bipolar Support Alliance.

Strive to Receive an Adequate Amount of Sleep

People with bipolar disorder have problems sleeping, and irregular sleep habits can provoke a depressive or manic episode. Approximately twenty-five percent of those with this condition sleep too much or take long naps, and about thirty-three percent have insomnia under their normal mood states. Try to schedule regular daily activities such as walking or exercising along with setting an alarm to wake up at the same time every day.

Maintain Hope and be Proactive

Physicians often try various combinations and doses of medication before they find the right cocktail. Be aware of what symptoms the drug is targeting and ask questions. If the medication is not working or side effects are too disturbing do not stop taking the medication before discussing your options with a physician. Being a good client means having an open discussion with your physician along with taking charge of your health.

Suggestions for Loved Ones Friends and Society

Do Not Miscalculate the Perils

Because research has shown:

1. The yearly average suicide rate of those having bipolar disorder is ten to twenty times that of the general population.

2. At minimum twenty-five to fifty percent, of those diagnosed will attempt suicide.

3. In the sufferer's lifetime, the majority or eighty percent will have at least one attempt at suicide and suicidal ideation.

4. In the weeks before their death, seventy-five percent who succeeded in committing suicide mentioned having suicidal thoughts and feelings.

Listen seriously to what this person is saying and discuss how you can help. Sometimes a little release of stress works at others hospitalization may be the solution.

The Illness does not Define the Person

Those that are bipolar accept the illness as being a part of their identity; however, one piece of the pie is not the whole. When someone is diagnosed bipolar, of course, the illness is a part of their life, and some have more signs than others; therefore, coping with symptoms plays more significant role.

Stereotyping someone with a mental illness leads to errors and misunderstandings. There are doctors, politicians, scientists, lawyers, celebrities, artists, teachers, students that have this illness, and the list continues, because mental health has no favorites.

Try not to use Common Place Phrases

Many people use common phrases such as "stop and smell the roses" because it is easier than directly facing the situation, and allowing words to reflect what you hear and see takes effort. Those that are struggling with emotional difficulties are often manipulated with these clichés in place of real interest and as with most people they appreciate the attempts when others express their true thoughts, feelings and concerns.

Do Not Give Up Hope

Those who are experiencing an emotional crisis take what others have to say seriously, and this is why friends, loved ones and society must never give up hope. People in turmoil cannot quite see the world clearly, and their vision of the world is blurry, trusting in others at times to guide the way. They need us to believe in them and in a future that does not center on hospitalizations, medications and physicians.

Bipolar disorder is a long-term condition that must be thoroughly managed throughout the patient's life. In the majority of cases, the condition can be treated with medications, psychological counseling, and patients monitoring their mood along with following a treatment plan.

Chapter 8
Highlighting Schizophrenia

Schizophrenia is a chronic debilitating brain disease that has affected people throughout antiquity. At times, those afflicted appear to be emotionally healthy until they communicate their thoughts, feelings and perceptions. At the present time, the National Institute of Mental Health states that more than 1.1 percent of world's population has schizophrenia, approximately 3 million cases in the United States. Males have a tendency to develop signs before women and symptoms occur at similar rates in all ethnic groups around the world. This illness impacts men about 1.4 times more than and women, does not, usually, occur after the age of 45 and is infrequently diagnosed in children. In 2002, the economic cost of treating and managing this disease was 62.7 billion dollars, and undoubtedly has increased at the time of this writing. The human cost is much greater because 10 percent of these sufferers are triggered to commit suicide (Hor & Taylor, 2010).

Tragically the condition, usually, begins in early adulthood and those diagnosed may hallucinate by hearing voices, seeing images that other people do not hear or see. A person who has schizophrenia may insist that someone is in control of their thoughts, can read their minds, or are plotting to harm them. Symptoms such as hallucinations and delusions, usually, start between ages 16 and 30. These terrifying beliefs can cause the patient to withdraw or at times become extremely agitated. When in crisis and while in their deepest moments of despair, the sufferer communicates in a nonsensical manner sitting for hours without moving or attending to the environment. Families and society are affected by all forms because many have difficulty physically caring for themselves or maintaining employment, thereby, rely on others for assistance.

The Basics of Schizophrenia

Schizophrenia is a mental illness identified by illogical, incoherent thoughts, bizarre speech patterns, hallucinations, delusions and unusual behaviors. Some researchers view Schizophrenia from a developmental perspective stimulating optimism that prompt, concentrated treatments may render greater assistance to those afflicted, and believe full psychosis represents a late stage of the disorder (Gilmore, 2010). Schizophrenia is an incredibly complex disease that a few scientists identify symptoms as being a group of different disorders (Cloninger, Arnedo, Svrakic, Dragan, del Val, 2014). In the past, researchers studied the illness by exploring the brains of those with a diagnosis after death. However, substance abuse age, medication, various diseases, aging and life stress, often changes or damage the organ making it difficult to distinguish where the disease originated. Researchers understand very little about the fundamental causes of schizophrenia and do not know how or what cells in the brain are affected.

The History of Schizophrenia

Historical documents that describe Schizophrenia are referenced to times before Christ and as far back as the second century to the old Pharoahs of Egypt. The heart and the mind were one and the same, to the ancient Egyptians and diseases were seen as symptoms of the heart. Madness in ancient times was a phrase that the community used randomly to all forms of mental deterioration. The symptoms were not thought of as being an illness but were identified as being a divine punishment or demonic possession. Evidence for this conclusion originates from the Old Testament in the First Book of Samuel, where King Saul became 'mad' after ignoring his religious obligations and angered God. David strumming on his harp, to relieve Saul's distress also suggests that some considered there to be a successful treatment of emotional illnesses. (1 Samuel 16.14, 16.23 KJV) In ancient times ideas that relate to mental illness were that the symptoms were caused by evil spiritual possession, and the treatment was to exorcise the demon. Therapies ranged from exposing the person to certain types of sounds, to releasing the spirits by drilling holes in the sufferers' skull.

During this time, everyone that was not considered normal was primarily treated the same even if the condition was due to emotional illness, mental retardation or a physical deformity. A few investigators have looked into the ancient Greek and Roman literature and concluded that the ordinary folks seemingly had an awareness of mental illness. However, no one has found a syndrome relating to the current diagnostic criteria for schizophrenia in these communities. In the epics of Homer and Greek mythology mental illnesses were also thought of as being a punishment from the gods. It is meaningful for people to understand that not everyone in ancient times thought 'madness' was an illness or a curse. Socrates (470-399 BC), the Greek philosopher states that, "according to the evidence provided by our ancestors, madness is a nobler thing than sober sense ... madness comes from God whereas sober sense is merely human." The concept of mental disorders being a subject of scientific inquiry occurred during the time of the Greek physician Hippocrates (460-377 BC). This doctor suggested that mental deterioration was a result of someone having an imbalance of the four bodily humors and illnesses could be treated by rebalancing these humors with treatments, such as blood-lettings, purgatives and diets. In the fourth century BC, these treatment methods represented a significant advancement from the belief that mental illnesses were a punishment God. Aristotle (384-322 BC), the Greek philosopher and Galen (129-216) the Roman physician, expanded on the humoral theories. This development helped to play a significant role in establishing humoral theories and was considered to be the Europeans prevailing medical treatment plan (Shorter, 1998).

The philosopher Cicero (106-43 BC) and the physician Asclepiades of ancient Rome shunned Hippocrates' humoral assumptions. They believed that symptoms of depression (melancholia) were related to emotions such as grief, fear, and anger, not from the excess of "black bile." Unfortunately, the leadership of Asclepiades and Cicero began to decline in the first century. Celsus the dominant Roman physician re-established the concept of madness being a sanction from god, later reinforced by the growth of Christianity. Religion became the key to curing madness, in The Middle Ages, and some monasteries became hospitals for treating mental illness. During these times and in arabic medical and psychological research bizarre psychotic behaviors and beliefs similar to a few of the symptoms of the present day schizophrenia were reported. A leading medical textbook of the 15th century, Serafeddin Sabuncuoglu's Imperial Surgery addresses no disease akin to schizophrenia. However, Avicenna (980 – 1037) in The Canon of Medicine, described a state somewhat similar to the symptoms of schizophrenia called Junun Mufrit. He explained this cruel madness and distinguished it from other forms such as rabies, mania, and dementia.

The humoral theories of Hippocrates were indeed absorbed into the Christian belief system, and the blood-lettings and purgatives continued along with faith and prayer. Prior to the 19th century, accounts of schizophrenic symptoms were rarely found in historical records, although irrational and uncontrolled movements were recorded. In the Ancient Egyptian Ebers Papyrus, brief reports indicate schizophrenia-like symptoms, but other documents did not show any connection. The Ancient Greek and Roman literature describes psychosis. However, there is no record of an illness that matches the principles for modern schizophrenia. The term may be a modern day disease given the sparse historical testimonies, or it may have been hidden in books by related diseases such as mania or melancholia

The scientific discoveries of the fifteenth century, such as those of the physician and anatomist Vesalius (1514-1584) and the astronomer Galileo (1564-1642) began facing the authority of the Church. Steadily the focus of attention and investigation drifted from God and the heavens to man from the earth. This experimental shift in focus did not promptly provide any improvements in the treatment of mental illness and hippocrates' humoral theories continued into the eighteenth century. John Locke (1632-1704) from England and Denis Diderot (1713-1784) from France were empirical researchers who provoked the status quo by disagreeing and agreeing in concert with Cicero. Their thoughts were that reason and rationality were produced by sensations and feeling states. The physician Philippe Pinel (1745-1826) of France began viewing mental illness as being an effect of psychological and social stress. Simultaneously, the Tukes, a father and son team from England founded in 1795 the first hospital for humane treatment for the insane, in the British Isles, the York Retreat. The Medico-Philosophical Treatise on Mental Alienation or Mania by Pinel in 1801 also requested a more humane way to the treatment of mental diseases. Pinel's treatment plan includes having reverence for the person that provides a trusting and confiding relationship, provide regular activity in a soft, quiet environment, and casting off the Hippocratic treatment methods.

Schizophrenia during the first part of the 20th century was thought to be a hereditary disease and patients were at the mercy of their genetics. The condition was first established as a distinct mental illness by the Dr. Emile Kraepelin in the 1887, a German physician, was one of the first to classify mental disorders into separate categories. Dr. Kraepelin pegged the phrase "dementia praecox" to people who had symptoms that link to the current day diagnosis. He called the disorder 'dementia praecox' (early dementia) to differentiate it from other types of dementia. One example is Alzheimer's disease which, often, appears later in life and Kraepelin suggested that dementia praecox was fundamentally a disease of the brain and especially a subset of dementia. He used the term dementia praecox because his research focused on working with young adults and was first to make a distinction between dementia praecox and manic depression. Kraepelin in 1919 concluded that the causes of dementia praecox, including the present day schizophrenia were "mapped in impenetrable darkness". The concept of madness has been observed for thousands of years; however, the term "schizophrenia" is less than 125 years old, although, the disease is considered to have followed the humankind throughout antiquity.

Eugen Bleuler, in 1911, a Swiss psychiatrist formulated the word schizophrenia. Originating from the Greek terms "schizein" (to split) and, "phren" (mind), translating into "splitting of the mind." The name was designed to describe the partition of responsibilities between personality, thinking, memory, perception and was to explain the fragmented thinking of people with the disorder. Bleulers description was not meant to convey the idea of a split or multiple personalities. He also understood that the affliction was not a dementia because those with the symptoms of schizophrenia improved at times. However, during this period, there were many psychiatrists and researchers in the field who did not accept the splitting or fragmentation theory. Eugen Bleuler was the first to define the signs as "positive" or "negative." The characteristics describing Schizophrenia were The Four A's: Autism, Affect that is flat, Association of Ideas that represent an impairment and Ambivalence (McNally, 2009). Bleuler changed the name to from Dementia praecox to schizophrenia because Kraeplins description was inaccurate in naming the state a dementia. Both psychiatrists partitioned schizophrenia into groupings that were fixed on observations of symptoms and predictions of recovery (Kuhn, 2004).

Kurt Schneider, a psychiatrist in the early 20th century, explained the types of psychotic signs that feature schizophrenia (Schneider, 1959). Despite the fact that Schneider's first-rank symptoms have contributed to contemporary diagnostic criteria, their relevance and precision have been questioned.

Schneider's first-rank symptoms include:

1. Delusions of being controlled by an outside force
2. The belief that thoughts are being broadcast to other people
3. A belief that thoughts are being inserted into or withdrawn from one's mind
4. Hearing voices that comment on one's actions or thoughts or that have a conversation with other voices.

Inducing malaria became a common type of treatment for schizophrenia at the beginning of the Twentieth century because "fever therapy" and conditions that induced fevers were observed to alleviate symptoms. At times, physicians experimented by injecting sulphur or oil in trying to induce a fever. Several discouraging, approved remedies included hydrotherapy, sleep and gas therapy, insulin shock therapy, electroshock treatment and prefrontal lobotomy or the removal of the part of the brain that processes emotions became famous. These treatments were more successful at controlling behavior than alleviating suffering or curing the illness (Whitaker, 2010). In WWII Germany, at the time of the Nazi era, a widespread assumption was that the schizophrenia was a hereditary condition of a defective human, leading to genocide and forced sterilization. Thousands of people that were labeled "mentally unfit" had sterilization procedures in the United States, Scandinavia and Nazi Germany. The relative silence about these therapies suggests an embarrassment and twentieth-century psychiatrists until the 1950's then focused on psychology and psychological treatments.

A Viennese neurologist Sigmund Freud (1856-1939) who is well known to be the founder of psychoanalysis shaped much of the twentieth-century psychiatry. By the end of the period and as a result of his leadership, the majority of psychiatrists in the United States concluded that the symptoms of schizophrenia were due to unconscious conflicts beginning in childhood. Except for the psychotherapies and with the advent of antipsychotic drugs, the use of the previous unsuccessful treatments became gradually unpopular. In the 1950's the first antipsychotic drug, Chlorpromazine (Thorazine) became available that identifies with the modern day era of hope and promise for schizophrenia patients, their loved ones and medicine. In these modern times, molecular genetic research and advanced brain imaging techniques have established that schizophrenia is a biological malfunction in the brain. Psychological and social pressure plays a vital role in creating a crisis event and health professionals need to consider different pathways to treatment and work in harmony. Because of, the appearance of antipsychotic medication, considering the disease in a bio-psycho-social fashion and the shift of attention to being in the community patients can at last, at times lead a content, peaceful life

Contemporary Beliefs on the Causes of Schizophrenia

As in the past, the word Schizophrenia has more significance to being a source of confusion that leads to social stigma than providing any scientific explanation. Deprived of being aware of the exact cause of the mental illness, scientists and mental health professionals can only ground their classifications of them on observations that some symptoms tend to co-exist. As scientists attempt precisely to describe the different types of emotional illness, characteristics of the different types of schizophrenia continue to develop.

1. Schizophrenia is rare and develops only in one percent of the population; however, having a family history of psychosis highly increases the risk. This disease occurs in approximately ten percent of individuals who have a parent or sibling with the disorder and the greatest risk occurs when an identical twin has the diagnosis. The unaffected twin has almost a 50 percent chance of developing the disease. The genetic element extends beyond the family environment because children from schizophrenic parents who were adopted at an early age developed schizophrenia at a higher rate than the general population (NIMH, 2008).

2. The documentation that schizophrenia is a biologically grounded disease of the brain has rapidly increased over the past three decades. This evidence is supported by experiments involving dynamic brain imaging systems showing precisely where the wave of tissue interference that takes place in someone who, unfortunately, has a diagnosis (Brunet-Gouet & Decety, December 2006). At this particular time, one single gene has not been shown to be of importance for developing schizophrenia. Although, some studies publish a link between specific genes and schizophrenia, other reports have found that those genes do not automatically increase the risk (Cloninger, Arnedo, Svrakic, & del Val., 2014)

3. Researchers believe that no one single gene causes the disease, but rather several genes are linked to an increased risk, unlike individual genetic conditions such cystic fibrosis or hemophilia. Epigenetic development is thought of as a switch, turning off or on genes. The epigenetic evolution of a gene is the way it changes or reveals itself over a lifetime and builds upon environmental stressors. These factors can sometimes interfere with the developing brain (Gage, Hook & Brennand, 2014). Customarily schizophre-

nia manifests itself in young adulthood or during puberty when the brain experiences significant alterations that may produce psychotic symptoms, despite the fact that many of the environmental influences appeared earlier in life.

Environmental conditions, such as poor nutrition or exposure to a virus before birth and psychosocial or economic components all collaborate within an epigenetic gene expression. The effect of early childhood trauma, in recent years, has gained attention as being one factor in the development of the disease. Substance abuse is one specific environmental influence that has gained much attention by scientific researchers and the general public. In the last decade there have been studies relating marijuana usage to the onset of schizophrenia symptoms, possibly by bringing about the disease in people with a genetic sensitivity (McLaren, Silins, Hutchinson, Mattick & Hall, 2010). The National Institute of Mental Health supports the fact that scientists do not believe that substance abuse causes schizophrenia although many experts argue that the simultaneous presence of these two conditions is not just bad luck. However, the potential effects of marijuana on the treatment outcomes of schizophrenia, has been known for many years because substances abusers are less likely to follow their treatment plan.

4. Environmental and genetic factors both change brain structure. Brain-imaging technologies, like functional magnetic resonance imaging (fMRI), and positron emission tomography (PET) render a detailed map of the brain. The findings of these studies show that people with schizophrenia have changes in both the brains chemistry and structure. Modern research continues to claim that brain structure differences between people with and without schizophrenia differ especially in the frontal lobe. However, most neuroimaging studies have not included non-medicated participants, thus hiding the facts that it

may be medications that are causing the changes in brain structure.

5. Brain chemistry and structure perform a central role in schizophrenia. The brain uses neurotransmitters to communicate, and some investigators believe that complications during brain development in utero are the cause for these flawed messages (Gage, Hook & Brennand, 2014). Dopamine and glutamate are two neurotransmitters that some scientists believe are the main problems that link to the manifestations of symptoms.

6. Investigations firmly believe that the development of schizophrenia is an outcome of both genetic and environmental influences. Even though the precise cause of schizophrenia is unknown, scientists have discovered that the brains of those living with the disease are different from those without the illness. Both impairments of the growth and development of the brain and a progressive loss of structure or function of neurons seem to develop over time. However, scientists cannot yet determine whether Schizophrenia is a neurodevelopmental or neurodegenerative disorder.

The Hope and Current Research

A new research study in 2014 by the Washington University School of Medicine has singled out distinct gene arrangements that provide eight different types of schizophrenia. These scientists have found the method of how genes collaborate with each other pointing to different classifications of schizophrenia. Cloninger and his colleagues (2014) paired specific DNA variations in those with and without schizophrenia to symptoms of schizophrenic clients. In patients with hallucinations or delusions the researchers matched distinct genetic characteristics to symptoms and demonstrated that these interactions produced a 95 percent risk of schizophrenia. In another group of patients, the researchers discovered that disorganized speech and behavior specifically associated with a set of DNA variations that displayed a 100 percent risk of schizophrenia. Dr. Svrakic Ph'D., a member of the team, stated that it was when they organized the symptoms and genetic variations into categories they identified clusters of DNA variations that worked together and produced different types of symptoms.

Sometimes genes are acting in concert with each other to disturb the brain's function and structure, resulting in the expression of an illness. Individual genes have a very inadequate and inconsistent relationship in defining schizophrenia, but, groups of collaborating gene sets produce a remarkably high and consistent prediction for the disease. By organizing clusters of genetic variations and coordinating them with symptoms, it may be feasible to target drugs to a particular pathway that produces distress. These results indicate that the illness is not a single disease, but a collection of eight genetically different disorders, each having separate types of symptoms. This finding could lead towards improved diagnosis and treatment for the debilitating mental illness.

A second investigation in 2014 aimed to explore the observable changes in the brain that point to schizophrenia. Applying new stem cell technology, researchers in the lab of Fred Gage have discovered that neurons spawned from the skin cells from those diagnosed with schizophrenia operate abnormally in early developmental phases. This discovery, published in Molecular Psychiatry, correlate with modern day beliefs that events during pregnancy can contribute to the development of schizophrenia, even though the disease does not express itself until early adulthood. Dr. Gage, reports that the study hints to opportunities of constructing diagnostic tests for schizophrenia prior to the development of the disease.

Dr. Fred Gage Ph.D., who leads Salks Laboratory for Schizophrenia Research, explains that the defects in neural function were found early in the cells developmental phases were unanticipated. These researchers took skin cells from ten people, four clients with schizophrenia and six without the illness and coerced them to regress to an earlier stem cell type. The team prompted the cells to grow into very early stage neurons, which are similar to the cells in the brains of developing fetuses. They then tested the cells in two types of inspections called assays and found that cells from those with schizophrenia conflicted in a significant fashion from those taken from unaffected people. UC San Diego's scientist Dr. Vivian Hook, Ph.D., published a paper in Stem Cell Reports taking a neuro-chemical explanation of schizophrenia. Dr. Hook and her teammates collected skin cells from three schizophrenia clients, changed them into stem cells, and then adjusted the cells into brain cells. The outcome was brain particles that mimic the cells of the patients.

There is a chemical imbalance hypothesis that has been considered with schizophrenia and these schizophrenic copied nerve cells provide the data. These researchers discovered that the schizophrenic neurons produced atypical increases in some neurotransmitters. The cells were generating more epinephrine, norepinephrine and dopamine, than those without the diagnosis.

Dr. Hook explains the research also confirms the fact that stem cell copied neurons can excrete neurotransmitters, similar to cells in human brains. This concept could lead to investigations into different medications for schizophrenia and possibly answer lasting questions about diseases such as like Alzheimer's, ALS, and Autism.

The Symptoms of Schizophrenia

Mental Health professionals and researchers commonly describe symptoms of schizophrenia into three broad categories that characterize into being positive, negative, and cognitive expressions. Positive symptoms are those found specifically among people with schizophrenia but are usually not present among the general population. These symptoms include thought disorders, delusions, and hallucinations. Oftentimes sufferers may hear voices other people do not hear, or believe that someone is examining their thoughts, controlling their mind, or conspiring to abuse. Negative symptoms are those found in other mental illnesses and in the general population, however, these manifestations are intensified with schizophrenia. The expressions consist of blunted affect and emotion, lack of ambition or wish to achieve any goal and an absence of craving to form social bonds. These symptoms make day-to-day functions especially problematic and contribute to an inability to maintain employment, become independent and form connections or relationships with other people in the world. The three broad categories:

Positive Symptoms

Positive symptoms and behaviors are usually not seen in people without having a mental illness. The manifestations can wax and wane depending on life circumstances and whether the individual is receiving useful treatment. Individuals displaying positive symptoms often lack the ability to function in society and appreciate the real world. Positive symptoms include:

Thought disorders which are unconventional or atypical approaches in thinking techniques.

1. One form of a thought processing problem is when a person has difficulty establishing their thoughts or connecting them in a lucid, logical fashion. People may express themselves in a jumbled manner that is impossible for anyone to understand. Scientists and health professionals identify this as being "disorganized thinking."

2. Someone with a thought disorder might make up meaningless words, or "neologisms." Neologisms are newly cre-

ated words whose meaning is unknown to others, and the term is from the Greek word neo meaning new and logos meaning word. The adoption of neologisms in young children is usually benign but is suggestive of brain damage or a thought disorder in adults.

3. "Thought blocking" is when someone abruptly stops speaking and when asked why they cut short communicating they might say that the idea or subject matter escaped from their mind. Thought blocking is similar to the conscious process of deflecting thoughts or talking about particular topics and is common when someone is discussing a psychologically sensitive issue, but it is not a conscious choice. Those suffering say their thoughts have completely vanished. For example, someone might begin discussing a traumatic event and then stop talking midway through a sentence. When asked to continue, the person responds by stating that they completely forgot what they were saying.

The most-common explanation for thought blocking is schizophrenia. However, trauma, brain injuries, some prescriptions and drugs, such as marijuana, may also induce the difficulty. Treatment may include medication along with learning coping skills to help people focus on and manage their thoughts. Thought blocking differs from casual slips in memory that we all experience when the subject is quickly brought back into the conversation by a reminder or refocusing.

4. "Hallucinations" are symptoms occurring when someone hears, sees, feels or smells, something that is absent. Auditory and visual hallucinations are the most typical types that mental health care workers observe in those with schizophrenia. Auditory hallucinations usually lecture about behavior, commands the person to do things, or warn of danger. Many times they communicate with each other in different tones and offer opposing advice, creating fear, confusion and disorganization. Other types of hallucinations include smelling aromas (Olfactory) that no one else recognizes and have sensations touching their

bodies (tactile) when nothing is present. Those who are experiencing schizophrenia may hallucinate for a lengthy period before the family, friends and health care practitioners notice the signs.

Hallucinations may be the result of illnesses that affect brain function, such as a head injury, brain tumors, neurological diseases, medication side effects, or someone who is using psychoactive drugs such as LSD, mushrooms, ecstasy, or heroin.

5. "Delusions" are false beliefs that are rigid, highly resistant to change and do not identify with someone's individual culture. A person who is suffering from a schizophrenic crisis believes these delusions despite experts providing evidence that the convictions are not correct or rational.

Although delusions can have many themes, certain ones are more common, such as believing that friends and acquaintances can regulate their behavior via magnetic streams or that radio stations are broadcasting their thoughts. They may also think that people on television are supplying them with individual personal messages. Delusions of grandeur involve the belief they are someone else, such as an influential historical figure. Some may have paranoid delusions or delusions of persecution, thinking that people are attempting to hurt them, by tormenting, poisoning, following, or plotting to harm.

Delusions may also be the result of illnesses that affect brain function, such as a head injury, brain tumors, neurological diseases, medication side effects, or someone who is using psychoactive or stimulant drugs such as amphetamines, crystal meth, LSD, mushrooms, cocaine, cannabis, ecstasy, or heroin.

6. Movement disorders include excited, repetitive body movements or in the opposite extreme severe psychomotor slowing. A person with a movement disorder may repeat certain motions over and over, such as repeatedly jumping up and down, or they may become catatonic,

standing at attention for hours on end. When the arm is gently, place down by their side, it will slowly return to their forehead.

Observations of movement type behaviors in medical disorders has been frequently observed and include focal neurologic tumors, strokes, neurological diseases, metabolic syndromes, infections along with alcohol and benzodiazepine withdrawal.

Negative symptoms

Negative symptoms are difficult to evaluate and at times are mistaken for many other conditions, such as medication side effects, drug or alcohol intoxication, grief reactions, chronic pain, anxiety reactions or depression. Negative symptoms are disruptions to the usual expression of emotions and behaviors. People with these symptoms need assistance with daily functions, such as personal hygiene and may appear reluctant to care for themselves, however, these are problems that relate to the everyday world of those suffering from schizophrenia.

1. Difficulties with tolerating social situations

2. Inability to focus which inhibits starting or maintaining an activity

3. Poverty of speech meaning there is a lack of content or paucity of spoken words that are usually expressed slowly and monotone in quality

4. Blunted or flat affect is the clinical term describing a lack of emotional awareness and responsiveness, the difference being the degree of facial expression. Gesturing or using one's hands while speaking is rare, and there may be an inability to detect social cues during conversations.

5. Anhedonia or the lack of pleasure in everyday life is the inability to experience enjoyment from activities usually found satisfying (reading, working out, hobbies, listening

to music). Previous definitions of anhedonia highlighted pleasurable experience; however, current models emphasize various aspects of enjoyable behavior, such as motive or ambition.

Cognitive Symptoms

Like negative manifestations, cognitive symptoms are profound and may be challenging for professionals to recognize as being signs of schizophrenia. Cognitive Symptoms refer to thinking mechanisms and are often detected following psychological testing. Those living with schizophrenia often battle with executive functioning or the ability to understand knowledge and apply it to make decisions. Many struggle with organizing their thought patterns and working memory which is the capacity to use information immediately after learning it.

These symptoms can create dreadful emotional pain because they frequently make it impossible to earn a living or enjoy having a successful life. Cognitive Signs include:

1. Inability to concentrate

2. Scattered or slow thinking

3. Problems with understanding

4. Difficulties with remembering

5. Struggles with expressing thoughts

6. Troubles with paying attention or focusing.

Researchers continue to re-define the five classification types: disorganized, catatonic, paranoid, residual, and undifferentiated. These classifications have not shown to be helpful in diagnosing schizophrenia or predicting the outcome. Therefore, many practitioners are applying other methods to organize the forms of schizophrenia, and base their diagnosis on the prevalence of "positive" or active versus "negative" or passive symptoms, the co-occurrence of other emotional signs and the advancement in terms of the type and harshness of symptoms. One goal is to differentiate the types of schizophrenia based on these clinical symptoms that hopefully will help pin down the various causes.

What the Patients Report

People who suffer from mental afflictions report that the stigma and intolerance they withstand is worse than the symptoms of the illness. Stigma destroys lives because people suffer in silence, afraid to tell family, friends, colleagues and physicians about what they are experiencing. This isolation encourages feelings of shame and fundamentally discourages people from receiving treatment. The public rarely hears from this silent group, who tacitly moves on with their lives, posing no threat and suffering at times in silence. Unfortunately, society rarely becomes aware of people with Schizophrenia, who manage their symptoms and live for the most part healthy and content lives.

How to help someone who is having an acute psychotic crisis

- Speak softly
- Sit in comfortable positions
- Do not banter or use sarcasm
- Resist the urge to hug or touch
- Ask casual bystanders to leave the area
- Stifle the urge to express frustration, irritation or anger
- Take a passive attitude and avoid extended eye contact

- Be consciously aware that this individual is not capable of reasoning

- Maintain a quiet environment by decreasing stimulation and disturbances

- Be aware that the person may be very frightened of their feelings of not being in control

Many people live with this disease lead rewarding and meaningful lives. Treatment assists in reducing many symptoms, but most people manage manifestations by learning new ways of coping throughout their lifetime. Scientists are creating more powerful medications and employing new research technologies to comprehend schizophrenia's biological origins. It is our hope that maintaining this research focus will help cure, prevent and better treat the illness. Research in the past 100 years into the causes of schizophrenia including a wide range of biological (drugs), psychological, and sociological advances have found multiple pathways for treatment. In present times, those diagnosed with schizophrenia may indeed at times live a tranquil, content, productive life.

Chapter 9
Life with Chronic Pain

Chronic pain is a debilitating condition affecting an estimated 1.5 billion people worldwide. Along with merciless or recurrent pain victims may encounter depression, anxiety, and sleep disorders. Untreated, chronic pain can disturb family life and hinder everyday functioning. Nearly all chronic pain, nevertheless, can be greatly relieved with proper pain management; although patients with chronic pain usually undergo many different treatment options before finding an approach that provides relief. The American Academy of Pain Medicine affirms that approximately 35% of Americans have complaints of severe pain, and 50 million Americans are disabled partially or entirely due to this condition. Coping with pain is an extremely common symptom that causes people to make multiple appointments with their physician, and this problem is managed better by using a multidisciplinary approach requiring close integration with various health care providers. Pain has biological, psychological and sociological components.

A Brief History of the Study of Pain

For as long as mankind has been aware of pain, the health care professionals have provided reasons for its presence and explored calming agents to numb or stop the unpleasant sensation. This section concentrates on the historical archives of how pain is perceived across culture and time. A person's judgment of pain varies and relates to determinants as circumstances, environments and the individuals past history of experiencing pain (Otis, 2007).

Archaeological data and petrified poppy seeds imply that Neanderthals may have practiced using the opium poppy over thirty thousand years ago, possibly for pain relief. Paleontologists have discovered clay tablets recording back as distant as 5,000 BC., explaining how to garden and apply the opiate flower to produce joy and ease pain. The Greek writer Homer in 800 BC wrote in the epic, The Odyssey by describing men who drank opium in wine to relieve pain or forget their worries. Some older societies investigated analgesics and promoted the practice, while others saw the pain as being a vital, essential emotion. Practitioners' of the 19th century thought that the pain levels were a diagnostic agent, hypothesizing that a greater amount of personally noted pain bonds to higher inner energy. Discomfort was a therapy in and of itself and the forcing of pain on the sufferers was treatment to free the patient of sinister beliefs that were causing the unstable health status (Rey, 1998).

Since modern findings of the neuron and how they send and translate signals covering emotions such as pain several assumptions have been suggested as to the causes of pain, and its purpose or intent. Indeed within obviously defined societies, such as the ancient Greeks, there were opposing theories as to pains origin. Aristotle thought that the pain was caused by a sinister essence that pierced the body through damage or injury. Like Plato before him, Aristotle viewed pain and joy not as feelings but as "passions of the soul." Hippocrates concluded that the pain was an irregularity in the essential liquids, called humors. During this time, neither Aristotle nor Hippocrates wondered if the brain had any capacity to interconnect with pain processing and associated the heart being the primary organ for the perceptions of pain. Avicenna hypothesized that there were plenty of feeling sensations involving pain, touch, and excitement, in the 11th century. In Europe, before the scientific Renaissance pain was not adequately understood and it was reasoned that pain lived outside of the body, being a discipline from God and the prescription was prayer. Within the restricted society of the religious practicing Christians more than one opinion emerged, such as, pain lives because it is a quiz or experiment to test an individual's endurance. In this instance pain was a strike by god onto person to reaffirm their belief, or in the case of Jesus to give legitimacy and faith to a claim through misery.

René Descartes, in his Treatise of Man (1664), speculated that the body was more alike to a machine and that pain was a change that moved along nerve filaments until the disturbance entered the brain. This assumption converted the understanding of pain from a spiritual, mystical encounter to a physical, manufacturing sensation suggesting that a remedy could be obtained by researching and locating pain areas within the bodies rather than seeking submissions to god. This thought removed the center of pain awareness and attention from the heart to the brain. Descartes explained his argument by demonstrating a picture of a man's hand being hit by a mallet. In between the brain and the hand, Descartes delineated a hollow hose with a cord originating at the hand and stopping at a signal found in the brain. The strike of the mallet would provoke pain in the hand which would attract the cord in the hand and produce the signal resided in the brain to respond explaining that the brain had caught the painful information. Researchers started to seek physical therapies such as cutting precise pain threads to block the painful signal from traveling to the brain.

Long after the age of Descartes in 1975, the International Association for the Study of Pain investigated a general agreement for the definition concluding "an offensive sensory and mental activity linked with real or possible tissue injury, or explained in terms of damage" being the final definition. It is apparent from this definition that while they recognize that a pain is a physical sensation, the emotional disposition of a person, as well as the circumstances or condition associated with the pain also influences the perception of the harmful experience. For example, if a person experiences a painful situation connected with current or previous injury (disease, an accident, trauma etc.), a reoccurrence of related physical pain will not just cause physical trauma, but also the emotional and subjective trauma connecting to the first painful experience. Researchers have studied comparable injuries between two people, one person who identifies great emotional disturbance to the pain and a person who does not identify emotional disturbance. The person who associates a high disturbance will have more extreme physical pain than the person who does not connect a high emotional outcome (Springer, Sheridan, Kuo, Carnes & Molly, 2003).

Supplementary investigation has revealed that the existence of pain is molded by an excess of contextual conditions, involving vision. Researchers have observed that when a person sees the region of their body that is being aroused the person will describe a diminished significance of recognized pain. For instance, one study applied heat stimulation on a person's hands. When advised to watch their hand when the heat provocation was administered they experienced an analgesic result and recorded a greater heat discomfort threshold or less discomfort. Additionally, when the appearance of their hand was visually increased, the analgesic impact also rose and vice versa. This study illustrated how the judgment of pain relies on visible information (Mancini, Longo, Kammers & Haggard, 2011).

The application of fMRI to examine brain activity strengthens the bond between visual awareness and pain perception. It has been observed that the brain areas that communicate the perception of pain are the same areas that encode the extent of visual information. One distinct region, the magnitude-related insula of the insular cortex operates to recognize the size of the visual stimulation and integrates the idea of that size across many sensory modes, involving the judgment of discomfort. This section also overlaps with the nociceptive-specific insula, the piece of the insula that selectively prepares pain nerve cells, driving to the determination that there is an intercommunication and bond between the two areas (Moller, 2011). This interaction explains to the individual how much relevant pain they are feeling pointing to the personal judgment of pain based on the visual provocation.

Conditions that Cause Chronic Pain

The typical causes of chronic pain are inflammation or injury influencing muscles (myalgia), nerves (neuropathy), and/or joints (arthritis). Pain symptoms associated to joint damage involve osteoarthritis which is the most prevalent reason of persistent joint discomfort, and rheumatoid arthritis which is when the body's own protection mechanism attacks the joints. Pain associated to nerve damage involves Diabetic Neuropathy appearing in painful feet; Tic Douloureux (Trigeminal Neuralgia), a disease that includes severe facial pain; Postherpetic Neuralgia, the irritating pain that may accompany shingles; and Post-Amputation pain, which occurs following the removal of a limb.

A distinct kind of chronic pain is psychophysiological and does not relate to illness or damage that is currently known requiring more investigation. Sufferers with this pain have genuine distress, but no cause of pain can be recognized or the level of pain overshadows any known plausible condition. On account of the organs inside the body not possessing pain fibers like the joints, skin, or muscles, organ injury may be indicated by chronic, throbbing, or aching discomfort that has the label visceral pain. Cancer of an organ (for instance, the bowel, kidney or liver), inflammation, or infection can cause visceral pain. The treatment of chronic pain in adults is an embarrassment to health care professionals, from inadequate preparation about any features of pain to a common view that people requiring opioids for chronic pain are guilty until proven innocent. Unfortunately for all concerned, even oncologists receive essentially no education in pain administration (Forman, 2014).

Chronic pain is connected with various illnesses and disorders. People suffering from any of the following illnesses may experience some of the cognitive and emotional symptoms that are linked to chronic pain. These illnesses or conditions include:

- Arthritis
- Sciatica
- Back Pain
- Fibromyalgia
- Clinical Depression
- Migraines and Headaches
- Irritable Bowel Syndrome
- Chronic Fatigue Syndrome
- Myo-facial Pain Syndromes
- Complex Regional Pain Syndrome (CRPS)

Chronic Pain Syndrome

Chronic Pain Syndrome (CPS) is a constellation of signs which usually do not respond well to the medical model of care producing quite a challenge to people in the medical professions. CPS is a poorly defined illness as some researchers believe that a consistent pain lasting longer than 6 months and others have used 3 months as a minimum standard for the diagnosis. Still, yet other researchers suggest that any pain which persists longer than the average healing time should be considered chronic pain. In general, chronic pain is defined as any pain that lasts more than six months versus acute pain which is a pain that last less than thirty days. Once again, any pain that lasts between a month and half a year is classified as sub-acute pain and is not considered to be a chronic condition.

Chronic pain syndrome (CPS) is a problem that presents a challenge to healthcare providers because of its, unclear cause, and poor response to the medical treatment model. The pathology of chronic pain syndrome (CPS) is complex, involves many factors, and still is poorly understood by those in the medical community. Some researchers have suggested that CPS might be a learned behavioral response that begins with a noxious stimulus that causes pain (Moller, 2011 Singh, n.d.). For example, a tooth extraction or surgery that causes pain may relate to some behaviors that are rewarded externally or internally. Internal reinforcers are relief from personal factors associated with different emotions (guilt, fear of work, sex, responsibilities). External reinforcers include such factors as attention from family members and friends, socialization with the physician, medications, compensation, and time off from work. Thus, this pain behavior is reinforced eventually occurring without any noxious stimulus.

Chronic pain can seriously affect people's lives in many different areas such as relationships, work, hobbies and performing simple daily activities. Emotional symptoms are depressed mood, a reduction in energy level or fatigue, decreased activity level and decrease in libido, along with coping styles related to excessive use of drugs and alcohol to manage the pain. What helps is for people to try to keep areas of their life in balance. In order to cope adequately everyone needs to realize that pain causes physical and emotional distress. In most situations, chronic pain sufferers can overcome the anxiety and fear that is brought about by chronic pain by learning ways in which to manage these emotions (Prince, 2014). By concentrating on a balanced approach when handling everyday tasks or duties, chronic pain sufferers can learn to manage the pain constructively. For example, be careful when taking on daily tasks, doing too much or not enough can result in added stress and increase pain. If people are taking medication, always take the medicine at the same time every day to prevent any unnecessary increase in pain level. When emotions relate to pain the amount of stress and anxiety that is created varies, therefore, cognitive behavioral therapy can help the chronic pain sufferer successfully cope and accumulate methods to manage everyday stressors. By learning effective coping strategies, people can find the drive and determination to live happier and more productive lives.

Cognitive and Psychological Symptoms

Chronic pain not only affects the sufferer physically, it can also have pronounced cognitive and emotional effects. Therefore, the psychological ramifications such as having difficulty processing information, as well as the physical discomfort, can be difficult to manage. With chronic pain, people may be subjected to: forgetfulness, difficulties in performing everyday tasks, problems with communicating, and a lowered ability to concentrate. Because of the prevailing pain of the disorder, fibromyalgia provides an excellent example of what kinds of cognitive and emotional difficulties can emerge from this diagnosis. For example, the fibromyalgia patient often suffers from forgetfulness, inability to concentrate, reduced attention span, and the inability to respond with any quickness or adeptness when performing certain daily tasks. These kinds of cognitive problems are linked to the anxiety and depression symptoms that are associated with the disorder. Pain certainly can have profound psychological effects on the lives of the sufferers. For example, in the case of fibromyalgia, patients usually experience widespread pain which is a pain that is exacerbated by any type of pressure. This condition can give way to such symptoms as tiredness, insomnia, problems with swallowing and joint stiffness. The researchers Mork, Vasseljen, and Nilsen in 2010, investigated whether physical exercise and high body mass index (BMI) influence an individual's risk of developing fibromyalgia. The study included 15,990 women, none of whom at baseline had fibromyalgia or any other physical impairment. By 11-year follow-up, the incidence of fibromyalgia had reportedly occurred in 380 women. The authors noted that a weak association existed between exercise level and fibromyalgia risk; however, women who were obese or overweight had a 60% greater risk for developing fibromyalgia than did women of average or normal weight. An individual who is overweight or obese has an increased risk of FM, particularly among women who also report low levels of physical exercise.

Pain and Gender Differences

Across many distinct ailments females report that they endure more pain than men. Nearly all human investigations of sex variations have matched the number of females with the number of men who state they are in discomfort. However, almost all have not studied intensity levels and numerous studies have not involved sufficient people to be effective in identifying variations between the sexes in pain awareness. One investigation combined data from 11,000 cases from pain rates that were entered in electronic medical records at Stanford Hospital between the years 2007 and 2010. Patients were directed to rank their pain on a range of zero (no pain) to 10 (worst pain). For nearly all illnesses, females described higher pain rates than males and were on average, 20 percent above male accounts. Females with lower back pain consistently recorded higher pain rates than males and also expressed the feeling more pain in the neck and sinuses, which are results not detected in prior investigations. Females attach different numbers to the level of pain they notice opposed to males for some unexplained cause.

Prior investigations imply a few factors which may add to the difference in judgments of pain level, involving psychological factors, hormones and genetics, which may differ between females and males. Pain systems may function uniquely in females and males, or females may encounter more severe forms of illness than males. Future investigation is required to ascertain the precise reasons of pain judgment variations, which would be the first to target for more efficient pain management. Biological markers for pain, such as proteins or genes, would take some of the subjectivities out of evaluating the existence of pain, but the description of these markers is going to be a future challenge.

A Few Tips on How to Learn To Live With Pain

Emotional stress can be influenced by a number of factors with respect to chronic pain. When beset by stress or anxiety, the chronic pain sufferer needs to consider: The degree of pain that is felt on a scale of 1-10, sleep patterns, triggers that bring on pain, ways they are coping with the pain, and the amount of psychological and emotional support they are receiving.

Look for Natural Ways to Cope with Pain: Managing pain-associated anxiety is ideal for keeping pain under control and enhancing the immune system functioning. The chronic pain sufferer can enjoy a better quality of life by using alternative treatments, such as Cognitive Behavioral Therapy, eating healthily, and following a regular regimen of exercise. Therefore, finding natural alternatives to relieve pain is preferred over dependence on medication, which can reduce the sufferer's overall enjoyment of life.

Exercise is one of the best ways to reduce pain. Chronic pain can be helped, as well, by following a healthy, nutritious diet. Exercise produces endorphins, which are mood-elevating hormones that are useful in combating pain. To reduce pain, the endorphins work in conjunction with analgesic-type receptors in the nerve endings, spinal cord and the brain. Exercise is probably the best way to treat pain as the endorphins that are produced during a workout are usually many times more powerful than analgesic medications and are non-addictive. Chronic pain sufferers can reap the benefits that are provided by endorphins by taking part in daily or regular exercise. The endorphins are proven pain relievers which can reduce anxiety and the existences of the symptoms associated with stress and effectively manage chronic pain.

Try to Make a Few Behavioral Changes. People need to examine how they are currently feeling to better manage pain. For example, if people feel frustrated or irritated then it is helpful to recognize the feelings and then examine the behaviors that go along with having the emotion (irritable, angry, sad). It is helpful to examine behaviors to assess the need to possibly initiate a change in the emotion and/or behavior.

Pain Medications.

There are two main types of medications that are prescribed for the reduction of pain. Health practitioners recommend people use drugs that fall under the classification of analgesics or NSAIDS (nonsteroidal anti-inflammatory drugs). They may also suggest antidepressant medications in some cases, as well. Among analgesics, acetaminophen (sold under the well-known brand of Tylenol) is often used to reduce pain. While analgesics are made specifically to relieve pain, NSAIDS are designed to reduce both pain and inflammation. Therefore, NSAIDs are often used to manage arthritis pain as the discomfort is brought on by swelling and inflammation of the joints. The most popular NSAIDs that are sold as nonprescription, over-the-counter medications are ibuprofen and aspirin. NSAIDs not only relieve pain and reduce inflammation and swelling, they also thin the blood. Therefore, they have been found to be helpful, in low doses, in preventing heart attacks. On the other hand, frequent use of NSAIDs can cause stomach upset and/or kidney difficulties. Therefore, patients should inform their doctors what medications they are currently taking to avoid any adverse drug interactions or side effects. Women who are pregnant, asthma sufferers, individuals with kidney or liver problems, people taking medicines for high blood pressure, and those individuals who have had ulcer problems in the past should be careful about taking NSAIDs and consult their physician.

Various Treatment Approaches to Decrease Pain

1. Herbal Medicines
2. Chiropractic Therapy
3. Physical and Occupational therapy
4. Acupuncture, Massage, Yoga, Trigger Point Therapies
5. Cognitive Behavioral Therapy, EMDR, Hypnosis, Meditation and Visualization Techniques

Focusing on the Positive

Pain affects not only memory but how people think and feel about life in general. It is understandable that the more suffering people feel the more cynical, angry and negative their outlook of the world becomes (Caudill, 2008). How to learn to live with pain is no easy task. Try to realize that you are not feeling well and then attempt to discover new ways to self sooth and comfort. Try to view yourself from a healthy and positive perspective by acknowledging all of your sound working physical parts, such as, "My left arm feels terrific." This technique, if practiced consistently works by changing your overall outlook on life, instead of focusing on the negative you are now focusing on the positive. Psychological interventions do indeed help manage pain. Consider, asking your physician for a referral to a health psychologist, to assist in learning new ways to cope, and get back into enjoying life's treasures.

Humans have perpetually attempted to explain why they endure discomfort and the origins of that pain. Even though the pain was long ago assumed to be the product of malevolent gods, it is presently perceived as having a neurological beacon. Nevertheless, the judgment of pain is not fixed and can be influenced by several factors in including the circumstances surrounding the painful provocation, the visual perception of the provocation, and an individual's personal history of experiencing pain (Siegel, 1998). Contemporary research has collected substantial amounts of evidence that advances the conclusion that pain is not just the physical event, but a biological, psychological and sociological phenomenon, embracing a culture, nerve cell stimulations, the environment of the event and past personal experiences.

Chapter 10
The Effects of Terror

Post-Traumatic Stress Disorder is a debilitating ailment that results from someone experiencing a terrifying situation. People with PTSD have tenacious terrifying perceptions and recollections of the event in which they may appear emotionally indifferent or feel numb. PTSD previously labeled as battle fatigue or shell shock was brought to public awareness by war veterans, although it can emerge from a variety of traumatic events. The situations that cause signs are events that endanger a person's life, the life of a loved one or being an observer of destruction, such as a bombing (NIMH). The symptom manifestations are more severe if the incident that triggered the eruption is inflicted by a person, such as molestation, as opposed to a natural disaster or tornado. PTSD can occur at any age and sometimes is characterized by having traits associated with substance abuse, anxiety and depression. Manifestations range from being mild to severe, some may become quickly annoyed or have violent eruptions, and in stubborn cases, sufferers may have difficulty socializing or maintaining employment.

Prevalence is the percentage of people in a community that have an ailment during a given time and it signifies the existing instances of a disease in a group of people. Prevalence measures can be affected by many conditions including disease occurrence and the duration of the disease. Prevalence includes new cases and people currently living with the disease and the longer people live with a disease, the higher the prevalence. These estimations can vary by demographic factors such as gender and age. It is essential to temper prevalence estimates with the time at which they were estimated as estimates can change over time. Furthermore, when explaining prevalence approximations, it is necessary to keep in mind that prevalence can not only vary over time, but, place and individual people. PTSD estimations among 5,692 participants were investigated by The National Comorbidity Survey Replication (NCS-R), between February 2001 and April 2003. The NCS-R assessed the lifetime prevalence of PTSD among adults in the US was 6.8%. The lifetime prevalence among males was 3.6% and among females was 9.7%. The original study, in the early 1990s comprised of interviews of a US sample of 8,098 ages 15 to 54 years. In this initial representation, the prevalence of a lifetime was 7.8% in the overall population suggesting approximately a 2% rise in the condition. Although much more research is needed, studies have reported that females are twice as likely as males to experience PTSD (American Psychiatric Association, 2013).

A Brief History of PTSD

PTSD has a past that is as striking as the ailment itself and there have been reports for thousands of years. The history books explain in detail of the Romans, Greeks and Egyptians soldiers who snapped and ran in combat situations because the warriors of remote times were no less afraid of death. One Egyptian combat soldier named Hori wrote about the emotions he endured before going into battle: "You're determined to go forward, shuddering seizes you, the hair on your head stands on end, and your soul lies in your hand." The Greek recorder Herodotus explains the battle of Marathon in 490 B.C., mentioning an Athenian soldier who went forever blind as the warrior standing near him was killed, though the blinded soldier had no injuries. Paralysis, deafness, and blindness are also familiar patterns of "conversion reactions" that are well-documented among veterans of modern times. The truth about PTSD is that it is a contemporary diagnosis with symptoms that have an ancient record.

Herodotus additionally writes of the Spartan leader Leonidas releasing his men from entering the action on account of recognizing that they were emotionally worn down from previous battles. During the fight of Thermopylae Pass in 480 B.C., Leonidas explains "They had no heart for the fight and were unwilling to take their share of the danger." Herodotus additionally writes of the Spartan leader Leonidas releasing his men from entering the action on account of recognizing that they were emotionally worn down from past battles. During the fight of Thermopylae Pass in 480 B.C., Leonidas explains "They had no heart for the fight and were unwilling to take their share of the danger." Herodotus goes onto describe a Greek warrior named Aristodemus, hanging himself in shame because he was so defeated by comrades ridiculing him and tagging him with the nickname "The Trembler." Conditions describing soldiers' reactions during combat changed very little, one thousand years later. The Anglo Saxon Chronicle gives an account of the conflict in 1003 A.D., in which the English commander Alfred becoming so overwhelmingly sick that he began to retch and was not fit to lead his men. During the attack of Gibraltar in 1727, a fighter who was a member of the security team of the city maintained a journal. In it, there are remarks of occurrences in which fighters wounded or killed themselves, further characterizing them existing in a state of severe physical exhaustion causing them to fail to understand even the simplest commands. These warriors would refuse to drink, eat, work, or fight, despite frequent whippings.

During the American Civil War, military health practitioners diagnosed countless cases of emotional instability due to the stresses of living in the military and the terrors connected with warfare. These accounts include a wide range of physical ailments that are currently recognized as being caused by emotional turbulence, including paralysis, blindness, trembling, self-harm and heart palpitations (also known as "exhausted heart" and "soldier's heart.") Civil War physicians began to notice that soldiers on regular furlough often collapsed with an emotional breakdown at home, yet exhibited no displays of mental debilitation before they had left the camp. During the first three years of the Civil War and not understanding how to treat PTSD, military practitioners only ushered the severe cases out of active service. Richard A. Gabriel, one of the leading historians of PTSD states "They were put on trains with no supervision, the name of their hometown or state pinned to their tunics and others wandered about the countryside until they died from exposure or starvation." Gabriel's investigation further outlines that the enormous number of emotionally disturbed soldiers roaming around the countryside was so large that there was a public outcry. On description of these numerous public objections along with the urging of physicians, the first military infirmary for the emotionally disturbed was opened in 1863. However, the administration made no attempt to treat the psychiatrically injured after the war and the hospital was shutdown. The discounting of the impacts trauma was linked to accusing the victim of having ulterior motives and the assistant surgeon general in 1864 echoed this opinion by stating that most who bore signs and symptoms of emotional war injury were in reality, malingering. The Russian Army of 1905 was the first in recorded history to conclude that mental breakdown was a direct consequence of the stresses of war, and requested to consider this mental collapse as being a valid medical condition. Gabriel reports that the Russian goal to diagnose and treat combat shock symbolizes the origin of military psychiatry. The Russians' influential contribution to the problem was the acceptance of the principle of proximity, or frontline treatment. While this concept is accepted by nearly all military branches today, the Russians were the first to treat psychiatric victims close to the front, with the intent of restoring sufferers to action. However, the documented percentage of those who returned to fight implies the method was not very promising as there was less than 20 percent success rate.

The ruthlessness of WWI created enormous appraisals of men having psychological scars and sadly what little had been known about PTSD was ignored. The single American inquiry related to psychiatric distress that anyone identified was under the command of Gen. John J. Pershing who documented that American fighters had an abnormally high incidence of mental breakdown. (Jones, Hyams & Wessely, 2003). Psychiatrists began associating the high psychiatric distress to the modern weaponry of large-caliber gunnery and it was thought that the blast of the shells produced a shock that disturbed the physiology of the brain, and thus the phrase "shell shock" came into fashion. By the conclusion of World War I, Americans psychiatrists abroad were starting to understand that psychiatric victims were not experiencing "shell shock." These psychiatrists thought it was emotions and not brain injury that was most frequently making soldiers crumple under a wide assortment of symptoms. Regrettably, physicians continued to view symptoms as being due to the sufferer having a weak character. It was during World War II when it became obvious that not only the "soft" in spirit were crumbling emotionally (Lembcke, 2013). This change in understanding reflects in the psychiatric vocabulary that took place near the conclusion of World War II in which "combat neurosis" changed to the title "combat exhaustion" eventually pointing to the modern day diagnosis of Post-Traumatic Stress Disorder.

The History of PTSD as it relates to Environmental Trauma

Samuel Pepys was an Englishman from London during the 1600s, and his journal provides an excellent account of the development of PTSD. In his description of the Great Fire of

London in 1666, Pepys characterizes people's terror and disappointment, mentioning the inability to preserve their homes or to even quench the flames. Pepys writes, "a most horrid, malicious, blood fire and so great was the fear that it was enough to put people out of their wits." Novelist Charles Dickens was involved in a railroad disaster, in England, on June 9, 1865 and experienced symptoms which in modern times would be associated with PTSD. Dickens recounts the horrifying picture in a message: "Two or three hours' work, amongst the dead and dying surrounded by terrific sights..." Later in his record he mentions being "unsteady" declaring, "I am not quite right within, but believe it to be an effect of the railway shaking." A few years before he wrote the novel, Man's Search for Meaning, Psychiatrist Victor Frankel survived the confinement of four Nazi concentration camps during WWII. In the book, Frankel says explicitly "an abnormal response to an abnormal situation is normal behavior" (Frankl, 1997). Unfortunately, this notion has not yet developed into being a popular view. PTSD symptoms can be detected among survivors of the holocaust, of automobile collisions, of sexual attacks, and from natural disasters.

The Biology and Physiology of PTSD

PTSD manifests biochemical alterations in the body and brain, that are different from other emotional conditions such as major depression (Kato, Kawata, & Pitman, 2006). Many physiological appraisals of PTSD are similar to those of someone having a prolonged stress reaction, such as:

1. The heightened corticotropin-releasing factor (CRF) concentrations, which are hormones and neurotransmitters involved in the stress response.

2. The effects of the catecholamine's within the central nervous system such as epinephrine (adrenaline), norepinephrine (noradrenaline) and dopamine.

3. There is a decrease in the hippocampal size of the brain.

In animal studies, as well as, human research, the amygdala is heavily implicated in the creation of emotional recollections, particularly fear-related memories. The position of the amygdala is within the temporal lobes of the brain and performs a fundamental role in the processing of memory and emotional responses. Neuroimaging studies in humans reveal both morphological and functional appearances of PTSD and the usual controls and balances on amygdala activation are impaired, so that the governing impact on the amygdala is severely disrupted. Inhibition of the amygdala creates an untamed cycle of reoccurring fear conditioning, in which minor provocations are more likely to be assessed as dangerous (Rothschild, 2000). The means for quenching minor responses are neutralized thereby reducing the threshold for fearful reactivity. On account of the extreme activation of the amygdala by environmental events, people view harmless situations as posing a threat. This activation generates outputs to different brain areas that have a number of functions: spatial learning, memory consolidation, memory of emotional events, autonomic fear responses, and fight or flight reactions. Additional animal and clinical investigations of the amygdala and how it relates to fear conditioning may give way to supplementary therapies for PTSD (Bremner, 2006).

Over the past decade, biological research is beginning to look at what is different from the chronic stress response, such as hypothalamic, pituitary and adrenal functions in relationship to gene expression. The aim of early treatment with medicine after exposure to emotional trauma is to soothe posttraumatic responses and inhibit the development of PTSD. Evidence of the neuro-circuitry underlying the human alarm response may assist physicians in identifying medications that are most apt to be useful. The pharmacological hurdle is to distinguish where and in what way to treat and to rein in the amygdala along with the consequential responses that are set in motion.

Social and Gender Implications

Upon review of the global history including the evolution of Post-Traumatic Stress Disorder, it is clear that at least one severe social stigma perseveres, that having "a weak character" is linked to one possessing the illness. By the same token, those grappling with symptoms are also struggling with attempts to get the guidance they need despite the complex, social embarrassment attributed to the diagnosis. Numerous epidemiologic studies confirm that a posttraumatic stress disorder is twice as common in females as in males. There are also gender differences in the kind of trauma exposure, presentation of symptoms, and comorbidities. A few of these variations are clearly societal and not biologically based, however, there is also explicit evidence that the biologic models altered in PTSD may strengthen or be tempered by sex hormones. Rachael Yehuda and associates (2009) conclude that there are a few PTSD gender variations in biologic irregularities detected in people with PTSD; however, there are more similarities than dissimilarities.

There are a plenty of thoughts of why PTSD is more prevalent in females than in males because different types of traumas carry varying risks for symptom development. Many epidemiologic studies confirm that females with PTSD are more likely to have depression and anxiety disorders, in contrast to men because having a history of anxiety disorder or depression at the time of injury is a risk factor for the emergence of PTSD. There are also distinctions between males and females in how they portray the manifestations. Although many disorders existing simultaneously with PTSD are common in both genders, males are more likely to have substance use disorders (Schnurr, Lunney & Sengupta, 2004). Females are more prone to having symptoms of avoidance and numbing, and males are more likely to have the associated characteristics of impulsiveness and irritability. Much of the heightened pervasiveness of PTSD in women is mediated by the type of trauma and comorbidity rather than only biology. Rape, in both males and females, presents one of the highest risks for exhibiting signs and is prominently more common in females than in males.

Sarah Inslicht, Ph'D., a University of California professor introduced a few findings during the 2012 "The Brain at War" symposium on investigations of how males and females acquire, and unlearn the fear reaction. Experts call these methods fear conditioning and fear extinction. The preliminary conclusions of the study infer that females with PTSD had higher fear-conditioning reactions than males which implying that there may be variations in how males and females learn to fear. Greater fear conditioning in females might indicate a pre-existing vulnerability or occur in a gender dependent style. Professor Inslicht, Ph'D., cautioned that the study is in the initial stages and what may be exciting is to learn how people stifle the fear response which is key in the recovery process.

The Three Main Therapies for Post-Traumatic Stress Disorder

There are accepted therapies for PTSD; however, discussing and exploring ways to cope with past traumatic experiences can be difficult because people usually keep their thoughts and emotions to themselves, rather than explaining the phenomena. Talking with a therapist frees the impact of the trauma, assists in recovery, decreases symptoms and most importantly provides victims the sense of not being alone in the world. Treatment usually lasts for a minimum of six months with some therapies lasting longer, especially if there are other emotional health problems that hinder recovery. Psychotherapy, especially cognitive-behavioral methods, are effective in the treatment of PTSD although there are limited investigations in gender differences, in response to therapy.

Successful treatment methods including gender differences are destined to be a useful area to explore in future research.

Cognitive Therapy

After experiencing a traumatic experience a survivor might find fault with themselves for circumstances in which they had no control, for instance, a soldier may have guilt about the decisions made during a firefight. Cognitive treatment guides people who feel guilt understand that the traumatic event was not completely their responsibility and the goal is to support the recognition of how thoughts produce stress that shape symptom development. Sufferers discover ways to recognize and cope with thoughts that are anxiety or fear inducing and with the aid of a trained therapist; people will learn to substitute these thoughts and behaviors with ones that are more precise and less distressing. Cognitive behavioral therapy educates people on how to regulate feelings connected with the anger, guilt, and fear. This treatment encourages sufferers to recognize and adjust to how they remember the trauma and its effect on healing, and the purpose is to assist victims in understanding how certain thoughts create stress that ultimately produces symptoms.

Exposure Therapy

The aim with exposure therapy is to reduce the anxiety about the traumatic event via behavioral methods. Exposure treatment focuses on the notion that people learn to dread emotions, thoughts, and circumstances that evoke a traumatic experience. By repeatedly discussing the trauma, they will discover ways to gain command of thoughts and emotions in relationship to the event. Some may concentrate on memories that are less upsetting, before addressing the traumatic event. With time individuals learn that they do not have to fear memories, which, at first may be challenging because it might seem odd to think about the stressful event on purpose. Gradually people will feel less overwhelmed and with the help of a therapist clients can alter how they respond to stressful memories. This is desensitization and the process enables one to cope with trauma situations gradually over time. A therapist may ask to retrieve many memories at one time, while, communicating in a place where they feel safe as feeling secure makes the process comfortable. This is the "flooding" technique which encourages people to learn how not to feel overpowered by their emotions and promotes practicing various ways to relax, such as focusing, mindfulness or breathing techniques when facing a flashback.

EMDR

EMDR or Eye Movement Desensitization and Reprocessing is a distinct type of treatment for PTSD. Like other types of therapy, EMDR assists in changing how people respond to the memories and recollections of trauma which research has confirmed that the method minimizes symptoms. While thinking of or discussing memories, the center of attention is on different stimuli like eye movements, hand taps, and sounds. The therapist will move his or her hand near the persons face as they are instructed to follow this movement with their eyes after discussing a memory of the trauma. Contemporary research implies that the eye movements may not be a vital part of treatment and neuropsychologists are investigating in what way EMDR operates in correlation to brain functioning (Jeffries & Davis, 2013).

The Effects of Terror

Immediate Effects: Fear triggers the fight or flight response and people decide whether to let the fear take control, or make a split second decision to run. Do they fight? Do they try to minimize the impact of the fear? Does the fear roll them over to the point of not being able to respond and they freeze? By Peering back in the past some may be pleased while others have misgivings about how they managed the crisis, and treating symptoms depends on how people think and feel about how they responded during that moment of trauma. While fear is not at all a desirable emotion, understanding the way people respond to it is fundamental and the knowledge that understanding provides helps to realize that they are capable of taking sensible steps even in the toughest, most terrifying situations (Ropeik, 2010).

In the immediate aftermath of a terrifying event, it is expected to experience fear; however, people perceive, process, and react to terrifying events differently. These individual reactions depend on past experiences, expectations of the present, and future concerns of this traumatic event reoccurring. Initially, most people would tend to wonder if the same type of event could happen again, and would try to think of different ways protect themselves in the future. Sometimes there is a replaying of the frightening event in the minds as if it is a tribute to pay homage, and then gradually the fears and memories fade.

<u>Short Term Effects:</u> In the first few days or weeks after the terrorizing incident most people would feel some stress provoking aftereffects and experiences distinct personal thoughts and emotions. These feeling states are those that a person tends to be aware of whenever they are in a difficult life situation and should seem familiar. As mentioned, individuals feel something different after experiencing a traumatic event and these reactions can be terror, anger, guilt, shame, anxiety or depression. Some will feel less of these aftereffects, and when they do, they will experience them less intensely and these short term symptoms are common, even when they are strong and seem ridiculous. Those who have these powerful feeling states have learned throughout their lives to cope with the high levels of stress which usually subsides within a month or two. If the bothersome thoughts and feelings decrease in intensity each day they will subside with time and without the need for professional assistance.

<u>Long Term Effects:</u> Long term effects may appear immediately, a few months later, or take years to emerge because the core problem began in childhood where a terrifying event was most likely originally experienced. As children, people develop their own distinctive style of protecting themselves that worked at that time. As adults, some still have childhood ways of protection hidden in the back of the mind and they modify the way they emotionally protect themselves based on the degree of security they feel about the world. When someone experiences trauma the way the adult learned to emotionally protect themself is challenged and he or she is tempted to return to childhood thoughts about maintaining safety. If people had a nurturing fearless childhood this revisiting might only mean that they seek out family and friends to receive comfort. However, if they had an abusive childhood or experienced a traumatic event, the return to childhood ways of protection might mean following a coping style that does not work as an adult. One of the most damaging effects of experiencing terror is the return or regress to the way they protected themselves as a child because this leads to an inability to function in the world.

How to Cope with Terror or Extreme Fear

<u>Immediate Effects:</u> If people feel the initial effects, it may be helpful try to remember the way in which you handled the incident, and how you coped with the feelings, and then try to believe that you can count on these abilities to apply in the future. By thinking of how well you coped with this event, you will become aware that you will be able to cope with any future stressful event.

<u>Short Term Effects:</u> Avoid being critical, and do not emotionally punish. Notice how often you experience terrifying emotions or flashbacks. You may want to learn new strategies and techniques to soothe yourself, like change who you spend time with or find ways to minimize overwhelming emotions.

Try spending time with family or friends, writing in a journal or attempt learning a new physical activity. These intense emotions should gradually diminish within a month or two.

<u>Long Term Effects:</u> If the emotional distress does not fade, if the intensity increases or if the distress interferes with the daily routine, professional assistance is recommended. Be kind and accept the fact that you are going through a difficult time at the moment, and decide that you are going to find ways to manage this problem.

PTSD and the Emotional Effects of Terror

Fear is a part of life whether it is fear of war and terrorism, or the general fears, like those of intimacy, abuse, inadequacy, a physical disease, surviving a natural disaster, or living with chronic pain. There is no right or wrong way to respond to terrifying events, and how one reacts varies from person to person. Understandably some respond with feeling helpless and not wanting to believe. Over time, these feelings may escalate to extreme anxiety, fear and despair and some may relieve the event in the form of having flashbacks, have difficulty concentrating, experience extreme fear, and have an increase in health problems. In conclusion, for people who have lived through a trauma it helps to be with caring friends and family. Take care of yourself physically, by eating well, exercising and getting adequate sleep

Chapter 11
Questions of Normal

Life has its ups and downs as just about everyone has moments in their lifetime where they doubt their emotional balance. No one lives a normal life because the concept does not exist and it cannot be accurately measured. However, there is an emotional steadiness that people try to maintain and therapists often urge patients to ask themselves if they sense "their normal." As people age, they begin to understand that their lives are for the most part relatively calm and somewhat predictable.

Abnormal psychology concentrates on irregular behavior, its description, organization, specification, and treatment (American Psychiatric Association, 2013). The field's recorded history is only 100 years old even though the literature pertaining to abnormality is well documented throughout the ages. To completely appreciate the range and importance of modern abnormal psychology one must acknowledge psychopathology and its roots, its unmistakable evolution, and the analytical principles of abnormality, which in application attempts to heal those experiencing symptoms from different dysfunctions.

Tales from biblical accounts depict sufferers experiencing symptoms that are comparable to present day ailments such as depression, schizophrenia and bi-polar. One of the earliest identified examples for mental disturbance in primeval civilizations was animism, which asserts the belief in the influence of the spirit world and someone in mental distress was thought to be possessed by a malevolent or evil spirit. Archeologists have documented evidence of a procedure termed trephination dating back to 3000 BCE (Velasco-Suarez, Martinez, Oliveros & Weinstein, 1992). This corrective treatment consisted of drilling openings into the head to free the noxious spirit and while this approach seems primitive in contemporary society, in a time when the spirit world penetrated all life, it was for the era a rational method.

During the evolution of the scientific progression of psychiatry, it was in 460 BCE when Hippocrates thought that emotional disorders were caused by an imbalance in the physical state of four liquids found within the human body. While incorrect, his interpretations were important strides toward modern medical reasoning as other ancient biological ideas affected other Greek practitioners to diagnose with preference to superstitions, legends, or religious affiliations. This progressive step of Hippocrates includes the connection made between mental dysfunctions directly emerging from biological conditions that stimulated innovative reasoning. At the start of the twentieth century, two psychological viewpoints surfaced: Somatogenic and Psychogenic. Somatogenic viewpoints maintain that an abnormal behavior has physiological roots, contrasting to psychogenic beliefs who declare that the origins of dysfunction were emotional or psychological in nature. The knowledge of hypnotherapy evolved into a remedy for hysteria, and ultimately appealed to Sigmund Freud, who presented his theory on clashing unconscious directives and their persuasive impact on thoughts and behavior (Feist, 2008). Freud eventually associated hysteria to unconscious processes and although his concepts lacked scientific evidence this was the first complete theory associated with abnormal psychology.

What is Normal?

Definitions of normality vary by circumstance, time, country, and person all of which adjust according to changing societal standards and norms. People frequently recognize normal in contrast to abnormal and to be normal in the purest form is good while abnormal is bad. Those who do not conform to the common standard have the label of being sick, abnormal, eccentric or disabled which points the way to stigmatization. Normality is the state of being average (Bartlett, 2011). Intrapersonal normality is behavior that is typical for an individual and the behavior is consistent with the most common practice for that person. Researchers call conforming to the norm thoughts and reactions that are the most common in society. Normality endures because the concept has a basis on societal norms and whether someone is normal is up to how people view themselves in contrast to the views of society. While attempting to determine and quantify normality is a significant start, all definitions face the dilemma of whether researchers are describing an idea that even exists, since there are so many diverse ways of identifying the idea.

When abnormality makes someone feel uncomfortable it is an exceptional person who will laugh it off to relieve tension as society's rejection of being different and feeling the pressure to normalize may cause shame. Mental illness is particularly misunderstood and this lack of knowledge oftentimes taints opinions of the one seeking help. The medical communities and families try to help those seeking help live a standard life; however, the pressure to appear normal creates conflicts. Society influences defines the concept of normal affecting millions of people that in turn has real world consequences. The treatment of every single mental illness from anxiety and depression on through bipolar and schizophrenia originates from how society views "normal" and "abnormal." This may be the time to rethink the terms as they apply to the behaviors and emotional states of human beings (Frances, 2013). Most people guide their actions by peer standards and then measure the suitability of behaviors by how far away they are from social norms. However, the perception of the norm may or may not be the most common behavior. In some cases, the individual may falsely believe the social norm is one thing when, in fact, very few people may hold that opinion. The social norms that affect individuals are not all the time common for everyone because behaviors that are abnormal for nearly all people may be thought of as being common for a subculture or subgroup (Reiss, 2009). For example, normal college student behavior may be to study and obtain good grades, but for a subculture of athletic students, normal behavior may be to go to practice and pursue athletic activities. Subcultures may actively deny "normal" behavior, instead substituting society norms within their own group.

Many people believe that being average is ideal as there are influences from external sources to conform, as well as, pressures from the fundamental desire to feel accepted. Sometimes someone will appear emotionally healthy while he or she may be struggling and experiencing the world in a different manner. A person with a mental health problem has all the freedoms, but may not be able to show and experience common thoughts, emotions and behaviors. These peculiarities may not be associated with their sense of identity, especially if they are unwelcome anomalies. Nearly everyone wants to be emotionally healthy and strives to be regarded as such because not having a bond with the general population leads to feelings of loneliness and isolation. Applying a label sets in motion the belief they may not have as much in common with the world at large, and this makes most people feel ill at ease. To diagnosis someone means that people have a label along with the accompanied social ramifications which include being a part of or not being a part of a larger community. This concept also sets in motion the scene for someone to be included, excluded by the larger society. Therefore, applying a diagnostic label stigmatizes people into believing that they do not have as much in common with the larger population and are alone. When abnormality has a diagnostic label, it is understandable for that person to accept some components of the sick role or have the stigmatization that also springs from some physical ailments. Taking on the role of being disabled has both interpersonal and societal consequences.

Four Factors related to the Definition of Normal

1. There is no deviation from the research or statistical norms. Researchers measure many facts, such as knowledge, weight, height, and eye color in which most people fall within the middle range. How would the world be if all were considered normal? Do all people need to be the same or average?

2. There is no deviation from social norms. Every culture has established standards for acceptable behavior. These standards usually change with time, vary from situation to situation and from culture to culture.

3. There is no maladaptive behavior. Meaning, any behavior that affects the well-being of the individual or the community in which they live. This includes any severe behavior outside of the norm of the culture, such as an attempted suicide.

4. What are the levels of personal distress? Personal, subjective feeling states.

Labeling and the Diagnostic and Statistical Manual of Mental Disorders

Numerous theoretical models in psychology stress the significance of therapeutic alliances while these forms overlap each approaches causality from a distinctive viewpoint. The psychosocial approach focuses on how people adjust to internal opposing conscious and unconscious processes throughout a time period while interacting with their surroundings. The psychosocial approach discusses the effects of impacts on behavior and frequently concentrates on social connections, environment along with internal memories, concerns and struggles. The biological model recognizes a physical connection to mental illness and dysfunction. This theory evaluates the physical and biochemical roles in the human body, particularly within the brain, as being a method to learn how these roles associate to abnormal behavior and the unobservable atypical thinking processes. The sociocultural model approaches the influences of familial, cultural and social environments on people and their effects on mental dysfunction and symptoms. This model considers the situation as a stressor and trigger, which intensifies possible dysfunctions thereby provoking abnormal behavior. Sociocultural models concentrate on the importance of social rules, norms, communication, social relationships and religious convictions (Comer, 2007).

A vast number of disciplines have attempted to define the concept of normal with the results being that there is no one meaning of normality. The prevailing enigma of answering 'What is normal?' is questions related to biology, sociology, psychology and philosophy. The most extensive effort to sort out normality from abnormality comes from clinical psychology, in the Diagnostics and Statistics Manual. Diagnostic tags are proliferating and mental disorders seem to be adding ever more territory, at the same time many people with and without diagnosable ailments are forming their own original ideas on what is normal. The Diagnostic and Statistical Manual of Mental Disorders (DSM-IV) consist of a persuasive symptom based identification process that consists of efforts to include life stressors and environmental triggers. The symptom focus allows convenience for the diagnosing to be swift because symptoms can be easier to obtain than life crisis points or event histories. Some of these life crises and event histories may conjure up what may be a brief and common unusual mental state in response to an environmental situation. The DSM points to how normality is dependent on the symptoms, how normality may change throughout history, and how it may relate to value judgments (Horwitz, 2007; Skopalová, 2010).

The American Psychiatric Association has revised its diagnostic and statistical manual and the subsequent version, DSM-V, will be out in the year 2014. Labels may increase and mental disorders may add more sections, but to call this a psychiatric power clutch is exaggerating. The true drive behind the generation of labels is the growing capability of technology to view people as they have never been able to in the past (Davis, 2014). Nevertheless, the idea of a change in the normal calls forth unease as to force normality is to persuade conformity. To increase diagnostic categories produces anxiety and some question the idea of anyone being emotionally fit. Judges of psychiatry complain that many cases fit in no obvious section and people are given labels like "anxiety disorder not otherwise specified." Such clients nevertheless frequently continue to be at risk for many serious complications and these conclusions are the result of expanding these categories. The mental health critics also object to the profession medicating people who have no diagnosis.

Researchers, as well as, clinicians in medicine have narrowed typical reactions, like quirks and peculiarities to become difficulties people dread and insist upon wanting medications to transform (Frances, 2013). Critics state that physicians are attempting to move someone from a common, but disfavored personality state (active) to another common, but rewarded state (calm). However, such a view is a swift jump from judges who are analyzing a narrow view of normalcy to declaring that all physicians overmedicate. Labels can be important even when medication has no part in therapy. For example, a woman complains that her child is too busy. Does the child have ADHD, or is the child interested in just pursuing many projects at the same time? There is no evidence in the literature that states that the generation of diagnoses has done any harm to an individual's identity. Parents who might have once thought of a child as being unusual, once diagnosed may view him as having Asperger's and may also become increasingly aware of a few strange tendencies in themselves. A diagnosis even if imprecise can produce comfort along with providing a way of doing things for directing the problem at hand.

What is a Chemical Imbalance?

Research technology is modifying the perception of psychiatric ailments. Methods of examining brains, neurons, and cell connections, along with using powerful computer models, associate with many observed fluctuations in function with disease and disability. The nerve associations' people form, the neurotransmitters that develop, the symptoms people suffer may be linked to a vulnerability that associates with a disorder. Life is a bio-chemical and bio-electric process that occurs for a limited period of time, and then ends in death. There are situations, such as a crisis, which can cause a reaction in the brain that creates a release of a chemical. The relationship these chemicals have with each other creates a feeling. It is how people perceive and react to the crisis that defines what emotions arise and the intensity.

Life stressors create an emotional crisis that can generate a chemical reaction. Therefore, there are many levels of emotions and how people respond to the crisis relates to the body's physiological-biological life. It is the individual that is in the crisis that controls how they respond to the tension. The feeling of being emotionally centered occurs when the chemical relationships (brain controls), and the how people manage life's stressors (which they control) balance. Treating a chemical imbalance often requires a combination of several different methods. In the event of a depression or anxiety related chemical imbalance, prescription medications may be ordered to either direct the production of neurotransmitters or compensate for the lack of transmitters. The medication helps to reduce the symptoms over time, allowing for the client and physician to move toward a more permanent solution. Therapy is helpful in treating the underlying cause of the imbalance, especially when life stressors are the primary cause. Learning how to manage anxiety is essential for a full recovery, as prolonged periods of stress can diminish the body's ability to absorb nutrients efficiently. Treatments often include lifestyle changes such as daily exercise to stimulate the production of endorphins and chemicals which help elevate mood, using supplements to infuse the body with nutrients that provide the building blocks for neurotransmitters, and adjusting dietary habits to ensure the body receives adequate nutrition.

When people ask a therapist if they are normal, they are assuming that therapists have an easy way to measure the concept. There is no such clear way to determine normal because normal is ever changing in life and depends on life transitions, age, culture and the community in which they live. For example, the next time people leave the house observe others and pay attention to all of the different types of people there are in the world. There is no one personality type that professionals view as being normal (Hur, Roese & Namkoong, 2009; Wachbroit,1994). The notion is a concept, a conclusion that cannot be measured. If one ever wonders if they are normal, the answer is it depends. Emotions allow people to experience strength, compassion, love, joy, sorrow, envy and a full range of feelings and sensations. Mental Health Professionals possess their own ideas about who needs help and these ideas are in dispute because they cannot be measured or quantified.

Am I Normal? A Self Measure

If people consider themselves being better than average, improvements with counseling are likely, though the costs may outweigh the benefits. If people view themselves as average, they could benefit from counseling and/or some professions include medication. If people feel worse than average, I think they should seek professional help. This is just my opinion because people are in charge of the decisions involving their situations in life. Although, I feel a bit sad about this belief because those who are worse than average could benefit and ultimately feel better and improve the quality of their life. At this stage, to achieve the best treatment outcome, therapy and medication may be included in the recommendations.

In the feeling state areas below, people can be considered better than average, average, or worse than average. (Circle each category to obtain your overall rating)

Happiness Scale

- Better: I am happy many times during a typical day, and this joy is a consistent, steady feeling.

- Average: I am at times every day where I am happy, but think at times these moments require effort or coaching.

- Worse: I have happy moments, but I think that I need much more pleasure in my life. I am generally sad.

Depression Scale

- Better: I never feel sad for any length of time.

- Average: I feel sad now and then, perhaps for a few days at a time, but not more than a couple of times a month.

- Worse: I am often sad and may fear that the sadness will never end. I have thoughts of despair and lack hope. (If there are any suicidal thoughts, receive help immediately by calling the local crisis hotline or 911)

Loneliness Scale

- Better: I receive the human, social contact to satisfy my needs for other people.
- Average: I do not feel intensely lonely or feel this way more than once a week.
- Worse: I sometimes feel intense loneliness, deprived of human contact, emotional support and care.

Love Scale

- Better: I resolve most disagreements and argue less frequently as the relationship unfolds.
- Average: I have disagreements and they are often not resolved. Verbal abuse is rare, and there are no threats of violence or physical abuse.
- Worse: There are many arguments involving verbal abuse, physical abuse, sexual abuse or threats of violence.

Fear Scale

- Better: I am almost never afraid unless I am in real danger.
- Average: I feel the fear and anxiety regularly, but the situation is tolerable and I am not in danger.
- Worse: My fear is so frequent that it limits my activities and my ability to enjoy life.

Self-Acceptance Scale

- Better: I am aware that I like myself, at times genuinely accept myself. (I have that internal proud strut like feeling)

- Average: I do not necessarily accept myself, but I do not hate myself either.

- Worse: I have periods of self-hate where I cannot even look myself in the mirror or, look into someone's eyes.

Safety Scale

- Better: I rarely worry about my safety and feel safe in my surroundings.

- Average: I occasionally worry about my safety, even when my world is safe.

- Worse: I worry about my safety daily, regardless of how safe I may be in the world.

Feeling Accepted Scale

- Better: There is at least one person in my life who knows and accepts me for just being me. I have friends who know a lot about me.

- Average: I try to gain acceptance by fulfilling other people's expectations at times. I hide qualities which I think other people may find offensive.

- Worse: I think that I do not deserve to be accepted. I may try to gain acceptance by doing what I think others like me to do, just in order to please.

Identify an area where discipline is lacking and determine where you stand in the present, acknowledge and accept this starting point, and then create a training program to improve. It takes different exercises to build discipline in improving communication, sleep, work and food habits. As people navigate through difficult times toward a better future, it is useful to examine some tried and true ideas regarding life. Encouragement is based on focusing on strengths rather than a weakness. The tools of encouragement are ideal for creating a stimulating learning environment which relies on mutual respect and dignity. Receiving encouragement is a key factor in restructuring and improving anyone's ability to change their lifestyle.

Why People want to feel Normal

Behavior fluctuates across a broad spectrum between familiar and standard, and its abnormal equivalent, but, determining the point at which behavior strays from normal and develops into abnormal is challenging. Hansell and Damour (2008) believe that abnormal reactions are frequently an exaggerated common state with diverse hues of gray between it and its normal counterpart. Attaching more difficulty to differentiating between the two is the shifting palette and social forms of humankind as it progresses through time. Relativism is the thought that normalcy and abnormality are determined within the parameter of the society and time in which the behavior occurs. Therefore, an understanding of behavior is continually shifting and related to the group, cultural, and historical meanings surrounding and directly preceding the behavior Responses and reasoning considered abnormal in one place and time may not at all be abnormal or surprising in a different culture and time. The position of distinction of the pathology is to some extent inconsistent.

As quoted, by Helen Keller "Character cannot be developed in ease and quiet. Only through experience of trial and suffering can the soul be strengthened, vision cleared, ambition inspired and success achieved." Icons like Helen Keller are not afraid of failure or rejection because the path to the goal seems clear enough and might even be a stimulating challenge. Others may occasionally make some progress; however, most of the time people have difficulty getting into a flow state by not being aware of the roadblocks. This lack of progress often occurs with long-term goals that require an action, like transitioning into starting a new business or losing weight. To create a happy life that is truly worthy people will have their own self-approval as acceptance from others is irrelevant. Self-approval will open the support mechanisms of the universe which will flood their world with plenty of validating evidence. Some believe normalcy is a condition that is desirable, although they are rarely able to explain to me the reasons why. Thinking in this fashion leads them in the direction of abandoning the dream in order to fit in and be common.

From the first animistic approach relating to spiritualism to the leading technology of medical science, psychology has proceeded to identify and implement new knowledge and approaches to influence the dysfunction of unusual behavior, and in its development, moves onward to scientific investigation. During the development, declarations marking the fields focus resulted into six core thoughts that facilitated a more precise description of the field. To promote a more precise description of abnormal psychology, six core ideas were formulated. These ideas combine the significance of circumstances, the continuum between normal and abnormal responses, awareness of social and traditional relativism, recognizing the advantages and disadvantages of diagnosis, understanding complicated causality and the importance of the mind-body association. The six core ideas assist those in understanding that abnormal psychology is a science that strives to guide and help people and defining diagnoses is a necessary component (Hansell & Damour, 2008). Numerous theoretical models highlight the value of taking a comprehensive therapeutic viewpoint that fosters a more consistent and accurate recognition of the enigmas surrounding abnormal behavior, such as using bio-psycho-social treatment approach strategies.

For those who ask, "Am I Normal" I would like to remind them that there is no measurable standard, just what is typical for the world in which we live and individuals must at times adjust accordingly. The desire to be normal can be just too overwhelmingly dominant in someone's life. When people realize that there are many others who feel the same way, much of the pressure to fit in is let go, and research findings show that people become happier as they age. To some extent as people mature they begin to relax, just be themselves and there is a tendency to grow out of this wondering if they are normal phase. However, those who are most valued are individuals who step out of the box and amend the rules. These are not the ones who make minor improvements, they are not the norm, and they are not the average. Why not strive to be a bit abnormal, focus on strengths, focus on thoughts, ideas and beliefs and some of you may end up with a way to improve the world.

Chapter 12
Parenting, Childhood Fears and Happiness

In psychology boundaries are the limitations or the personal emotional distance that people place on others that are present in all relationships. The description of a boundary is subject to many interpretations, however, establishing a personal boundary instructs people on how they can communicate with one another. Boundaries are personal, emotional states that many learn to impose on others to preserve a sense of self-love, embedding a psychological dividing line between their self and another person (Katherine, 1994). They are like the physical boundaries that are present between countries and one example is the saying "don't cross this line," in expectations that someone will support this request. However, everyone is conscious of the fact that now and then this appeal is not respected.

There are countless troubled adults in this world, but the unhappy ones are those that were horrified by an event or an adult in their life when they were a child. This includes all significant adult figures, parents, siblings, teachers, preachers and any person that is affiliated with the creation of a traumatic experience. Many adults call this behavior discipline, stating "I was only trying to teach them....." Adults who were treated abusively as children often wisely choose safe and caring partners, yet most find it hard to trust these partners even after many years of receiving loving kindness. In the adult year's safety and security worries continue to gnaw away in the back of their minds affecting the quality of many if not all relationships. It is no wonder that frightened or angry children will become fearful or hostile adults, just waiting in anticipation for the next person (or circumstance) to strike. If people have self-love they respect their thoughts, feelings and beliefs along with feeling a deep sense of pride, declaring that they have the right to have ideas, speak them and expect others to be respectful. Those that love themselves have a type of emotional strut recognizing and accepting the fact that they have some weaknesses, but for the most part pardon themselves by learning from past mistakes. Learning how to love ones-self originates in childhood through nurturing from parents who showed and communicated the benefits of being kind, caring, trustworthy and honest, right along with accepting the child's minor imperfections. In other words, people learn techniques including how to set a boundary for emotional self-protection along with discovering how to love through parental modeling (Lindahl, Bregman & Malik, 2012).

The Connection between Fear and Discipline

Strict discipline instills fear, a powerful, primitive human emotion that alerts us to the presence of danger that was a critical emotion that involved our ancestors' ability to survive. Fear can be divided into two components, biochemical and emotional. The biochemical response to fear is universal occurring when all mammals face the perception of being in danger. Physically the body responds in distinct ways including sweating, increased heart rate and producing higher adrenaline levels. This biochemical reaction is likely to be an evolutionary development or an automatic reply that was crucial to survival centuries ago (Adolphs, 2013). This response is the fight or flight reaction occurring when the body prepares to either enter a situation by confrontation or avoid by evasion. The emotional perception of fear is highly individualized although the physical response is universal to all mammals, the comprehension of fear may be sensed as being positive or negative to humans. Some people are at times judged to be "adrenaline junkies" succeeding in performing extreme sports and others search for fear-inducing response states. The repeated exposure to high risk conditions leads to mastery, acclimation or in laymen's terms adapting that diminishes both the fear response along with the resulting euphoria. The adjustment to high levels of stress has a cumulative effect leading the adrenaline junkie to seek out ever new and bigger thrills that can be a socially acceptable or unacceptable way of coping with the fight response. Others have a negative response to the perception of fear and avoid anxiety producing states at all expense, thus being an example of the flight response.

Internal, personal boundaries protect people from becoming emotionally unsettled in comparison to the external boundaries that protect countries from invasion, though the goals of both are to keep antagonists out (Means, 2005). Internal, personal boundaries are akin to having an emotional "bubble wrap" stretching a bit during conversations. They are different from the fixed, rigid external boundaries that countries establish, for example, the walls of China are well known to be constructed of stone. The ability to execute an internal boundary hinges on how people value their sense of self, their thoughts, ideas, and beliefs relying on one having the capacity to possess self-love. In general, humans define relationships by how much they care for another and by how much they want to maintain their sense of self. Once again this emotional "bubble wrap" is present in all relationships: family, friends, coworkers and all contacts people make in the world. Placing limits and accepting limits that others impose will ground the relationship on the path leading towards mutual respect. Those who feel emotionally vulnerable or who desperately seek approval from others are most susceptible to losing their sense of self because the protection, the emotional boundary was not noticed, properly set, or possibly not even communicated. It is important to be cautious about making too many compromises as the "bubble wrap" can expand to the point of breaking causing a questioning of thoughts, feelings and identity as this uncertainty leaves an empty space in self-esteem. Emotional boundaries are indeed flexible, although they can break under stress or when making too many compromises much easier than the rigid concrete walls of China.

The adults role in creating boundaries for a child

The role of the adult is not to control the child, but, is to protect the child by keeping them safe by preparing them to enter the adult world. Many would say that discipline has gone by the wayside in recent years, yet there are many ways to manage a child and under no condition should this entail fear (American Psychological Association, 2014. Discipline should be applied when the child learns because children need to know what mistake was performed, otherwise they are going to enter into a fight or flight mode resulting in not learning how to cope with the problem. There is a relationship between fear and trust as where there is fear, there is less trust and if adults want to create trust, than reducing fear is an important activity.

Take, for example, a child who fails to look both ways before crossing the street. The adult places the child in a time-out, gave a firm warning saying that they might be hurt by a car and finally explains how they did not want this to happen because they would feel sad. This reaction is something the child can understand also realizing the importance of learning this behavior, along with how to prevent being placed in a time out. The child also learns that the adult might be hurt because most, if not all very young children do not want to hurt the adults in their life. On the opposite end of the spectrum, if an adult were to hit or severely punish the child they would become fearful, not understand, and attempt to learn all the ways to resist punishment. The learning part about self-injury and how this would hurt important figures is missing. Looking both ways before crossing the street preventing potential injury is not in any child's instinct, it has to be learned.

The definition of emotional abuse is the systematic tearing down of another human being and like most forms of violence emotional abuse has a basis on power and control. Emotional abuse is the least understood type of injury, although it is the most prevalent and very destructive (Rees, 2010). The victim or child in this example comes to view him or herself as being unworthy of love, respect, affection and cannot trust. Behaviors can be forced on a child, of course, but they will not understand why and will just feel the fear of the discipline and want to learn how to cope with that fear because this is instinctual and has a biological component. A child matures during puberty and if important adults terrified them into behaving, serious behavioral and emotional problems may begin at this time. Often the severe emotional damage to injured children will not surface until adolescence, or even later when many abused children become abusing or fearful young adults. Learning how to cope with the fear may lead to resistance later on down in the child's life because now the child is big enough and mature enough to prevent, resist and protect. As adults the point is to teach a child something, which is not to teach them how to cope with fear associated with learning how not to trust. An adult who was abused as a child has trouble establishing lasting stable personal relationships and may have difficulty with closeness, touching, intimacy and trust.

Adults who grew up neglected or abuse have to battle with two emotionally opposing forces: To accept life in the caring for others style (co-dependent), or the opposite direction, accept the fact that they are going to be the manipulators of the world striving to get their own needs satisfied at the expense of another person's self-esteem. Those who do not respect or accept limits are the energy zappers of the world that can emotionally wear anybody down, and if protective boundaries wear down enough people will start to feel like and be victims of emotional abuse, just as they were when they were a child. Sometimes anger and resentment results, at other times depression or anxiety symptoms emerge and these sufferers often tend to weaken and injure important people in their life. The fortunate ones are able to process the pain, place themselves into therapy to work through the anguish of abuse with a kind caring therapist and bounce back with their identity, self-worth and self-acceptance restored (Katherine, 2000).

Learning lessons from life

There are real world consequences for every individual action and with that being the case, adults may not need to pay too much attention to a child's minor misconduct. For instance, if a young child is being a bully, he or she will discover at some point that they are disliked and undesirable. Having no friends in itself can be a punishment. Many lessons learned from living will, in fact, work as long as adults do not try to teach their child through unnatural consequences, fear and abuse. Continuing with the above example, if a child is very young and being a bully, it is not wise to hit or instill fear in that child, rather explain to him or her that no one will like them if these behaviors continue and intervene if you witness the event, by removing them from the situation. Fear and discipline only confuse the young child and it is wise to first look for the real world consequences. When adults want to teach a child something explain to them the reasoning in words and behaviors that they can understand.

How adults can set a boundary

Setting Boundaries is the First Step to Regaining Control of Life.

If relationships are abusive and people find themselves being submissive they must accept a portion of this state as being their responsibility, in view of the fact that adults have more options. People can ask themselves if it is truly worth the pain and suffering to be with someone who is abusive and not respecting their self-worth. It might seem like learning how to walk again because this is indeed a new learning activity and change can be threatening. It takes courage to face fears, but perhaps some of these fears are of the imagination, but, for the first time in life people might notice that there is another option. One alternative is to find a compassionate therapist who can help assist with being a path leading towards finding self-love.

Learning to Set Limits will affect your Partner

This setting of limits is different for friends and partners who need to make their own adjustments because this creates a significant change in their mindset. Honesty with concern is the best strategy, but as quoted "to thine own self be true."

Direct Communication is the Key

Misinterpretation or lack of communication turns molehills into mountains. Using clear, simple language in a direct, respectful fashion creates a feeling of satisfaction only because people spoke their peace. If friends raise an eyebrow, try not to assume understanding because honestly people do not know what others are thinking, even though we all might wish we had these remarkable mind reading abilities. Make people do some emotional and intellectual work by insisting that they verbally communicate thoughts directly, which can be accomplished by simply asking them what they mean by that raised eyebrow.

Reflections in the Mirror

Accept, forgive and take responsibility for mistakes because everyone makes them at times in life, no one is perfect. Most people have not set out to control what someone else is thinking or doing, however, sometimes due to circumstances this happens. Learning to stand up for oneself is not about being right or wrong because this is learning how to effectively communicate. Forgive, apologize and people will oftentimes receive that joyful feeling of not only accepting themselves they also may notice that warm, fuzzy feeling of inner joy when someone else forgives them for making that mistake! Accepting the mistake and owning up to the errors takes strength and courage.

Strive to Satisfy

When people surrender it allows others the opportunity to attack boundaries and says to them that it is their responsibility that allows others to take control over improving the situation. Surrendering absolves all responsibility for self-care, setting the scene for an abuse. At times people forget that there is another choice, strive towards making oneself happy.

The purpose of this chapter is to discuss fear, limits and happiness and we have explored a few ways adults can teach children how to learn and follow rules, however, do not ignore the hundreds of other techniques. Scaring and hitting a child are two different behaviors, but they are both abusive and unnatural. Remember frightened children will become the frightened adults who have great difficulty trusting others because they are in fear, waiting for the attack. Adults who use fear and discipline as a tool to get children to do what they want them to do are bullies, severely damaging the ones they love. This is the relationship between fear and discipline.

Children will learn the lessons required to move into adulthood as long as adults are there to offer guidance and increasing the amount of adults who understand this concept will create children who are happy, emotionally healthy, respectable adults.

People who have had a healthy, nurturing childhood grew up feeling grounded by learning how to protect their self-worth creating a sense of feeling internally proud and in charge. These adults were taught how to set emotional boundaries by learning how to say no because they felt nurtured and loved as in their childhood experiences there was no need to scavenge for affection, or try desperately to please, just to gain affection and attention. They sensed love for their thoughts, beliefs and feelings, just for being in the world, even when they made mistakes (Whitfield, 1994). Thank these adults and parents for their modeling and thank these grown up children for having the ability to model this behavior to other people in the world, as it just makes the world a better happier place.

Past Experiences, Life Transitions and Happiness

Throughout life without reservation humans can count on conversions or transitional stages sporadically drifting into their world and undoubtedly they will accumulate learning from these experiences. A few of these transitions are positive, leaving an abusive home, graduating from school, winning the lottery, a marriage, birth of a child, and some are negative, living with a chronic illness, injury or death of a loved one, or facing a natural disaster. One factor associated with success is that determined people are skillful at learning how to adjust to this fast paced ever changing world and this capacity to adapt guides them on the path to having a more gratifying, enriched fulfilled life.

Investigations have revealed that gaining wealth, an education, a big house or an expensive car do not alter happiness levels as much as people would like or might anticipate. Several various types of researchers have observed the lives of those who have won the lottery noticed year after year that these people are no happier than those who did not have the experience (Lyubomirsky, 1997). Social psychologists call a hedonistic adaptation implying that there is a baseline level of the feeling, further explaining that the effects of happiness are short-lived, as humans tend to revert to their baseline level once they have received something external or material in quality. This baseline level differs among individuals and can be attributed in part to genetics explained by watching the varying temperaments of infants, parenting explained by being raised in a nurturing environment and the culture of their society or community group. However, there are ways in which people can practice increasing the baseline level as attitudes or perceptions can be adjusted, such as making a conscious attempt to enjoy the day. Trials along the way can be seen as being opportunity's to grow as a human being and enjoying a high quality of life does not depend as much on material comfort and money or on satisfying the emotional demand for a fleeting sensation of feeling happy (Diener & Larsen, 1993). Happiness is a blurred sensation which can signify different ideas to different people and a piece of the psychologist's quest is to distinguish all of the different applications of the concept. Most agree that happiness is an emotional state of well-being characterized by positive feelings fluctuating from contentment to intense joy.

Psychologists of all types aim to apply research methods to answer questions that link to defining happiness and ways in which it can be achieved. It is well known that happy people are physically and emotionally healthier. The data suggest that people can increase their level of happiness with activities like exercising to release endorphins, and different habits, such as listening to music, reading a good book, playing video games, painting and craftwork (Lyubomirsky, 2001).

This book views mood disorders like depression through a bio-psycho-social lens, indicating there is no single cause because biological, psychological, and social factors all contribute to mood fluctuations. The bio-psycho-social model proposes that everyone can benefit in varying degrees from developing habits and practices by applying health psychology principles.

Primitive man survived in clans and was profoundly reliant on social arrangements for security and access to shelter and food. People live with this concept even in modern times as the mind seems to be instinctively drawn to compare with friends, evaluate social status and many possess a drive to discover ways to advance. One unfavorable outcome of having a comparing to others thought process is that people form a mindset that has its' basis on being at a disadvantage or in poverty. This sense of deprivation occurs when someone focuses on what other people have, leaving them with the belief that they are unlucky or left out which stirs feelings related to sadness, anger and thoughts of inferiority. Another way of approaching life is nurture a mindset that focuses on abundance by emphatically instructing the mind to concentrate on the positive aspects of life which will create the sense of other people caring associated with safety, producing a sense of belonging and feelings of contentment.

If someone is forced to adapt, even if unsatisfied in life they are entering into territories of the unknown that may be even more stress provoking than the unsatisfied life. Nevertheless, the opportunity to change is always possible and those who do not have the ability to trust may miss out on the chance to increase happiness and improve their quality of life (Buss, 2000). Many people are afraid of change because of a preference for routine and stability as transition disrupts self-confidence. Fear inhibits people from taking risks and when this fear relates to a positive development it usually has a link to concerns of not being able to achieve success. Some are overly concerned about not being capable "enough" or of being judged, as if dignity is solely measured by the notion of success or winning. One certain transition in life correlates with adulthood or growing older and this passage at times brings with it an isolated feeling which connects to feeling a sense of loss with what was once in the past. With each transition people must learn novel ways of coping and facing this new way of being in the world which can be anxiety provoking because it tests ones' ability to adapt. To cope well with life everyone needs to be open to the challenge of examining their thoughts, feelings and beliefs of the world in which they live (Bridges, 2001). Fear warns us of danger, but, one way to cope with an illogical fear is to pretend that the worse scenario happened, and then backtrack in your mind to logically solve the problem. Even though this is a fantasy people are learning a new way to acquire knowledge, problem solve and cope.

Serenity involves nurturing a way of remaining calm and composed carrying with it the sensation of being grounded even when the world is in chaos. Maintaining composure involves not becoming trapped in life's ups and downs by not clinging to positive situations or avoiding painful ones, as these conditions are not constant in life (Carter & Stewart, 2007). Serenity means to accept the certainty that passionate ups and downs are elements of life produced by biological and psychological cycles, situations and outside events. People can achieve balance by becoming more aware of when they may be entering into a 'fight or flight' state because this allows time to process the information and not feel compelled to behave hastily or run in the either direction. The unconscious compulsion to be a success or to dodge a sense of failure can influence ultimate goals. Serenity involves resting and relaxing thoughts accomplished by taking a few deep breaths, emotionally stepping back and then consciously making a rational decision. Humans have an uncanny ability to be able to delicately redirect thoughts, focusing on feelings associated with goals or intentions.

For something unique to occur in life there is something lost and allowing change to take place to the broadest extent means allowing errors to be made along the way. Those who do not acquiesce to the fact that they will make mistakes will not be able to adapt well with life transitions and will not be capable of enjoying life to its fullest extent. What is indisputable is that everyone is going to be forced to adapt, as transitions are a guarantee until the day we die. Human beings are unique because of possessing the internal capacity to increase the feelings connected to a sense of empowerment as we have the choice to learn new, distinct approaches to adapting to novel situations. There is data that states having religious faith assists with stresses and struggles of everyday life, and to answer the question is there a relationship between happiness and joy, in the Biblical sense the answer is no. Happiness is not an emotion that many strive to attain and keep, no one is happy all of the time, but some people are more satisfied and content. Being joyful requires feeling connected with the environment, with people in life, with nature, with appreciating the arts (music, creativity, books) and it demands an acceptance of life as it is in the moment. At times life does not treat us well, financial devastation, getting sick, a divorce, having a chronic illness, being disabled, death of a loved one, or adapting to growing older, and these challenges are normal parts of life which people will have to cope with in varying degrees.

Some think that joy is an intentional commitment to be happy, to take pleasure in being in the present, despite life's transitions being an internal, continual emotional phenomenon. During times of joyfulness, physiological and biochemical changes take place resulting in having a sense of well-being, completely altering negative viewpoints. Joy is an approach or a faith that comforts even in the most sorrowful of times. Joy arises from within as it is an internal belief and in the biblical context is not an emotion as the feeling is not based on something good happening, but is a position of the mind or spirit. Everyone has the opportunity to change their approach in how they think about a topic whenever they learn something new the subject. Whether the shift in thought is easy or not depends on the individuals' capacity to stay open to the notion of wanting to discover something unique, despite opposing views on the matter. This may sound confusing, but people have to be open to the idea of learning something new which in turn will change thinking, reasoning and mood. For example, most people feel rather strongly about war. The central question about war is: "Is it the right way to act?" How many people can honestly say that if this question could be answered once and for all, would they be willing to accept and follow the truth? The practical question is to what degree someone is invested in holding onto old beliefs, despite being aware of the new material. Questioning and altering a value or belief can be at times an easy task, however, people have thousands of beliefs and can only change one at a time, so this transition can be a lengthy process. In order to challenge a belief, look at the evidence, investigate the facts and then alter thinking about the belief. For example, some may think that consuming a Big Mac is to some extent a healthy meal, but went onto read many books on nutrition and discovered differently. This person now believes that this meal is not nutritious thereby changing their thinking associated with learning more information.

In contrast to changing thoughts and beliefs, challenging feelings can be extremely complex, especially when someone is in crisis or confronting a transition. Feeling states mount up over a lifetime of experience and attempting to change a feeling can seem as if this is working against everything ever learned. Some have persuaded themselves into thinking that what they think and feel is right; therefore, this must be a necessary belief in life. Most everyone has met people who are chronically anxious, angry or sad, and we describe them in this fashion on account of their permanent, unpleasant mood states which can be easily recognized by the way they speak and their behaviors. Negative emotions are the cumulative results of experiences in life and the treatment is to incorporate novel positive encounters to offset the negative ones. It takes time and energy to develop these perceptions and individuals hoping to change need to become open to the notion of wanting new, positive adventures and also welcomes them into their lives (Seligman, 2003). It is possible to change beliefs and thoughts with acquired facts and instruction, although it is difficult replacing a feeling state without professional support.

Research on what causes happiness states that it does not have much to do with material gains or high achievement and it appears to be an individual's viewpoint on life, the quality of their relationships and having the capacity to give and receive (Helliwell, Layard & Sachs, 2013).

A Few Tips on how to brighten the day

1. Choosing to Smile, consciously deciding to have a good day produces endorphins and other uplifting chemicals associated with the brain. Nothing can dampen the mood when people understand the methods involving bringing on joy and applying this technique can bring on fleeting happiness; however, practicing regularly throughout the day will increase baseline happiness levels and effect the consistent sensation linked to Joy.

2. Meditation and Imagining. Receiving something that is wished will increase happiness of short duration; however, it is important to avoid confusing this fantasy with reality. With training, meditation in the pure sense will produce lasting joy.

3. Positive Thinking. Making it a goal to think positive frequently brings a happy feeling to the surface quickly and fostering a positive mindset can certainly enhance mood and produce temporary happiness. Despite the problem, situation, or circumstance, people do get to decide whether they want to feel happy, depressed or anxious. The solu-

tion is to exercise this method and make it a daily goal to appreciate the simple pleasures in life.

4. Feeling Grateful is a deeper emotion and consciously practicing, focusing on what you have in life will increase a baseline level of happiness, such as, health, employment, family, friends, home, etc.

5. Notice Immediate Surroundings. As people become more aware they will find plenty of evidence that happiness is in many situations. Individuals will increase the capacity to feel happiness by checking and noticing the positive pieces of the surrounding environment. This approach can be fostered by asking the question, "What is good about this moment."

6. Become Active and support a conviction or become active on a lesser scale by practicing random acts of kindness. Helping others increases the endorphin like chemicals and being active in a cause helps you feel empowered thereby assisting in managing life's storms.

In conclusion, joy is a feeling state that lasts, and happiness is fleeting. Joy includes an internal, conscious belief and happiness attaches to the external world. Happiness is a feeling state that people have for a short time, for example, when they buy something that is desired. Joy brings a sense of contentment when in the middle of a life storm and happiness is not present in a life storm. A person's low genetic baseline level of happiness which is the personality style in which they were born, along with surviving past childhood traumas, can improve with positive experiences and over time anyone can increase that internal feeling of consistent joy.

Chapter 13
The Psychology of Helping

Most people want to help others at points in life because it is kind and generous to support a fellow human being who is in distress. Aiding someone who is in crisis can be difficult; however, helping someone in their time of need has benefits since it gives both parties a sense of connection that leads to contentment. The caretaker senses that they are a part of the world that enhances the life of another, consequently shaping the world into being a better place. Nevertheless, it is important to reflect on helping behaviors by examining two questions: Who are the people that always seem to be available and present? What are the sacrifices in providing support? This chapter will be discussing three areas:

1. How anybody can provide aid to another person who is appearing depressed, irritated or troubled and in absolute need of comfort.

2. Co-dependency and the people that continually appear to relish helping others who are in need.

3. In what manner can people make sure that by offering support they are not placing themselves at risk?

What is a Crisis?

When someone feels anxious or depressed it does not indicate that he or she is in severe distress or suicidal. An emotional crisis or emergency condition only last hours to days, in unusual cases weeks because is usually short term in quality. A few people in crisis are at risk of acting impulsively, which may involve risk taking behaviors, health harming actions and perhaps a suicide attempt. A suicide attempt occurs at the point when the usual problem solving strategy is not sufficient to maintain a calm, objective mood. Assisting someone in need is a social practice, a voluntary action that has the intention of assisting by sharing information, comforting and/or rescuing. Occurring with these voluntary actions receiving a reward can be expected or not expected. In psychology, assisting actions follow the altruistic model, which means the behavior is selflessness in principle, and there is a concern for the welfare of another human being. However, at times there can be a more selfish motive such as pleasing friends, receiving money or gaining something such as prestige.

Latané and Darley (1970) detailed a step-by-step description of how people choose whether or not to help in an emergency. The five steps are:

1. People must be consciously aware or notice that a circumstance is a crisis. Now and then minor life events, such as how much of a hurry a person is in might hinder people from noticing someone else in trouble. In their research, Darley and Batson (1973) reasoned that seminary students who were rushing to give a presentation were much less likely to help an obviously injured fellow scholar groaning in a doorway than those who were not rushing. The students personality scores were not a predictor for aiding nor was the theme of the sermon as half of the students were about to give a teaching on the tale of the Good Samaritan.

2. Onlookers must evaluate the condition or event as meaning a crisis. When many people are present they are more likely to believe an emergency situation is not serious. This happens because people watch to observe someone

else's reaction and when they recognize the bland expressions, they think there must be no threat. Latané and Darley (1970) reinforces the above hypothesis by asking people to sit in a room where white smoke began pouring out of the vent. The more people that were in the area the less likely anyone was to solicit help and the longer they took to render support. People in groups will influence each other that nothing is wrong and obtain false reassurance from each other.

3. Someone must accept responsibility. When there are multiple bystanders, there is diffusion of accountability, the phenomenon whereby each person understands duty to help decreases as the number of eyewitnesses' increases. Everyone believes that someone else will take action, and as a result, no one helps.

4. There must be a fundamental understanding of how to help. A person must know what type of support to provide, or they will not be able to assist.

5. Someone must choose to carry out the desire to help. Even if someone knows what kind of help to give, they may elect not to intervene because he or she feels incapable or are too fearful of the costs.

The term codependency came about over forty years ago, originally applying to the spouses of alcoholics. Historically, the idea of codependent appears straight out of Alcoholics Anonymous, sharing the understanding that the present knowledge of alcoholism was not entirely the problem of the substance abuser, but also includes family, friends and coworkers. Codependent stands for co-alcoholic. Labeling a person codependent came about primarily by people in the mental health profession relating it to the older psychoanalytic concept to someone who has a passive, dependent personality who attaches to a stronger character. The original book by Melody Beattie, "Codependent No More" in 1986 subsequently broadened the term to include the idea that the codependent fixates on another person for subsistence and admiration. In contemporary times, professionals further explain that any adult from a dysfunctional family or someone who has a parent in poor health may be at higher risk of becoming codependent.

Investigations reveal that the characteristics of codependents are prevailing in the general population and the term has begun to find its place in the world of cultural expression. Codependency is an emotional connection with someone who is manipulative, or has an unhealthy ailment that typically associates with narcissism or substance abuse (Sadock & Sadock, 2000). Codependent people receive sustenance by the inadequacies or limitations of another person, and this position regularly involves setting a weaker priority on their own shortcomings. They are greatly absorbed with the needs of other people. Codependency can take place in any relationship, involving work, family, friendship, romantic, peer or people in the community. As mentioned, codependent was a term used to describe the thoughts and behaviors of partners associated with chemical dependency, persons living with, or in a relationship with an addicted person, but, further research describe similar patterns in people who have an association with someone that has a psychiatric illness.

Now, the term further expands stating that having a dysfunctional nuclear family can lead to someone becoming codependent which results in adapting to dysfunctional relationships. A codependent has the helping someone else addiction because they need to be needed, and at times will cause the other person to continue to be in need of assistance. The specialists who work in this field label this way of life enabling. The enabler will purposefully overlook someone abusing a substance but will call in sick for someone who has an addiction, they will delay encouraging a sick person to undergo treatment, and at times others will hinder a child's efforts to become independent. In a general sense, codependency is an addiction to people, situations and behaviors (Miller, 2008). These people have the false idea of attempting to improve their own internal feelings by externally guiding people, behaviors, and circumstances. In every area of life, the codependent's central focus links to control or lack of it.

Codependent Characteristics

Codependency may be identified by denial, low self-esteem, excessive compliance, or control patterns and narcissists are natural magnets. A codependent person has a standard way of behaving, feeling, and thinking about themselves and others that produce uneasiness. They are self-destructive because they usually answer to people that are harming themselves and injure themselves in the process (Miller, 2008). Co-dependents aspire to take care of a person who is undergoing pain, but the caretaking corresponds with habitual thoughts and actions that are self-defeating.

Years of studying interpersonal bonds in relationships have increased awareness that codependent reactions arise from the effect of learning by modeling family members who promote the behaviors. This is an acquired response that can be passed on from one generation to the next. This behavioral conditioning affects the ability to have a healthy, mutually satisfying emotional connection. Codependents share a link with those who have a "relationship addiction" by virtue of forming or maintaining relationships that are unilateral, emotionally damaging and/or abusive. These habits can cause someone to hold onto destructive relationships and can they disrupt relationships that may otherwise have worked. There are repeated rescue attempts to allow the needy individual to continue on a destructive course as they gradually become dependent on the unhealthy caretaking. As the dependence develops, the co-dependent feels a sense of compensation and satisfaction from being needed. Just as soon as the caretaking harmonizes with failure and they acknowledge this compulsive behavior, the codependent believes there is no choice and are unfit in the relationship, but, powerless to break off from their series of behaviors that creates them (Hemfelt, Minirith & Meier, 1989). Consequently they view themselves as being a victim and continue to have an attraction to weakness in love, work and friendship relationships.

A codependent may suffer from a 'Messiah Complex' where they recognize a difficulty and see themselves as being the only person who can assist. On occasions, people who are codependent take on the role of martyr, because they tend to set themselves up as a "victim," yet, are frequently hunting for approval. During times of conflict and when they stand up for themselves in an argument, they feel guilty which produces a sense of need as they cannot stand not being helpful and the sensations associated with being alone. When the dependent person continues taking instead of giving back, co-dependents become severely annoyed, as they have a subconscious belief that there will be compensation for their charitable behavior. This anger may smolder below the surface and usually is not verbally communicated, because angels have the reputation of being pleasant. However, the co-dependent's rage seeps through in passive aggressive or self-destructive behaviors. This is the result of placing the needs of others before their own and in doing so they, unfortunately, ignore taking care of their own needs. A spouse may cover for the alcoholic partner, a father may make excuses for a child being a bully, or preventing a friend who needs emotional support away from calling a counselor (Beattie, 1986). A codependent therapist or psychiatrist will never think their clients' therapy as being complete. This is one primary reason why it is advised to spend the first few counseling sessions assessing the problem and establishing a schedule to achieve the work.

The only remedies for codependency entail finding the real, healthy sources for positive self-esteem to displace the negative ones. There are many codependency recovery workbooks that can be truly helpful in the recovery process. They have to learn how to wean dependent people off of their help, which may result abandoning the relationship. Although very painful, this is better for both people as this is forcing both to find better sources of fulfillment. It is a growth to finding productive and fulfilling activities that do not involve satisfying needy people. There are many ways to be productive without attachment to a chronically emotionally bankrupt person (Schein, 2011).

As discussed, codependent people are in search of recognition. They acknowledge other people's needs ahead of their own, which produces a sense of being helpful as they cannot bear the idea of being alone without assisting down and out people. They tend to set themselves up as being a victim when arguing, and when they do defend themselves, they feel guilty. By recognizing other people's needs before their own, they fail to take care of themselves. Co-dependent behaviors can prevent people from finding peace and happiness with the most influential person in life.... themselves. As people age, most realize that there are people who are givers and then there are takers of the world. Sometimes, people teach others to be takers, by doing everything for them, and insisting that they do not need any help in return. In other words, they are playing the superwoman or superman role in relationships. At times, givers attract takers (and vice versa) as the negative and positive attraction in magnets. Givers are truly grateful recipients, whereas takers have a sense of entitlement. True givers consider other people's needs and the importance of balance with getting their own needs met. Takers are not even aware that others people have needs. Givers experience extreme joy in giving. Takers feel resentment or a sense of obligation while giving.

The benefits of helping

Children who help or volunteer are less inclined to developing risk taking behaviors. One research study, conducted by the Search Institute, examines the lives of 47,000 children in fifth through 12th grades across the United States (Benson & Roehlkepartain, 1993). The study indicates that children who volunteer just one hour or more a week were less likely to have at-risk behaviors, and tend to have a more optimistic outlook on life. Even children who are coerced to help or volunteer are more likely to grow up to be adults who demonstrate empathy and compassion. Communities with many volunteers are more stable and peaceful places to live, which in turn encourages others to volunteer. Whatever the cause, helping especially in terms of volunteering services improves the health, happiness, and in some cases longevity.

Rules for Helping

1. Examine the genuine wish to help verses believing as if this is a duty, or a life calling.

2. Only listen to what is being said, without reacting to fixing the problem.

3. Focus on the emotions until this person can problem solve

Tips for Helping

- Try not to reason for the person that is requesting assistance. It is not polite to furnish advice, explanations, or interpretations. These types of statements can be taken as an insult as some may think that the helper is assuming that the person in need cannot think for themselves. Wait to be asked for advice and give it very carefully.

- Do not probe for intense, sensitive feelings. If this person clearly asks for help on a highly emotional level then do not produce levels of emotional connection that are outside of the ability to manage. Nevertheless, if the helper believes that the person in pain merely wants to communicate their feelings than the helper must be prepared to sit through, observe and listen.

- Keep the focus on the task at hand as this protects the helper from getting absorbed in the problem. When someone is experiencing a problem that has a lot of emotional attachments try to pay attention to the emotion, not the problem. Tell this person that you commiserate with how badly they feel. If they are angry try to persuade them to explore the anger and talk-out the problem, while neither agreeing nor disagreeing. For example, if this person is afraid stay with them to listen and give support.

- Remember your place in the situation. This person came to you because they wanted help, and could have decided to go to a friend, preacher, a therapist, a parent or sibling. They chose you, so be honest, even if a stranger. Be aware of personal boundaries.

- Strive to understand. There are three elements of helping when people experience negative emotions: empathy, understanding and analysis. Therapists offer analysis, friends show compassion and fun, and strangers can provide support and empathy.

- Signs of Restlessness. Many people when agitated shake, pace the area, wring their hands, or continually move their legs up and down. Persistent restlessness is a sign of extreme emotion and disorganization. If the person in distress is becoming increasingly agitated it is essential to attempt to help them calm down, so they can concentrate and not feel out of control. It might be too much to manage if all of that passion and confusion were expressed. If the agitated behavior continues, it is time to change the subject and perhaps ask them to go for a walk. They cannot think clearly enough to problem solve.

- Be aware of knowing when the support is not working. Know the limits and do not be afraid to explain them. There are times when compassion and caring may not be enough to improve the situation. If the helper becomes frustrated or anxious, remember that people cannot truly help unless they want to, and they cannot want to help if they are running out of emotional energy. Sometimes the best response is too lovingly say, "I do not think I can help with this anymore."

- The person in crisis may ask where they can turn. Reveal to them all the information known about community resources, and take the time to help them find the sources that can help address the issue. Explain that they are not alone and that you are happy to help in other ways.

Understand some people just always seem to feel sad or angry and some people with codependency always want to help. Do people need a friend, counselor, minister or family member? Take a moment to think about relationships. Ask a question, "Do I usually have fun with people?" or "Do I always seem to be discussing some problem that needs to be fixed?" Let relationships be friendships as it is not healthy for people too always want to help. If someone is always asking questions like: "What is wrong, you look a little down?" "You are not looking good today, should we talk?" Then they are not proposing a relationship but are offering some sort of helping hand, maybe a codependent relationship. If people are not having any play or leisure time with other people then relationships have taken on another role, such as a therapist or minister. The specific problems that can emerge with these types relationships are harmful and too numerous to mention. Try to withdraw cautiously or insist that the relationship change into something you can both count on to be fun and entertaining. Ask these questions, "What am I getting from this relationship?" and "Do you always want to help?"

Chapter 14
Love and Intimacy

Humans are social animals and want to believe that they deserve to be in love because most want to have a sense of feeling bonded with another human being. The closer someone is to another person, both physically and emotionally, the more united and intimate the connection grows. Love is a hot subject of conversation and there is undoubtedly the urge to become intimate, but what is love? Why do people in all communities even have the passion? What is the biology and physiology of love? Do humans always appear close with their partner? In what ways do we gain affection?

Intimacy is a bond with someone that evolves over time, and there are various distinct forms: Intellectual intimacy is when there is a sharing of opinions that allow both parties to appreciate the process of exploring different topics through discussion. Sharing activities produces the second example of intimacy which relates to experiencing a mutual pleasure, whether it is playing a game of baseball or participating in a quilting group. Psychological or emotional intimacy is when there is the exploring in depth of thoughts, feelings and beliefs. Sexual intimacy is a driving theme in many conversations that involve physical contact of all forms which may, or may not embrace the notion of love. Love and intimacy are separate concepts.

The ancient Greeks identified four kinds of love: "Eros" is romantic and/or sexual desire. "Storge" in Greek relates to family or familiarity love. "Philia" love associates with friendship. "Agape" is selfless or divine love. Plato's philosophy discusses platonic love as being unblemished, at times non-sexual and centers on the essence or nature of love. Even in contemporary times, people spend a substantial amount of energy hunting for soul mates, and a few search their entire life just to experience the type of love envisioned by Plato. Psychological perspectives of love introduce Freud's notions of the way people choose their partner which has a basis on the relationship they had with their parents, at times, associating love with a regression into irrational behaviors. Romantic love forms in the mind a yearning for the fancied partner creating a psychological dependence similar to the one that exists between a newborn and their caregiver. Strong bonds require a penetrating psychological and physiological relationship and the absence of either can at times truly be life-threatening. Reliable, resolute romantic relations have numerous positive impacts on survival and health of mammals including their offspring.

The Evolution and Biology of Love

The biological explanation of love has been examined by evolutionary biology, neuroscience, anthropology, and psychology. Since Darwin's time, there have been thoughts about the development of human engagement in relationship to music being a potential signaling method for attracting and judging the robustness of prospective partners. A few investigators suggest that the ability to experience love emerged from a signal that the partner would be a good parent which would ultimately assist in transferring these genes onto later generations. From the viewpoint of evolutionary psychology, the experiences and actions connected with love can be studied in terms of how they were formed by human evolution. For instance, some propose that the language decisions during development were a "mating signal" that provided possible partners the ability to assess reproductive health. Evolutionary psychology can be a starting point for additional investigation in which cognitive neuroscience should attempt to localize courting adaptations in the brain. Evolutionary psychology has offered many interpretations for love, one signifying the fact that children are for a long time reliant on their parents for survival; meaning love is a mechanism, to encourage parental support. Jeremy Griffith (2011) a biologist, defines love as having an "unconditional selflessness" implying that cooperative abilities originate and evolve from our ancestors. Investigations often cite the bonobo, the great apes called pygmy chimpanzees to support the belief that human ancestors were interdependent, coordinated and lived in groups.

Another biological evolutionary interpretation for explaining the concept of love is that sexually transmitted illnesses decrease fertility, harm the fetus, and increase childbirth risks making it favorable to have a long-term relationship, limiting the danger of contracting the disease. Sexual passions and orgasms occur to cause all animals to be profoundly driven to engage in sexual intercourse for the purpose of creating offspring. These desires are so powerful that it is challenging to suppress even for those who have taken vows of celibacy, as the passions act against the deliberate decision, resulting at times in improper sexual conduct. Everyone makes arbitrary decisions, but themes of survival and reproduction are too significant to be totally dependent on a person's conscious choice. Emotions developed to inspire people to do what is healthy despite what they believe, as romantic love unfolded to motivate men and women to form bonds for survival of the species. Biological principles of love focus on a mammalian drive, similar to thirst or hunger that were formed to track down fancied partners that have a significant impact on social behaviors that have genetic and reproductive outcomes. Unquestionably hormones, neurotransmitters, and pheromones regulate love and how people think and act when in love is determined by their perceptions. The traditional belief in biology is that there are two significant drivers, sexual appeal and attachment (Buss, 2003).

Three educators of psychiatry from the University of San Francisco present a general outlook of the scientific assumptions and decisions linking to the function of the limbic system in love, social bonding and attachment, in their book General Theory of Love (Lewis, Amini, & Lannon, 2001). They raise the position that the nervous system is not independent but in harmony with the environment. This compassion, which they term limbic resonance, is the ability associated with the anatomical aspects of the sections of the brain that link to all other creatures. Their work strengthens earlier investigations of the value of physical contact and affection in cognitive and social development earlier conducted by Harry Harlow on rhesus monkeys that raised awareness of the physiological consequences of isolation. Romantic and parental love is profoundly satisfying because both connect to human survival and thus have a physiological role relating to evolution. The ability to examine the neural correlates of individual emotional states with brain imaging techniques has enabled neurobiologists to learn about the neural roots of romantic and parental love. Both kinds of attachment activate areas in the brain specific to each, as well as the sections of the reward system that correspond with areas abundant in vasopressin and oxytocin receptors. Both types of love deactivate regions affiliated with social judgment, negative emotions, and the ability to assess other people's aims and emotions.

Research led by Semir Zeki and Andreas Bartels of University College London (2000) found that at minimum two regions of the brain become more engaged when in love. These areas are the foci in the media insula, which the brain links to instinct, and a section of the anterior cingulate cortex, which relates to the feeling of euphoria. To understand the biophysical response to love, researchers must explore the brain and understand the patterns of arrangements. One of the central structures associated with love is the limbic system as it identifies the parts of the brain linked to an emotional reaction. The limbic system contains several structures, including the thalamus, the hypothalamus and the basal nuclei. Although all of these structures are important, functions of the hypothalamus concern both sexual and behavioral experiences. The pituitary gland and hypothalamus manufacture the endorphins which are peptides commonly known as the feel good chemicals and they function as some medications, such as the analgesics and sedatives. Exercise releases endorphins and people commonly hear the avid jogger express enjoying a runner's high, which ultimately the body starts to crave, explaining the drive to run. There is a release of endorphins during sex that accounts for the tranquilizing effects after experiencing an orgasm. Lastly, touching releases endorphins illustrating why a moms hugging and cuddling soothes their crying infant because these substances produce a relief from pain creating a feeling kin to euphoria. It is this irresistible ecstasy that people sense at the moment they begin to recognize that they have fallen in love.

Research in the neurosciences investigates chemicals that exist in the brain that relate to how people feel when in love. These chemicals include testosterone, estrogen, oxytocin, serotonin, dopamine, norepinephrine, nerve growth factor, and vasopressin. Adequate brain levels of testosterone appear to be essential for both male and female sexual functioning. The detection of serotonin, adrenaline, and dopamine occur during the temptation or attraction phase of a relationship, and oxytocin and vasopressin seem to have a link to long term bonding marked by powerful attachments. These scientists examine distinct chemical substances such as oxytocin in connection to their roles in the emotions and behaviors of those in love. Some researchers believe that the chemicals triggered for romantic love and long-term attachment relates to the activities in which people share, rather than individual personality characteristics (Fisher, 2000).

Author Diane Ackerman discusses in her book, A Natural History of Love, the value of the hormone oxytocin when someone is in love. Known as the cuddle chemical, Oxytocin, encourages caressing between lovers heightening the desire during lovemaking, because it stimulates the smooth muscles and excites the nerves that intensify during sexual arousal. Oxytocin links to the feeling of being close that is felt after intercourse, possibly explaining why some fall in love with someone that is not available, yet falsely link the feeling of closeness with the release of oxytocin. Pincott (2009) reasons that the release of oxytocin through touching that includes hugging, cuddling, stroking, kissing, or sex may also correlate with the release of other physical hormones. It is true that oxytocin operates together with other neurotransmitters, such as testosterone that may impact how the neurotransmitters norepinephrine and dopamine effect the reward sections of the brain. The discharging of all the various hormones and neurotransmitters makes it hard to determine which chemical is the most influential when it relates to love (Marazziti & Canale, 2004). However, biological determinants are unquestionably essential for love to occur and to maintain the love.

Human attachment or bonding seems to operate on a push-pull mechanism that subdues emotional distance by deactivating systems utilized in the brain for critical social assessment and negative emotions. Love bonds people through engagement with reward circuits, demonstrating the power of love to motivate and invigorate. However, the biological investigation of love must move ahead and look for physical insights that can be found by examining the global literature on love to assist the humanities. Researchers conclude without any reservations that people react to the feeling of desire with their whole body and agree that this is a biological and psychosocial phenomenon.

As stated earlier, in the early stages when someone is around an object of desire, there is a discharge of adrenaline known as epinephrine that is both a neurotransmitter and hormone that is released from the brains adrenal medulla during the "fight or flight response." The sympathetic nervous system initiates this reaction allowing people to make the decision to either fight the situation, or "flight" meaning to avoid and run off. During this response, the brain becomes increasing more alert, the pupils dilate, heart rate increases and there is stimulation of the sweat glands, all of which describe the thrill and power of those in love. To understand the mechanisms of falling in love, analysis requires much better observations pertaining to a real-life courtship, covering the measurable features that impact partner selection, the sexual outcomes of individual differences along with emotional, cultural and cognitive roles.

One Anthropologist and research professor at Rutgers University, Helen Fisher, thinks that three fundamental, different, but interrelated emotional arrangements in the brain negotiate mating, breeding, and the rearing of children: lust, attraction, and attachment. All emotional networks associate with a particular neurobiology in the brain; all are connected to a distinct repertoire of performance, and each developed to address a specific aspect of reproduction in mammals (Fisher, 2000). The sex drive, libido, or lust is identified by a yearning for sexual gratification and connects essentially with hormones, estrogens and androgens. These urges developed to assist people in attempting sexual union with any suitable companion.

The attraction system is marked by elevated energy and the centering of attention on a selected mating companion. Attraction also links to feelings of exhilaration, intrusive thoughts about the sweetheart, and the yearning for emotional connection. Helen Fisher (2000) explains that an attraction connects in the brain essentially with higher levels of the neurotransmitters dopamine and norepinephrine and low levels of serotonin. This network emerged to enable males and females to discriminate among possible mating companions, maintain their mating potential, leans towards genetically higher individuals, and will track these people until insemination had been achieved. The attachment system or "companionate love" is identified by conduct that may involve protection of a mutual territory, mutual nest construction, mutual grooming and feeding, separation distress, and shared parental tasks. Attachment is also marked by feelings of calm, safety, contentment, and emotional connection. Attachment links in the brain primarily with the neuropeptides oxytocin and vasopressin. This emotion system developed to motivate people to maintain their affiliations long enough to perform their parental responsibilities. For each system, the neural paths can be suspected to differ among people and change over one's lifetime. The independence of these emotion systems may have emerged among our ancestors to empower males and females to take advantage of various mating approaches at the same time. With this brain structure, people could form a bond with one companion and also exercise a clandestine adultery to take advantage of unique mating opportunities. However for present-day humans, these distinct brain networks have complicated our existence, contributing to global patterns of infidelity and divorce and the rise of clinical depression that associates with romantic rejection.

The Psychology of Love

The brain releases endorphins, neurotransmitters that reward people in the same way opiates or heroin induces a euphoric state and the release of these natural opioid chemicals occurs during sex, physical exercise and entertaining life events (watching a comedy, reading a comic book, laughing with friends). Endorphins are physically and emotionally addictive and answer the question of why people crave attachment states. There is also a basic desire to feel connected with other people in life as modern day humans are social beings that continue to instinctively follow each other in groups.

There are many other physiological responses and chemicals/hormones released, along with the endorphins creating a "love soup", as love and intimacy link to peoples' individual biochemistries.

In his hierarchy of needs, Maslow's' theory explores the concepts of safety, security, love and belonging is powerful because this structure enables us to understand the fact that love is not just a superficial physical concept, but is essential for emotional health. Skinner's account of positive reinforcement explores operant conditioning provides insight into how psychology demonstrates and strengthens love. Michael Boylan (2008) views love as being on a path leading towards acting good behaviors that can be witnessed around the world, and he notes that people support loved ones who struggle with problems that probably would be overlooked if they were a stranger. The thought that love is an incentive for good symbolizes the nature of the human psyche. Robert Rowland Smith's (2011) view of love and sex as being a braid that conveys increased significance to sex, transforming sex from a biological drive to something wonderful that people experience in order to feel a bond with another person. The prevailing belief is that there are two influential forces related to love, attachment and sexual attraction. Adult attachment operates on the same principles that influence an infant to become bonded to their parents. Love is a sensation and to understand the definition science has to develop a wider application that links to the evolutionary role to feeling states. One major purpose of emotion is to stimulate motivation, as when people encounter a strong positive or negative feeling they become driven to do something that is useful or to evade something that is dangerous.

For the first time, at the instant people meet the attraction can have an immediate effect and has the description of being electric, stupefying and shocking to the system. When questioned, some say "everything else in the room faded" or "when we locked eyes I could not take my eyes off of him."

What is this biological response? Palms sweat, breathing gets shallow, the skin feels hot, pupils dilate and the amygdala which is the center of the brain that processes emotions, blazes with action as adrenaline levels rise. At the same time dopamine, a mood enhancing neurotransmitter linked to passion increases along with oxytocin, the hormone relating to bonding. With all of these biological processes happening at once, it is not difficult to understand that the pupils in the eyes dilate to take in more of the picture, and people often smile at cartoons of men producing an unbelievable reaction to an image of a woman who has large, showy pupils. Some researchers say that there may be an evolutionary basis for men's attraction to women having larger pupils stating men favor big looking pupils because they are a symbol of arousal and receptivity that are reminders of youth and fertility, holding in the subconscious male mind this sight to behold (Gerulf & Savin-Williams, 2012). These are the elements of love at first sight.

Psychology at times examines love from the social and cultural aspects. One common psychological view considers love being a mixture of companion love, which is an attachment and a sensation of intimacy that is not associated with physiological arousal, and passionate love which is an intense longing characterized by physiological arousal. Love leads to a mixture of many thoughts, moods, and beliefs that range from interpersonal attachment ("I love my wife) to pleasure ("I love that music"), and can involve emotions of great temptation and personal devotion. Love can also be a value representing mercy, empathy, compassion and affection that represents a selfless, faithful kind of interest for the welfare of other human beings. This type off love represents compassionate and devoted behaviors towards oneself, other people and/or animals. Intimacy in any relationship takes time, effort, and motivation, and all forms require action along with emotional work. Intimacy fluctuates throughout certain stages of the relationship, during times of crisis, and even during the positive transitions in life (birth of a child, buying a new house). However, people have specific behaviors that they are in charge of developing. Therefore, it is possible to achieve intimacy because of the interrelationship between physiological, psychological and behavior components.

The broad majority of Americans decide to marry because love carries with it a persuasive effect. However the divorce rate in the United States is expected to reach 67 percent in the next decade (Raffel, 1999). At this time, 80 percent of divorced men and 72 percent of divorced women remarry; although 54 percent and 61 percent, respectively, divorce repeatedly. As well, high divorce and remarriage rates are observed in many other cultures and it might be time to examine the fundamental science of this bittersweet emotion society describes as being in love. From deep within the passionate fires of the brain and mind comes the chemistry that conveys the magic of love.

Ways to Achieve Intimacy

1. Spend Quality Time with your Partner: Intimacy takes time to develop, and someone who is not willing to spend time with another person will obviously not be able to develop an intimate relationship! Communication is the key to success, therefore, explain that you want full attention.

2. Active Listening: Focus all of your attention on what your partner is saying and do not respond until you fully understand what they are trying to explain. Pay close attention to what the other person is actually saying. Communication verbal and nonverbal is what people are in charge of and expressing yourself clearly is one of the main factors in establishing any relationship.

3. Be Sincere and Speak the Truth: Without hurting your partners' feelings, be as clear and straightforward as possible. People, who are afraid of intimacy, do not share their sensitive side, attempt to take the risk and share a few

warm, soft "fuzzy" feelings. Acknowledge, evaluate and accept the sentimental side. If one is sad express it verbally as feeling sadness, rather than anger, irritability or frustration.

4. Have Pleasurable Physical Contact: This includes hand holding, kissing, eye gazing, back rubbing, and of course sex, as long as the physical contact is consensual.

5. Accept Your Partner: Relates to understanding and forgiving them for their imperfections. People cannot achieve intimacy of any kind if acceptance of each other is lacking. It is also necessary to have self-acceptance because it is difficult to trust anyone else if you do not have the ability to accept your own shortcomings. If there is a disagreement, learn how to acknowledge the fact that there is a discrepancy, accept it, and move on to another topic of conversation.

6. Take Individual Personal Time: This follows the saying, "absence makes the heart grow fonder". Personal time allows for the space to reflect on the relationship and this observation creates a greater desire to more intimate.

7. Schedule Play Dates: No serious discussions, no talk of work, no talk of the children or anything that is off the topic of just having fun. The time is only for the two of you to enjoy, have fun at the moment, as there is nothing wrong with being spontaneous.

Conversations can be quite awkward when relationships are just forming. Learning how to resolve differences increases the intimacy in a relationship, as it brings about the idea of accepting the other person for who they truly are. Couples do not always feel intimate with their significant others, and it is not an uncommon feeling, especially at the beginning of a relationship when people are just starting to get to know each other and feel comfortable. However, during stressful times not all couples are able to communicate effectively or accept their partner for their short comings, without an objective person to guide. This is the time when a couple may want to seek out-side assistance. At this time, the divorce rate in the United States is 50%, and this large of a number suggests that people are not working on ways, to achieve intimacy. Human biology has not changed as the endorphins continue to flow, the human social instinct has not changed, and people continue to strive to be included in the pack. However, what people do with each other, how people treat each other, and how much time people spend with each other has indeed changed over the years. People can choose to modify the behavior and can strive for different types of intimacy in all relationships. To make the decision to alter a communication style or a behavior opens the door for hope in a relationship and to achieve the love that they desire.

In summary, love and intimacy are good for emotional health and survival. The various physical and mental changes that have emerged by natural selection induce bonds that assist in raising children work remarkably well. Investigative research has decided that the principles of sociology, biology, and psychology are all essential in examining love, though, further study must be performed to define the concept, and determine how people may apply this information to everyday life. Brain scanning procedures, such as magnetic resonance imaging have been applied to study brain areas that appear to be associated with creating the human existence of love. With the divorce rates rising, and the idea of marriage evolving in today's culture, the value of examining the notion of love should not be ignored. It is in these studies that a society will be able to appreciate the love and its relationship to the stability of the human race.

Chapter 15
Food and the American Culture

The food Americans eat has evolved more in the last several decades than it has in the previous individual centuries combined. The apple, today, is not the apple of long ago. Rather than producing better patterns of nutrition to create a healthier environment for the planet, the food people consume has suffered a downward spiral in terms of nutritional protection. The topic of the day is how this food affects physical health and environmental sustainability. Food production and advertising, as it pertains to physical fitness and environmental protection has been replaced by economics, speed and uniformity.

Social scientists have described several conceptual theories of food preference behavior. General principles of study include both personal and environmental circumstances impacting the making or modification of eating behaviors. Social cognitive psychology investigates the interaction between environmental, personal, and behavioral factors. Food preference includes emotional, sociological, economic, and sensory viewpoints which link to health psychology and which utilizes a bio-psycho-social approach. There are positive and negative consequences related to food consumption because eating certain foods assists many people cope with negative emotions (Stewart, Adler, Laraia & Epel, 2012). In the long term, coping with tension by eating can truly reinforce negative emotions because people are not coping with the problem creating the stress and self-image and physical health might become more negative as weight increases. To shed weight, people must alter their thinking. Weight control is about creating a lifestyle change which is not going to occur for those who rely on short-term tactics. To achieve victory, people need to become mindful of the role of how food consumption impacts their life and discover how to use decisive reasoning using cognitive behavioral coping strategies that effect health and weight.

Health Psychologists believe there are many events that can influence attitudes about food and consumption habits. These factors include:

1. Social Components

2. Cultural and/or Religious beliefs

3. Biological and Genetic Conditions

4. Psychological or Individual Preferences

A hamburger and french fries started to develop into a staple food in the American diet during the 1950's as a result of the clever marketing tactics of fast food chains. Today, in the 21st century it is estimated that the average American consumes approximately three hamburgers and four orders of fries every week. For most, fast food is considered to be an ingrained part of life forgetting that what we eat is a choice and that decision affects physical health. Applying the well-known techniques of brainwashing were and continues to be heavily enforced and the industry's marketing techniques have been very successful. The idea of eating fast food has taken over and this concept is so instilled in people's lives that it is a consistent part of the American culture. Consuming fast food is now considered a standard healthy way of eating food. In 1970, Americans spent $6 billion dollars on fast food which increased in 2000 by more than $110 billion on the same fast food (Schlosser, 2001). This rise is due to the fact Americans are just making poor food choices related to marketing thus changing priorities. However, another reason for this increase in junk food consumption relates to sheer convenience. Fast food is not only served at the fast food restaurant themselves, but also drive ins, stadiums, airports, zoos, elementary and high schools, universities, cruise ships trains, and additions to the list are rising. There are very few places in the 21st century where people can go where they are not surrounded by cheap, unhealthy fast food. Why not eat fast food? After all, it is quick, inexpensive, and convenient. On any given day approximately one quarter of the American population eats at a fast food establishment and this relates to the ways in which people are coping psychologically with living in this fast paced culture.

The reason so many people decide to consume fast food, a substance virtually void of nutrition in many cases is both simple and complex. The simple explanation lies in the branding, and it is fast, so it just makes sense that in a society that moves at lightning speed people would also want to eat quickly. The more complex level is that there are many sociological forces at play in the undercurrents of the fast food consumption. Women have entered the workforce in record numbers over the last several decades as former housewives that lovingly cooked healthy meals are now busy working. How people nourish and support their body is much more complicated and fast food is a solution to feeding the family because these are meals can be obtained simply by speaking into a microphone. Time has become something people are short of and priorities have shifted, therefore, going in a fast food direction is one way to reclaim time. However the real cost factor in deciding to consume processed fast foods is making Americans physically ill.

People feel safe with uniformity and consistency and fast food restaurants along with food advertising apply this concept to the very core. Marketers using the principles based on psychology are aware that people in general love the familiar, as advertisers spend much time and money making sure their product is uniform with developing a hamburger that tastes the same, even in far distant lands. Customers are drawn to familiar brands as they offer reassurance and something related to that feeling of consistency, reliability and stability. Marketing has tricked people into believing that if they want to make life easier than eat this tasty, nutritious product. Fast food branding may not be as much about people enjoying the taste because popularity seems to be connected to the marketing of the product. Food advertising talks to children, when they watch their educational cartoons and movies teaching children that fast food is good for them, and they will receive a prize in the form of a toy. The average preschooler saw 2.8 TV commercials per day, children 3.5 per day and teens (12-17 years) 4.7 per day, all promoting fast food. Advertisers target marketing to children, 15% of preschoolers ask to go to McDonald's every day, and two-fifths of U.S. children younger than 11 ask their parents to go to McDonald's at least once a week. Of the 2/5's of children who ask weekly, 84% of parents admit to giving in to their child's demands. This indicates that children will not recognize having a life without fast food quickly explains how consuming these foods have become a part of the American way (Harris, Schwartz & Brownell, 2010). Targeting children in marketing is, in a sense, targeting adults because parents take the children, or the entire family, and purchase meals for everyone. This suggests that selling a kid's meal will turn into multiple meal purchases which are costly and guess who makes a fortune. Marketing children puts psychological pressure on parents who want to give their child what they want, to please and make them feel loved. The food industry spent more than $4.2 billion dollars in 2009 on the above advertising which is a no win situation for parents, children, physical health and medicine.

The subject everybody should be examining is what people are not placing in their body when fast food consumption becomes a routine. This food lacks fiber, vitamins, minerals and antioxidants, just to list a few human essential nutritional requirements. Drive Ins adopt the poorer cuts of meat that contain greater fat content, highly refined grains, heaps of added sugar and salt along with fillers to enhance the taste. These ingredients point to the extremely addictive properties of fast food that provides a hoard of calories satisfying the daily demands of an elephant. Fat is on the menu when it relates to these foods as oxidized fat and polyunsaturated fats accelerate plaque buildup in arteries as the transfat in fast food destroys the beneficial cholesterol and promotes the dangerous. These foods also have a high energy density which implies that people overeat because the brain cannot regulate the appetite accurately. The long list of ingredients includes many unhealthy substances that have associations with various cancers, heart diseases, diabetic diseases and of course contribute to the obesity epidemic. While there might be some nutritionally redeeming qualities, the risks associated with the physically harmful substances make fast food consumption extremely damaging to physical health.

Many investigators believe that sleepiness following meal consumption is induced by the reorganizing of blood flow from cerebral to the abdomen or mesenteric canals. This notion continues despite its clear disagreement with a popular neurophysiologic theory that cerebral perfusion is achieved under a wide assortment of physical situations. For example, while exercising there is a large quantity of blood flow that is redirected to muscles, yet, perfusion to the brain is sustained and recent documentation suggests that there is no measured shift of blood flow after consuming a large meal. Researchers suggest that the release of gut-brain hormones and activation of vagal pathways perform a role in producing fatigue through the alteration of sleep centers such as the hypothalamus (Forsythe & Kunze, 2012). Meal consumption alters hormones such as orexins and melatonin and raises central vagal activation. Lastly, sleep provides for "cognitive reinforcement" of the conditions that led to the energy acquisition of food that was in years past related to survival. Therefore, when drowsiness knocks people to the couch after a meal, they are arousing an ancient survival mechanism related to resting after tracking and attaining the food. Consuming a meal will dependably modify mood and emotional stability because eating diminishes arousal and irritability consequently increasing tranquility. However, this depends on the meal quantity, type of food chosen, expectations and habits. Exceptional meals are those that are too small, too large or unhealthy may also negatively influence mood. Sweetness and sensory signals to high energy density foods, such as having fatty construction can elevate mood and mitigate impacts of stress via brain opioid and dopamine neurotransmission. However, change in these pathways intensified by acquired sensitivity with prolonged exposure could point to overeating of energy-dense foods and obesity. Sweet, fatty foods low in protein may also produce alleviation from anxiety in people via the production of serotonin. In rats, foods of this sort appear to work as part of a feedback circle, via deliverance of hormones and insulin, to restrain activity of the hypothalamus, pituitary and adrenal glands during stress. However, this effect also correlates with abdominal obesity. A number of emotional traits predict people's desire to prefer sweet, fatty and salty foods when stressed (Moss, 2014). For example, emotional eating, depression and premenstrual sadness, all could point to the neurophysiological sensitivity to the reinforcing effects of such foods.

Taste preference and the sensory qualities of the food regulate meal selection. Additional factors associated in food choice involve price, availability, convenience, cognitive inhibition, and social familiarity. In addition, environmental signs and increased portion sizes perform a role in the choice and amount of foods eaten. Researchers have discovered that people mention taste as the main determinant of food preference. Roughly 25% of the US populations are supertasters, and 50% are tasters. Epidemiological investigations imply that non tasters are more apt to eat a broader assortment of foods and have a higher body mass index (BMI). Genetic variations in the capacity to recognize bitter taste are thought to play a part in readiness to eat bitter-tasting vegetables and for decisions to prefer sweet and fatty foods (Bartoshuk, 1991).

By discovering how to make healthier selections, people will be able to manage compulsive eating, binging, and weight gain. In addition to greater appetite control, there is also the likelihood of experiencing sensations of calmness, elevated energy levels and alertness from the foods consumed. For optimal physical health, it is smart to be informed of food selections. There is a connection between physical illness and the foods that people consume, and this is the health psychology relationship. As in generations past, many diets promote skipping basic nutritional requirements while opting for fasting or binge eating that may damage the body. These are the rapid weight loss plans that people read daily in advertisements. The best way to develop a long term diet plan is to make changes in eating habits that are acceptable in meeting daily nutritional requirements. The organic diet plan does not sacrifice items suggested in the six food groups. The current generation is suggesting that people adapt to eating high amounts of organic foods to maintain physical health. This avoids the harmful effects of eating processed foods which are those that are in a package, boxed and may contain harmful ingredients to prolong shelf life.

Genetically modified organisms are one more interest in diets which the average customer overlooks. There are numerous applications of GMO's, but the most prevalent use is in food production and the reasoning behind adopting this technology is profit motivated. These "food like substances" are in the mainstream food supply and many experts report that there is not sufficient, independent research support relating to physical and environmental safety. GMO's in food production have had the actual seed gene altered using genetic engineering techniques. The procedure, recombinant DNA technology, introduces DNA molecules from various sources and combines them into one molecule to create a new set of genes or seed. A biotechnologist transfers a novel piece of DNA from a bacteria into a known form (a corn seed), assigning the seed a modified or unique genetic structure. Transgenic organisms, a subset of GMOs, are organisms which have DNA that originated in a different species, such as the insertion of a bacterial gene into corn seed enabling the seed to produce a pesticide. At this point in time, it is very difficult to find foods which do not include some kind of genetic adjustment, and some are transgenic in quality

A piece if corn eaten today is of a different species than it was before this genetic alteration, and is not the same corn of years past. A popular headline, today, is the introduction of a gene into seeds to diminish the requirement for the chemical herbicide glyphosate or round up. It has now become standard practice to genetically engineer novel genes into corn, soy, canola and sugar beets to enhance growth (herbicide resistance), exterminate pests and reduce tilling of soil (Lemaux, 2008). This distinct genetic engineering technique produces a concern over the possibility of people ingesting pesticides from these products. Many researchers also wonder what harm the actual genetic engineering method may cause to physical health related to allergies and immune system function.

The name GMO is like the scientific statutory name, "living modified organism" as defined in the Cartagena Protocol on Biosafety, any living organism that possesses "a novel combination of genetic material obtained through the use of modern biotechnology". The prevailing belief of producing a GMO is to change the genetic structure of an organic structures biological map or its genome. This may involve mutating, eliminating, or adding genetic material. When a genetic substance from a different species (animal gene to plant gene) has the insertion, the resulting DNA of the plant or animal has the label recombinant DNA, and the newly formed species (animals or plants) are now transgenic. GMOs are useful in biological and medical research, experimental medicine (gene therapy), pharmaceutical drugs, agriculture (herbicides & insecticides) and food production (Golden Rice). The term "genetically modified organism" can include, targeting the introduction of a gene from one class into another. For instance, a gene from a jellyfish that has a fluorescent protein can be physically joined with a mammal that would reveal this fluorescence to recognize the position of the protein in the cell. These methods are valuable tools in many fields of study, including those who examine human pathological conditions or other living processes.

In food production genetically engineered crops have their origins in a laboratory and possess characteristics, such as resistance to pests, toleration to harsh environmental conditions, improve product shelf life, or involve the production of medication. There are hopes that GM crops will improve the plants nutrient content such as Golden Rice and someday enhance the flavor of the primary plant. Since their first introduction in 1996, one GMO has been modified to be resistant to the papaya Ringspot virus, some plants produce the Bt toxin which is an insecticide to ward off pests and others are tolerant to the herbicide glyphosate to kill weeds. Species that are genetically modified include micro-organisms such as bacteria and yeast, insects, plants, fish, and mammals. As a noun, genetically modified organisms are the sources of genetically modified foods, and are also widely used in scientific research to produce goods other than food. GM foods are the outcome of the genetic engineering of plants or animals, which most at this time have a hardiness to plant diseases (herbicides) and resistance to pests (insecticides). At this time, biotechnology is currently under high examination from people who grapple with this process in relationship to food production. The CDC stresses the importance of evaluating the allergic potential of genetically modified foods before they become available for human consumption. Research continues to investigate any possible harmful effects involving the health of people, animals and the soil.

There are the controversies centering around the genetic engineering of food that include whether producing them is ethical, should such food be labeled, is a biotechnology needed to address world hunger, what are the environmental effects and how do intellectual property rights (patent law) effect farmers and market dynamics. Following an organic diet will help avoid Genetically Modified Organisms and all of the unanswered controversial questions. Critics have objections to GM crops on various fronts, including environmental and economic matters raised by the fact that the present goods are answerable to intellectual property or patent rights (Shimoda, 2013). GM products are topics involving many debates with respect to

1. The safety of GM food in relationship to physical health

2. Plants developing a tolerance to pesticides which creates weed and pest resistance.

3. The possibility/probability of cross-pollination to organic crops or non-GMO crops.

4. The possibility/probability of interbreeding with "organic species" such as fish.

5. The belief that humanity needs GMOs to address the world's food & nutritional problems.

The American Medical Association (AMA) concludes that "there is no scientific rationale for the specific labeling of genetically modified bio-engineered foods. They further explain that the labeling of GMOs as a group and optional labeling has no value unless it coexists with buyer education". The AMA's position against labeling is that the Food and Drug Administration cannot call for labeling because of variations in the production method, if the GMOs are not different or do not profess a safety hazard. Both believe that it is unjust to label all genetically modified foods when only a few may constitute a health risk. However, the contemporary voluntary management of statutes does not according to the AMA do sound evaluation of discovering which GMOs are unsafe. Therefore goes the reasoning that labeling is of no purpose but the AMA suggests that additional pre-market management should be a concern. On one side, the AMA is telling purchasers that GMOs should be further examined for any possible health risks before food corporations sell them to the people. On the other side, the AMA is saying that it is OK that foods containing GMOs not have a label. It is illogical to recognize the lack of certainty about the safety of GMOs and to recommend pre-market testing, but disagree with consumers having the right to know which foods contain GMOs. Why disallow the consumers' ability to avoid GMOs, especially if they have not been proven sufficiently safe?

The U.S. Food and Drug Administration (FDA) and U.S. Department of Agriculture (USDA) have no formal definition for the use of "natural" on food labels. However, the FDA has no complaints with the use of the term on food labels that say "natural" if it is in a manner that is truthful, not misleading, and the product does not contain added color, artificial flavors or synthetic substances. "Natural" claims have become common on new foods and beverages. Natural and Organic are not interchangeable terms. People may see "free range" or "hormone-free" and "all natural" or "natural" on food labels, as there is no formal description. However confusing the advertising label may appear to people, these descriptions must be truthful, which means to follow the FDA guidelines, but do not confuse these labels with the term "organic." The USDA allows the usage of the label "natural" to be placed on meat and poultry products that contain no added color or artificial ingredients. The label must describe the use of the word natural (minimally processed, no added coloring). The meat may be from a feedlot and the animal fed genetically modified grain under this label. At this controversial time, the FDA and USDA do not recognize any difference between organic foods, modern, grown foods, and processed foods, which may be bred in a laboratory and contain GMOs.

When a person visits a doctor and is given medication, the prescribed medication has gone through systematic, independent testing before the physician prescribes a drug. The same governmental body, the Food and Drug Administration, oversees food security. The logical assumption is that any food that one finds in a grocery store went through independent testing for potential health associations before it enters the food supply. However, the FDA has minimal security requirements for genetically modified foods and relies on companies and promoters that are designed to avoid finding a problem that relate to health. There is an economic relationship between the FDA and the chemical companies that produce and promote this food. This connection most certainly causes a conflict of interest that relates to the US economy and profits for large scale agriculture businesses. The position the FDA records are that there is no difference between non-GMO crops and GMO crops and, thus, in depth testing is not necessary. There is, however, data that state this is not necessarily correct, and multiple requests from organizations have been presented to the FDA requesting additional examination on the safety of genetically modified foods. There are hundreds of documents explaining how FDA scientists are aware of the fact that genetically modified foods are quite different from ordinary foods. These documents report that consumption may lead to the development of allergens, toxins, disease, and nutritional deficiencies and recommend additional, independent research study.

Genetically modified foods are in common trusting places, and people in the US ingest them every day including those who try to pursue a completely organic dietary regimen. Present safety assessments are based on a "weight-of-evidence" design, at which point each GMO is judged on a single basis using a variety of determinants:

1. Does the gene encoding a new protein come from a commonly allergenic origin such as food (eggs, milk, hazelnut

or peanut), a respiratory allergen (dust mite or pollen), or a touch allergen (latex)?

2. How closely does the chain of the recently entered protein match that of a known allergen?

3. Does the protein encoded by the transgene bind from people known to be allergic to the origin of the transgene?

4. Is the stated protein extremely unyielding or can it be clearly broken down by digestion?

5. Is the protein stable and abundant in the new food?

GMOs are found in:

- Soy
- Corn
- Canola
- Tobacco
- Papaya
- Sugar beets
- Zucchini and Yellow Squash
- Honey and bee pollen that may have GM sources of pollen
- Dairy products (from cows injected with the GM hormone rbGH)
- Meat, eggs, and dairy products from animals that have eaten GM feed
- Food additives, enzymes, flavorings, and processing agents, including the sweetener aspartame (such as NutraSweet) and rennet used to make hard cheeses

The soil in which the seed sprouts into food can have a portion of the GMO, along with the pesticide. It is essential to understand precisely where seeds originate and the circumstances of how they mature in relation to individual' and environmental health. Common American produce starts in a soil that is lacking in nutrients; consequently the crops do not develop accurately and are vulnerable to complications because this compromises their immune system. Farmers have to cope with a significant obstacle of combating pests that invade the crops because the soil and the plant lack the nutrients to resist disease. This in turn, may influence the nutritional value and quality of the produce. Many researchers question the association between consuming this food and the harm it could create to someone's immune system.

With the advancement of GMO technology, many farmers have chosen to utilize GMO seed and apply chemicals to exterminate the weeds or pests destroying the produce. Plants are sprayed with insecticides and other types of pesticides that threaten the life of the produce and these chemical's transfer into people eating the produce. While many health experts claim that pesticides are harmless, there is also significant evidence claiming the opposite. It is a recognized fact that pesticides in farming or gardening environments can enter the bloodstream if they are inhaled or come into contact with the skin. Pesticides are fatal if swallowed. If this is correct while the seed is developing, than what is the change process that makes it safe for human consumption once the crop matures? Pets, farm animals, and wildlife are especially vulnerable to the toxic impacts of pesticides. How does this apply to physical health hazards with human consumption? A few of the side effects of pesticides include nausea, headaches, vomiting, and dizziness and some can severely damage the skin, nervous system, and respiratory system. What are the side effects, even if they are small doses that occur once these substances build up in the body over time? Scientists do not understand the answer to this question as there are no definitive studies being performed and minimal regulation from the FDA. It seems wise for people to make informed choices about the meats, fruits and vegetables they consume, and GMO's are worth time examining.

The Dirty Dozen Plus (2014 foods that have high pesticides levels)

- Apples
- Pears
- Celery
- Grapes
- Lettuce
- Peaches
- Potatoes
- Nectarines
- Cucumbers
- Strawberries
- Summer Squash
- Cherry Tomatoes
- Hot & Sweet Bell Peppers
- Spinach/Kale/Collard Greens

There is also a group of fruits and vegetables that retain the least amount of pesticides and are relatively safe to eat, despite the fact that they have been sprayed.

Clean 15 Least Contaminated Fruits and Vegetables (2014)

- Kiwi
- Mango
- Papaya
- Onions
- Cabbage
- Avocado

- Eggplant
- Pineapple
- Grapefruit
- Asparagus
- Sweet Peas
- Cantaloupe
- Sweet Corn
- Mushrooms
- Sweet Potatoes

The most contaminated products are the varieties where the skins are consumed, like grapes, apples and pears. With these food items, it is best to choose organic produce since everything about organic produce is safer especially in terms of pesticide consumption. In contrast, the least contaminated foods, like pineapples and bananas, are fruits that produce a cover and thus, there is a decrease in the number of pesticides consumed.

The word organic, when it relates to the Organic Foods Protection Act, is the process that farmers support to produce their goods and how they manufacture products (meat, vegetables, fruit, grains, dairy). Organic fruits, vegetables' and grains thrive in nutrient rich soil and must be kept separate from modern day produce. Farmers use limited amounts of pesticides, no petroleum-based fertilizers, and sewage fertilizers that involve minimal amounts of bio-engineered genes. Organic farm management may use, but stringently restricts the use of manufactured (synthetic) fertilizers and pesticides that includes herbicides, insecticides and fungicides. This farming method prohibits using human waste matter, growth hormones, livestock antibiotics, food additives and severely limits the amount of genetically modified contamination. Organic agriculture is a distinct style of cultivation that has environmental benefits because these techniques increase the richness of the soil by using nitrogen-fixing plants, or by spreading compost instead of synthetic fertilizer. They manage and control insects by planting a greater diversity of crops. Organic farming practices support soil and water conservation and reduce pollution because there is lower fertilizer runoff into adjacent waters. They use nature's fertilizers, such as compost or manure to feed the soil and plants. These farmers rotate crops, till the soil, hand weed and apply mulch to control weeds. To reduce pests and disease they use insects, birds, mating or traps. To farm in an organic fashion follows the belief that there is little need for chemicals to control pests, they do not inject their animals with any growth hormones and do not use man made manufactured fertilizers. These methods cost money that is what people are contributing when they buy organic foods.

Organic food continues to be challenging to find in local Shopping Marts and a short time ago buyers found them only in health food stores. As the demand grows quantities of organic foods have increased which has in turn generated confusion for buyers. This uncertainty is obvious as we observe people shop in the fruit and vegetable aisle. In one area of the store, there is a present day apple. In another area, there is one marked organic. Both apples are red, polished, and hard. Both contain fiber and vitamins both are free of cholesterol, fat, and sodium. How does one decide which one to buy? Most tend to go for the present day grown foods because they cost less. However, the question remains: Is organic food safer or more nutritious? Organic foods contain large amounts of essential vitamins, minerals, phytochemicals, and antioxidants which allow the foods to keep that fresh and juicy taste. Chefs from all over the world use only organic ingredients which allow people to recognize the improvement in taste. However, taste preferences are difficult to evaluate, quantify and measure. Research in this area is continuing.

Current ongoing research examine decades of scientific reports concerning the nutrient content of organic, non-organic and genetically modified foods. When food relates to nutritional quality, garden produce varies enormously and this is true whether the foods are organic, conventional or genetically modified. For example, one carrot may produce two to three times more beta carotene, which is the forerunner of Vitamin A than the one taking a seat right next to it in the vegetable market. The distinguishing characteristics in relationship to nutrient content are due to weather conditions, the ripeness of the produce at harvest and the genetic make-up of the different varieties. Many researchers' conclude that organically and genetically modified fruits and vegetables are similar in nutrient content, but this is an area that continues to be under serious investigation (Crinnion, 2010). Once again, when it relates to nutritional quality, produce varies enormously, and this is true if they are organic, non-organic or genetically modified.

It is extremely significant to understand that researchers have difficulty uncovering subtle effects of the environment and what people eat in relationship to health. A few studies include people who were eating either organic or genetically modified food and then scanned for evidence stating that the decision made a difference in health status. Many examined the food itself for the nutrient content, as well as, levels of pesticide residues or harmful bacteria. One recent investigation examined the effects of Organic, pasture raised cows' verses the Conventional factory farm animals confirming the belief that Organic milk is much higher in the Omega 3 fatty acids, therefore, healthier and recommends buying the pasture raised Organic milk. Many studies also report that when children switch to consuming Organic foods they excrete fewer pesticides in their urine along with Organic beef containing higher amounts of "the good fat" or Omega 3 fatty acids. The maximum length of most conventional food studies are fewer than two years and results can be easily dismissed as being inconclusive, as two years is not enough time to determine the health benefits or harm. What may have a positive effect on health is that most studies report less pesticide contamination on organic produce.

Only foods that are grown and processed according to USDA organic standards can be labeled organic. The United States require these foods to have at least 95 percent organic ingredients to obtain the department of agriculture's organic seal. Foods made entirely of organically produced ingredients can display a 100 percent label and will also have the organic seal. At this point, there are many growers who are marketing their own organic label along with the USDA seal. Taking a look at the sticker on the produce is a quick way to tell if the fruit or vegetable is non-GMO. If the number has 5 digits and starts with a 9, the produce is organic and non-GMO. If the number has any 4-digit number, the produce is conventional. Producers rarely use, but, have the option of using a 5-digit number that starts with an 8 to signify a GMO crop.

Advantages and Disadvantages of the Organic Diet

Nutritional Benefits

The organic food industry consists of the customers assuming that the organic food is healthier, containing higher nutritional content and fewer toxic compounds. Analysis on the nutrient content in organic foods change, due to variations in the soil, weather conditions, and the individual farming culture related to the organic farming method. The nutrient content of the produce varies from year to year and farmer to farmer. Nevertheless, reports of multiple investigations reveal that organic produce contains significantly higher levels of vitamin C, magnesium, iron, and phosphorus, than non-organic variations of the same foods. Organic foods are lower in pesticide residues and nitrates and higher in the above nutrients. With the exception of oats, wine and wheat, organic foods typically produce higher levels of important antioxidant phytochemicals (anthocyanins, flavonoids, and carotenoids). In vitro research of organic produce consistently shows that organic foods have greater antioxidant action, are more powerful suppressors of the mutagenic activity of noxious mixtures and repress the reproduction of certain cancer cell groups. Nonetheless, research of antioxidant action in humans has failed to confirm additional advantage. Investigations confirm that people who consume more fruits and vegetables have lower chances of developing a number of diseases. However, it is not clear if this effect correlates to the quantity of antioxidants in fruits and vegetables, to other lifestyle decisions, to other elements of these foods or to other determinants in people's diets.

Conventional meats contain growth hormones and antibiotics. Organic poultry, beef, eggs and fish provide the body with nourishing amino acids that are required to enhance lean muscle mass and contain no growth hormones or antibiotics. Conventional vegetables are grown with pesticides and retain water, however, eating organic produce will help eliminate edema or "water weight." Organic carbohydrates, meaning the fruits and grains, will increase cardiac energy as the liver processes these carbohydrates quickly to provide lasting endurance. The organic process increases energy levels and will help people with their ability to exercise. Organic vegetables are loaded with antioxidants eliminating the disease producing free radicals as they assist in removing them from the body. In conclusion, our body can metabolize, and utilize the nutritional content from organic foods much easier than in processed foods.

Physical Health

In 1996, the research scientists at the FDA prophesied that engineered foods would consist of rogue proteins that could be poisons that could give rise to allergies, nutritional insufficiencies and other illnesses. A tremendous increase in childhood food sensitivities in the US is often in the news, but most articles fail to think of a connection to a recent drastic shift in America's nutrition. To start the ball rolling in 1996, bacteria, viruses and other genes have been artificially injected into the DNA of corn, soy, sugar beets and cottonseed. These unlabeled genetically modified foods may give rise to risk factors, such as the triggering allergic responses, and data gathered over the preceding decade now implies that GMOs are giving way to greater sensitivity rates. Currently, there is minimal indication to support the increased rate of allergic response that has an association with consuming GMOs. This is because of the safety assessments to which GMOs are subjected to prior to marketing or selling them to the consumer. Pre-market research and evaluation is the most effective tool to protect the public, and suggestions from many are to conduct independent longer term studies on humans. It should be said that hard and fast avoidance of all danger to producing an allergic response is not feasible. For every bio-engineered food product, the effects of these ingredients are summarized and presented to the FDA to determine possible allergic reactions. In this fashion, the safety assessments that center on avoiding dangers that are anticipated and likely to produce an allergic response are very important. Research to examine more efficient methods of determining allergenicity is ongoing.

The compounds put to work with the modern day farming practices link to many known allergies and have also been associated with a few serious illnesses. The pesticides put to use in growing modern day produce consist of both synthetic and noxious chemicals which linger in the food after they are grown. Organic crops significantly reduce the chances of ingesting these chemicals. Apparent health advantages from eating organic dairy goods have been demonstrated in regard to allergic dermatitis. Disputes that GM crops bring about include an increase in antibiotic resistance, increase the presence of toxins, fungi, or toxic metals within the body and increase disease risks. Others state that a genetically modified food degrades the foods nutritional value, produces new allergens and has a direct association with developing many physical illnesses.

Weight Loss

Psychology studies the science of behavior and by what method and for what reason, people do what they do. For people attempting to manage their weight, psychology explores the following areas:

1. Behavior. Treatment includes recognizing established patterns of eating and uncovering ways to improve eating practices.

2. Cognition (reasoning). Therapy concentrates on recognizing self-defeating reasoning patterns that add to weight control problems.

A new trend is growing that promotes the belief that following an organic diet promotes physical fitness and weight loss. Physical health directly relates to the foods that people consume and following an organic diet is a popular weight loss program. There is no need for fasting methods or weight loss pills to suppress appetite or speed up the metabolism. However, there are concerns about the feasibility or practicality of following this theory. Current research for using this method for weight loss needs further evaluation and benefits correlate to the idea of consuming a diet that has a focus on fruits and vegetables. The results may take time to manifest, and reports suggest that people include other fitness measures, such as an exercise program for weight loss. Following an organic diet that consists mainly of fruits and vegetables is beneficial for decreasing pesticide consumption, weight loss, maintaining overall health and improving fitness levels.

Tips for developing healthy eating habits

1. Drink lots of water.
2. Give yourself support.
3. Make healthy food selections.
4. Only eat in particular settings.
5. When annoyed exercise instead of eating.
6. Think of eating like a lifestyle adjustment.
7. Watch and study about appropriate portion size.
8. Try to distract yourself from eating harmful foods.
9. Keep a record of consumption practices by recording the food that was eaten throughout the day

The culture of the organic farm management at the time of this writing is safer, nurtures the land and preserves the entire ecosystem. The methods used in organic farm production protect the structure and nutrient content of the soil that maintains the soils health over time. In the long run, a healthier atmosphere leads to the ability to take care of a physically healthier body. Organic farming diminishes pollutants in groundwater and brings about richer soil that assists plant growth and reduces erosion. Taken as a whole, organic farming decreases toxic pesticides that can have their final destination in drinking water. In more than a few US cities, pesticides found in tap water have reports of being at hazardous levels, for weeks at a time. This report is a straightforward declaration from the Environmental Working Group. Although, this is not to say that organic farm management techniques do not use certain toxic chemicals at times. In comparison to modern farming methods, organic farming utilizes 50 percent less fuel consumption and is better for the environment, says one 15-year study. A different study from Oxford University reports that organic farming may not be more favorable for the ecosystem and point out that organic products such as milk, cereals, and pork create greater green-house gas emissions than their modern day counterparts. However, this same study agrees that the organic farming methods of cattle produce lower emissions. When people focus on a whole food organic diet, they are free from wondering food origins and the mass production process is without a doubt transparent.

One common concern with organic food is the price because organic foods typically cost more than their conventional counterparts. Higher prices are due in part to more expensive farming practices. If people can afford it, buy local and organic. Farmers' markets carry reasonably priced locally grown organic and conventional food. If people cannot always afford the cost of organic foods, try to spend the extra money when it comes to what the Environmental Working Group calls the "dirty dozen": peaches, strawberries, nectarines, apples, spinach, celery, pears, sweet bell peppers, cherries, potatoes, lettuce, and imported grapes. These fragile fruits and vegetables often require more pesticides to fight off insects compared to hardier produce, such as asparagus and broccoli. Another downside of Organic products is that because produce does not have that wax cover or contain preservatives they may spoil faster. However, please take into consideration that people are also not consuming these compounds. Some organic produce may appear imperfect, may be of an odd shape, vary in color and differ in size. These foods exceed if not, meet the same quality and safety standards as those of modern day conventional foods and are nutrient dense.

Making a choice to follow the organic diet method has a cyclical impact, meaning a healthier food environment which gives birth to a physically healthier human being. Choosing to purchase organic products even if in limited amounts contributes to promoting the lands clean bill of health. Organic agriculture utilizes the traditional methods and the gentlemen farmers are the pioneers of organic food research who conduct the studies and shoulder the expense. A few Universities are developing organic research teams to assist farmers in the advancement of this agriculture but funding is sparse. Buying organic products will help support the cause to fund a quest to develop and improve innovations that promote physical health along with protecting the environment. Food is vital to the lives of all and has for ages been honored in song, poetry and art. Recently, industry has centered public awareness on the food people eat, and its implication on physical and psychological well-being. In the past couple of decades, social scientists and social psychologists have paid significant attention to the subject of food. Everything people consume influences how people think and feel about themselves. Food should give people a sense of being emotionally and physically fit because of its taste and nourishment to the body. When eaten in small or high amounts, however, fitness and physical condition can be changed, which can produce negative perceptions and emotions.

A Few Safe Food Practice Tips

1. Thoroughly wash Vegetables and Fruits. Washing with water helps take away the traces of pesticides and compounds, thus, removes the bacteria and dirt from the surface of fruits and vegetables. Some chemical residue may not be removed by washing and people can peel fruits and vegetables.

2. Buy Fruits and Vegetables in Season. Buy produce at the local farmers market and ask the manager at the supermarket when they receive fresh shipments.

3. Grow an Organic Garden and Create Compose. People will have no doubt of food quality or safety.

4. Carefully understand and read Food Labels. If a product says it is organic, it does not necessarily mean it is a healthier alternative. Organic products can be high in calories, fat and sugar content.

5. Choose many different Types of Foods from many different Sources. This activity reduces the chances of exposure to one pesticide and allows the buyer to receive a better combination of nutrients.

Organic produce carries significantly fewer chemicals and pesticide residues and buying organic products limits this exposure. Some buy organic products to decrease the consumption of food additives. The organic food regulations forbid or severely restrict the use of processing aids, food additives, and fortifying agents commonly used in non-organic foods. This practice includes the exclusion of artificial sweeteners, colorings, flavorings, preservatives, and monosodium glutamate. Others buy organic food because of concerns over the environment. These types of farming practices reduce pollution, improve soil quality and conserve water. Some simply choose organic produce because they prefer how the foods taste. Making a commitment to changing food habits is a start towards physically improving health. Beyond eating more fruits, vegetables, whole grains and good fats, there are the moral questions associated with food safety/security, a consumer's right to know, nutrition and land sustainability. Those that follow this diet nurture a belief that society should consider how foods are grown or raised, when they think about making healthier food choices. There are many benefits to organic foods that cannot be matched by eating a conventional, processed food diet. Eating organic foods is a rational, logical choice which considers the benefits of the physical body and the health of the nation. To follow the culture that associates with the organic diet plan is a choice that helps nurture the planet along with promoting physical fitness. This food processing method is well worth investigating and implementing into anyone's lifestyle.

Chapter 16
The History and Success of Therapy

Nearly all therapists want to improve their clients' awareness, which in turn encourages them to understand thoughts, feelings and behaviors in relationship to the problem. This knowledge in turn opens up the notion of having many options or choices to discover new ways to cope with difficulties in life. A few therapists think that this process is about transformation, but, therapists are more than only change advocates and treatment is more than just adjusting to change. This last chapter will be examining the history and types of therapy, how to assess the need for treatment, how to plan for the initial discussion and the benefits of employing the bio-psycho-social model.

According to a review of the research, carried out by the American Psychological Association (2012), psychotherapy is useful and produces long-term alterations in emotional health, and in turn, these improvements decrease the demand for health services. Nevertheless, data provided by the government and insurance industry state that the use of psychotherapy declined over the last decade while the application of medicines to approach mental and behavioral matters increased. Many have trouble comprehending the fact that going to therapy provides genuine, tangible benefits. Others view treatment as signifying an intrusion of privacy. A few people may be scrupulously independent and have concerns of losing that freedom, or have fears of the label "crazy" which unhappily is a view that continues to exist. Those in the medical and pharmaceutical businesses bombard the public with communications that lead to drugs being the solution to unlocking all of life's dilemmas. Health Psychologists assist people evaluate those situations with research-based information about how treatment renders a safe, efficient solution that has enduring improvements in mental and physical health. Therapy is effective for a variety of mental and physical ailments with effects being greater than those created by many health related practices. Recommendations remain to be the last option from experts in the health community despite research affirming that clients do unquestionably gain benefit. Therapy is an emotional method, and health psychologists are careful during these challenging brushes because of the importance that they set on the therapeutic alliance. Treatment is a dedication to increasing emotional and physical health and women manage to adopt the therapy connection easier than men, as this is one setting where they can go without concerns of repercussion. The aims vary and often involve decreasing stress, strengthening problem solving skills, or, empowering people to experience a meaningful, productive, purposeful life (Carlson & Heth, 2007).

Psychotherapy is a generic phrase pertaining to the healing interplay or approach arranged between a qualified specialist and a person, couple, group, or family. The challenges explored are emotional in quality and can vary in terms of their sources, triggers, consequences, and potential recommendations (Cooper & Leeser, 2011). Proper evaluation is reliant on the practitioner's knowledge which may increase or surface as the clinician gains understanding, recognition and comprehensive information. Therapy encompasses the interactive rules between a person or group and a mental health professional (psychologist, clinical social worker, licensed counselor, or psychiatrist) and the goal is to examine feelings, behaviors and thoughts thereby improving problem solving skills to produce a higher level of functioning (Norcross & Goldried, 2005). Psychotherapy also aims to heighten the sensation of overall well-being. Psychotherapists use a variety of communication methods that include exploring, discussion, experiential relationship building and performance enhancement, all of which have the intention of increasing mental health, daily functions and improving relationships.

The History of Therapy

The treatment of emotional or mental difficulties can be traced to primitive man, and the classical Greeks were the earliest to recognize mental illnesses as being a pathological condition, rather than a strike from the evil gods. Even though the Greeks understanding of the nature of mental illness was not always accurate, and their practices were somewhat unusual, they did recognize the treatment benefits of using encouraging and comforting statements. With the defeat of the Roman Empire, the Middle Ages brought the renewal of a culture embracing a belief in the paranormal or evil spirits causing mental illness and along with this belief spread the practice of using cruelty especially in securing confessions of diabolical possession. However, some practitioners such as Paracelsus (1493-1541) were advocates for psychotherapy in the treating of emotional distress.

Theoretically-based psychotherapy was first promoted in the Middle East during the ninth century by the Persian doctor and emotional mastermind, Rhazes, who was the head physician at the Baghdad Psychiatric Hospital. Although there is a scattering of writings, reports of the benefit of discussing problems it was the English psychiatrist Walter Cooper Dendy who originally coined the phrase "psycho-therapeia" in 1854. Contemporary, scientific psychology dates to 1879 by the opening of the first psychological clinic by Wilhelm Wundt, though, effort's to design techniques for evaluating and managing mental distress existed long beforehand (Boeree,

2013; Evans, Staudt – Sexton & Cadwallader, 1992). In an informal sense, psychotherapy can be declares to be in fashion throughout the centuries as people received emotional guidance including reassurance from specialists.

Contemporary psychotherapy was launched by the development of psychoanalysis, or the "talking cure" by Sigmund Freud. He explained the method around the crossing of the 20th century and produced insightful additions to the field with descriptions of infantile sexuality, the unconscious, the value of fantasies, and the design of the human mind. Freud's work with the troubled guided him to decide that emotional distress was the effect of holding recollections or thoughts in the unconscious mind. A few of his techniques regularly practiced were free association, dream analysis and transference. Psychoanalysis was essentially listening to the client and then presenting interpretations which would lead to recollections and bringing the memories to consciousness, consequently diminishing symptoms.

For the next fifty years, Freud's techniques of psychoanalysis and its numerous versions continued to be the primary approach utilized in clinical practice. Clinical psychologists focused on psychological assessment, and the use of psychotherapy was adopted into the field following the Second World War. Shortly afterwards scholars, such as, Alfred Adler and Carl Jung started to introduce new understandings about mental functioning. Many other theorists helped to improve the broad orientation, which includes multiple strategies based on Freud's central belief of raising the unconscious, conscious (Everson, 1991).

Traditionally, psychotherapy was a long process usually demanding years of processing, and as the treatment grew more universally accessible importance was placed on developing more concise techniques. The following notable methods of treatment were explained, not as a result of anyone having different thoughts from Freud, but were due to economic matters because psychotherapy was expensive. The humanist psychologist Carl Rogers emphasized a process known as client-centered therapy that focuses on the therapist furnishing unconditional positive regard. This interpersonal therapy was explained by Carl Rogers during the 1940s and focuses on the expression of sympathy, genuineness and acceptance from the therapist to the patient. Beginning in the early 1950s, the school of thought identified as humanistic psychology started to have a notable influence. Client-centered therapy persists in being one of the most broadly applied forms in the area of clinical psychology.

Behaviorism evolved into a central school of thought during the early years of the twentieth-century and words such as conditioning and association played an instrumental role. The use of behavioral psychology embraced teachings from animal psychology to treat behavioral and emotional distress (Mandler, 2007). Behavioral treatment regularly employs social learning, classical conditioning and operant conditioning to assist in reducing problematic behaviors. Behaviorism, today, may not be as prevailing though numerous practices are nevertheless quite common and over the years behavior therapy has been improved to include the importance of thoughts and feelings.

The cognitive reconstruction of the 1960s produced a significant impact on the use of psychotherapy as psychologists began to focus on how internal feeling states influence functioning and performance. Cognitive Behavioral Therapy improves as a system of treatment that stimulates people to recognize thoughts and feelings that guide their behavior. The blended cognitive-behavioral treatment process has evolved into being the primary treatment for various psychiatric conditions and is regularly practiced tackling a wide range of problems including anxiety, depression, addiction and phobias (Sundberg, 2001; Robertson, 2010). By the early 1970s, there were over 60 distinct types of psychotherapies, stretching from guided imagery (mental images and stories) to psychodrama. At this time, virtually all therapeutic modalities offer brief therapy designed to aid in managing difficulties of daily life.

The Types of Therapy

1. Psychoanalytic – This is the original method to be endorsed as being psychotherapy. Psychoanalysis fosters the verbalization of all thoughts, involving dreams, fantasies and free associations from which the therapist gives form to the sort of unconscious struggles that are producing the symptoms and personality difficulties.

2. Psychodynamic – A process whose fundamental focal position is to reveal the lost content of a patient's psyche in an effort to reduce emotional tension. Although its roots are in psychoanalysis, psychodynamic approach is short, less expensive and less time consuming.

3. Behavioral – Focuses on diminishing maladaptive patterns of behavior to improve cognitions, communications and spontaneous reactions.

4. Cognitive Behavioral – Seeks to understand maladaptive assessments of thoughts, beliefs, and responses, with the aim of reducing destructive negative emotions and changing problematic dysfunctional habits.

5. Humanistic – This therapy appeared in response to psychoanalysis and behaviorism and some experts consider the approach to be the Third Force in the advancement of psychology. The treatment attention relates to the emotional evolution of the client and has an emphasis on the subjective intent towards positive growth. Humanistic theory affirms that human beings have an innate ability to want to maximize their potential and have a desire to become self-actualizing. The responsibility of humanistic therapist is to establish an environment where this inclination would thrive. This treatment method has philosophical origins and a few features of existentialism.

6. Existential – Has a connection to philosophy essentially with the idea that people are isolated in the world. Standing alone produces isolation that leads to thoughts and beliefs of possessing a meaninglessness reality. These views can be overcome entirely by forming one's own values and purposes of life.

7. Systemic – Community psychology is one example of a systemic process that attempts to address life's dilemmas, not on an individual level, but as in a relationship to the group. These approaches cover family, marriage and group counseling in which communications, patterns of responding and dynamics are the center of the therapists' attention.

8. Transpersonal – Acknowledges the client in connection to owning a spiritual perception of consciousness.

9. Brief Therapy is a generic title that includes diversity of techniques. Brief treatment deviates from other forms of treatment in that it emphasizes concentrating the awareness on one problem and there are straightforward interventions. This process is solution-based and not problem-oriented as it is not as involved with what way a problem arose but with the principal factors maintaining the difficulty that hinder progress.

The Therapy Relationship

The therapeutic alliance is a collaboration where both therapist and client synchronize shared intentions and act unitedly on tasks that conceivably will yield a positive outcome. This partnership strengthens on one's capacity to have acceptance, compassion and trust, with the understanding that the relationship is a determinant for successful treatment. The attachment or therapeutic alliance between the therapist and client has been a focal point and measured many times throughout the historical evolution of psychotherapy. Cooper and Leeser (2011) emphasize the notion that the client is an active ally in the treatment process. Many therapists concur with the idea that it is the relationship and collaboration between therapist and client as being one of the answers if, not the key factor to successful treatment.

Past investigations have focused on patient characteristics that have had an impact on the therapeutic alliance, such as motivation level and the ability to develop relationships. Studies have shown that these traits and characteristics have an impact on both the connection and the therapy outcome (Black, Hardy, Turpin, & Parry, 2005). The research further explains that the clients' ability to form a relationship provides the foundation for the alliance, but it also appears that the therapists' ability to develop relationships is just as important. Empathy is an essential ingredient in the healing process. A therapist's empathy toward their client plays a role in developing the alliance, and its impact on the relationship is crucial. Moore (2006) suggests empathy is not only communicated verbally, but also with an increase in eye contact, body posture, tone of voice and listening skills. It is significant for therapists to think of not only the therapeutic alliance, but also the ways in which they show empathy as an influence on treatment outcomes. The literature does lead professionals to believe that a genuine bond between therapist and client can occur pretty quickly, even within the first 10 minutes, but on average it takes 2-3 sessions (Corp, Tsaroucha & Kingston, 2008).

There are numerous and varied reasons why people decide to go to counseling. Some have undergone traumatic experiences, which they would like to explore in a safe environment; bereavement, separation, challenging life transitions, or distressful events from the childhood. Others seek aid with learning how to cope with distinct psychological or behavioral habits that they would like to change; addictions, compulsive thoughts, difficulties with relationships or poor dietary habits. Many people try counseling to examine a prevailing sense that their lives are not quite satisfied, or to learn how to cope with feelings of hopelessness linked with enduring a chronic illness. Nevertheless, it is not at all essential to have a severe problem to obtain progress with counseling.

People may utilize therapy to form a purpose in finding meaning in life, or attempt to stir up the confidence to accomplish a goal (Frank, 1988). At times, clients approach treatment with having well-defined goals, such as, the alleviation of symptoms of one sort or another and then move onto contemplating other changes. These intentions are commendable, although, at this point, treatment no longer applies the psychiatric or medical standard. The therapy focuses on the challenges that everyone has in living, is optional and is directed towards accomplishment or self-realization.

Some do not want to be in counseling and are pressured into receiving treatment. "My husband says I have a problem." "My wife says I do not communicate." "The judge says I have to do six sessions." "My doctor said it all in my head." These are not ideal therapy situations, and it will take an accomplished therapist to be able to assist, and many do indeed profit. Nearly all want to attend counseling to improve the problem or find alternatives to coping with a distressful life event. A few experience emotions associated with stress, mixed with beliefs of receiving of hope in removing or finding new ways to manage the dilemma. The anxiety is often linked to how they believe they will be judged by the therapist. The hope relates to having a positive outlook about their future capability of achieving success.

How to evaluate the need for therapy

How do people recognize and evaluate the need to consult with a professional therapist? Many individuals have attempted to cope with the problem by themselves, discussed the problem with friends, co-workers, minister or anyone who was willing to listen. At times just talking out a problem with a sympathetic listener will help, however, if talking about the concerns has been of benefit it might be a good idea to assess the advantages of seeking professional guidance.

Health psychologists can examine the situation in a non-judgmental fashion and has the qualifications to aid with problem solving (Priebe & Wright, 2006). Most people will be investing a reasonable amount of time, money, and energy into treatment which means picking a therapist wisely, possibly a referral from a friend or a therapist that they have known in the past. Find a therapist that promotes an emotional connection, not one that is acting superior or indifferent, during the session. When someone senses this emotional bond treatment is more likely to be extremely useful and the treatment will be on the path to success. Therapy is more about the relationship and less about the technique.

Treatment and Time: People can determine whether they are prepared to attempt counselling by questioning if going into treatment is worth taking an hour out of the week to discuss the difficulty. If the reply is yes, then the person is presumably ready. If no, then they are not, however, there will always be an opportunity to re-visit the notion in the future. For nearly all of the population, the solution to this issue is that simple.

Treatment and Motivation: People postpone starting therapy for numerous reasons. Frequently some think that the challenges are obstacles that they should be capable of solving alone and others think no one else needs to be aware of their business. Isolated people do not have a firm support system and it is tough if not improbable for them to reach out to others to ask for assistance. It takes strength to sit in a vulnerable situation, particularly when talking to a professional. The reaching out demands motivation, and for many it is scary to accept having problems. If someone is apprehensive about scheduling an interview, he or she can view this process as signifying a once in a lifetime meeting, merely to evaluate if treatment is worth the risk. After all for most, the judgment to go to therapy is a choice. Nevertheless, it is necessary to realize that anything in life that is done for the first time is indeed anxiety provoking. If this image is kept in the back of ones' mind while stepping into the counselors' office they may understand that the therapist is also facing them, for the first time. Individuals who choose to make an appointment can decide never again to go back should they believe that this encounter was just too traumatizing.

Treatment and Success: It is reasonable to assume that patients will acquire a deeper understanding of themselves and their difficulties. It is also fair to expect they will discover new ways to manage problems, beliefs, emotions and life experiences. It is logical to anticipate that people will feel more empowered and in charge of life. Nevertheless, it is not possible to expect that treatment will resolve every problem in life. Life's' obstacles vary routinely corresponding to the conditions. With long term treatment, the capacity to cope with different obstacles independently will develop over time. Successful therapy facilitates change in the way people respond to events. It is the therapists' obligation to promote the exploration of discovering new approaches to coping and developing a deeper perception of the complexities in life. As the therapy progresses the process enhances a sense of awareness "an aha moment" that encourages thoughts of empowerment and self-respect.

There are especially stringent privacy rules concerning treatment and everything the therapist discusses is in strict confidence. Though, psychologists have a judicial mandate to report any firm and determined suicidal intentions, any threats to hurt someone and any physical or sexual abuse against a child or senior citizen. Throughout the process therapists, support people asking questions of any and all sorts, as clients are hiring them to help. Therefore write down issues and "ask away."

How to Prepare for Therapy – The Initial Interview

Counseling is effective for those who are facing a transition, enduring a loss, for those wanting to greet the day with more passion and for people who are coping with a severe psychiatric illness. People should weigh the benefits of therapy when they think their lives have no purpose, when the distressed feeling conflicts with their quality of life or when they want to improve an area that is in satisfactory working condition. The decision to explore treatment is for most a conscious brave decision to attempt to change or resolve a difficult life situation.

Clients customarily decide which subjects to examine leading to the therapist and client simultaneously planning the steps to tackle. After the first few sessions, there will be a review that covers other areas to investigate, methods to cope with the immediate difficulty and explore the approaches to problem resolution. Therapists should specify the approximate length of time it will take to examine and resolve the matter. However, there have been occasions in my profession when, I have asked a patient, "How can I help?", only to see that look of shock and awe. These individuals are unmistakably tongue-tied and nervous, which is surely understandable, and over time they increasingly unwind enough to explain. Although, some in a displeased nature, bitterly retort, "I don't know why I am here, this is your responsibility to tell me," that ultimately escorts us down the path of uncharted territory and sometimes ineffective treatment. The angry clients regularly feel the obligation to receive counseling through recommendations of their physicians, family, friends and preachers. Many are highly opposed to accepting treatment and at times fear being judged.

Unless the client is gravely disabled (suicidal, psychotic), regrettably, under these circumstances, the first session may be the last. Asking for help is a symbol of bravery. There are many thoughts as to why someone chooses to proceed and many view treatment as being a learning experience and an opportunity to grow. In reality, most make a deliberate choice to heighten the conditions of their life, which could involve arousing the motivation to run a marathon. People do not have to be seriously ill to attend, as some have trouble with maintaining happiness and joy from life while other's search for the driving force to perfect a healthy ability.

During the first few meetings, the client and the therapist are improving compatibility and are preparing for the commitment that it takes to create resolutions. In order to make a lasting change it entails having a healthy connection with the therapist and this may take time. People who do not realize this will sometimes leave promptly saying: "I went to therapy, and it didn't work." The abrupt leaving illustrates why identical problems may pop up throughout someone's life. These people frequently are asking for and wanting advice, not healing and they misinterpret the ideas and principles of treatment. With the hope that the same problem will not re-surface in the future, successful outcome relates to this relationship along with working through the core difficulty.

Therapy values the expression of emotions. What is also meaningful is if the level of revealed emotion explains to the therapist the corresponding value of each emotion (mild importance, moderate importance and intensely important). To adopt the feeling of anger as an example: One client may appear angry and rage often, but each eruption exhibits the same level of emotional pain. This individual receives much relief, though that is all and often confuses the therapist. Another person may seldom get angry, although they do mention anger whenever they sense it and they reveal whether the anger is high, moderate or minor. Because the feeling is clearly communicated and the therapist recognizes the predicament, this client receives added assistance in managing the situation. The next task is to examine and assist with managing or coping with the discomfort. Possessing an understanding of emotions and how someone communicates that information is significant in achieving resolution. Be prepared to examine the problem areas and circumstances leading up to making the decision to enter treatment.

1. Were there any precipitating events including the death of a loved one, divorce, lack of employment, or medical illness and how long has this problem been challenging.

2. Have there been any prior psychological treatments or psychiatrist visits including hospitalizations?

3. Be prepared to discuss developmental or childhood experiences along with explaining any emotional problems within the biological family.

4. Be ready to communicate thoughts, moods and behaviors.

5. The therapist will examine how people are taking care of themselves physically and emotionally.

A treatment plan is then reviewed and a preliminary achievement date should be given (customarily 4-6 months on a weekly basis for 45 min). If the counselor or client is wary about scheduling another meeting it is logical to think about rescheduling and call the office for additional appointments in the near future.

The Last Therapy Session

Counseling is beneficial, soft and at times firm in its approach; however, it entails the endurance and personal fortitude to work through the process. Therapy has many benefits and advantages for anyone who exercises the steps. Conceivably, many will display that strut and pleased sensation as treatment progresses, because everyone values "standing up straight and walking tall." To achieve success there has to be an acknowledged partnership because it takes time, energy and effort by both the person receiving treatment and the therapist. Therapy is a promise to make tough alterations in thinking patterns and performance. Effective counseling is a two way street because it demands time, enthusiasm and economic responsibility from the client to make shifts in behavior or thought patterns and then acquire new ways of managing thoughts, emotions and behaviors.

In summation, it takes courage and wonder to enter into the healing arena because this is one approach that traverses inner life. Therapy stimulates understanding the facts that people have choices, and then analyzes the various ways to accomplish goals connected with that choice. Once people experience and work through this process they will start to feel empowered and will become much more driven to take charge of their life. The last appointment includes a basic overview of how people think they improved and the evaluation can be accomplished by applying a percentage evaluation system. The conversation usually covers directions in which the person can individually "take on the world."

The Counselors Personality and Style

A therapist who is in the field over a stretch of time usually recognizes that years later they are still learning and discovering. This is on account of the reality that psychotherapy is not a practice of operational exactness, but is a progressive process that involves being with a patient and evolves over time. Like most treatments, therapy can be administered poorly, less well or very well, and it is important to keep in mind that a therapist who is a great fit for one person may not be with the buddy next door. A few investigations have found a small relationship between therapist experience and favorable therapeutic results; however, the majority of the data confirms the opinion that a more qualified therapist does not automatically generate more favorable outcomes (Hersoug, Hoglend, Monsen, & Havik, 2001). The ancient saying "practice makes perfect" does not appear to fit in the field of out-patient practice.

One essential ingredient for resolving difficulties and determining new ways to cope is the emotional connection or relationship people have with their therapist. Training is taught, learning occurs, sensations are examined, and thoughts are explored in relation to behaviors. Nevertheless, education, learning and exploring of issues are not perfect circumstances for receiving aid with managing a difficulty. It is very important to emphasize the significance of the client being able to emotionally relate with the therapist and to pay heed to this emotional chemistry (Donner, VanderCreek & Gonsiorek, 2008). The outcomes of obtaining progress towards reaching those goals in therapy depend on this connection.

One major ideal environment for the counseling situation is that the therapist must recognize the client being a whole person, not strange, irritable, or identify them with a psychiatric judgment. If therapists exhibit respect and courtesy and if clients receive these offerings, they will achieve progress in handling the problem. If genuine respect and recognition are not granted, and/or if the client cannot accept the suggestion of support, reaching success in counseling is severely jeopardized. This implies that the therapy may be a misuse of time, service and finances. Nevertheless, many professionals are oftentimes pleasingly surprised when the most opposing clients make a 180 degree shift and become most satisfied in managing their life. Progress in counseling does certainly correlate to the connection that people possess with their therapist (Høglend, 1999).

There are several rules such as those linked to privacy, recognizing sexual limits, thoughtful listening, and holding the client as being the center of the conversation versus the therapist speaking about their own concerns. Though, these are fundamental expectations of all therapists. What individuals need to assess is the therapists' temperament, their characteristics and communication style. Some therapists are more verbal than others, some practice specialized methods, some use amusement, others interpret, and a few are passive. The client should assess the therapists respect and appraise how much the therapist appears to care about what is being reviewed and then evaluate if the therapist suits their requirements. People deserve the best union as this is their time and everyone deserves the professionalism it takes to help reach a resolution (Silverman, 2005). If the client and the therapist are a fitting personality match, the issue lingers on to what are the client roles in accomplishing success, in counseling.

Many issues surface when clients are not successful in therapy. The general barriers are those including intoxication or abusing substances during meetings, clients that are not taking their prescribed medications or those that require medicines, individuals that cannot establish relationships, and those whose temperaments do not harmonize with the therapists. Counseling can be challenging for people with significant character disorders due to a lower threshold for emotional discomfort, as well as having an inability to be consistent in their thinking processes. People who do not have their primary needs satisfied and those that are extremely emotional likewise have a tougher time in treatment. Resource obstacles to progress are need of transportation, childcare difficulties, finances, and insurance. Additional research suggests that a person with multiple clinical symptoms may not have as much ability to retain information and work productively with the therapist. Hoglend (1999) states that counseling does help those that seeks it out. Overall, it seems that motivation, collaboration, active engagement and personality characteristics, along with a developing relationship all have a direct connection to favorable treatment outcomes. Nevertheless, all clients deserve the therapist's time, energy, caring and respect. Everyone warrants these prerequisites even if the individual is delivered into the office "kicking and screaming." Clients should find a trustworthy, private, atmosphere and a caring human being that will listen without judging and who does not have an air of superiority.

The Four Client Qualities associated with Achieving Success

1. **Desire** is the source of all accomplishments, not a fantasy, not a necessity, but a piercing, pulsating desire that rises above everything. Some people will proclaim that they want to make adjustments in their life but need the motivation or ambition. They will start by investigating treatment and indicate a hope for change, but will not or cannot deliver the energy required to carry out the means to succeed. The original aim to seek out therapy was because their life may have grown so uncontrollable that their life is in a state of emergency. In addition, these patients may further be in emotional pain over an extended period creating physical health problems.

   A stressful circumstance may be upsetting, but it may also be helpful. In many life situations, events may have to get serious before they improve for the transition to occur. Consequently, a crisis can be a life setback or trial, but it can also be a gateway to secure an improved life, because the discomfort provides an impetus towards personal growth and advancement. Without a definite desire for change, reforms are less apt to happen. When a person has both the wish to make modifications and the driving force to do so, this is half of what it takes to reach victory.

2. **Belief** is one of the most important building blocks to reaching success in any venture. If someone does not have trust in them self or in what he or she is striving to achieve then this makes reaching the goal nearly impossible. The more someone believes in their abilities the higher they increase the likelihood of being successful. The notion of belief in oneself appears straightforward, but there are

those who falter on account of the fact that they do not possess the hope that they can accomplish their goal.

One reason people suffer severe and enduring emotional pain is that they do not believe counseling or psychotherapy can be of benefit. They have viewed media presentations or read books that defame individuals who attempt counseling, or render therapists in an unflattering fashion. Some may deem counseling as being only for the weak and timid. These people usually fail in consequence of the evidence that they have little or no faith in the healing process of reform. The successful person realizes that it takes self-confidence to achieve a goal. Successful people understand that a certain measure of confidence needs to be put in a health care provider. They may also want to review any lack of trust with the therapist in the beginning stages of counseling because lack of confidence may have resulted from early childhood matters and be the original source of pain. Countless people have the hopes that the first few therapy encounters will fix everything negative going on in their life and the initial few appointments frequently do resolve troubles that people were already equipped to fix. Nevertheless, the problems that persist after the first few sessions are the mighty ones. What people want to accomplish in counseling should be precisely established during the beginning stages of the treatment process. The following steps would be to examine a reasonable time frame to attain the goal and then determine how to gauge the improvement.

3. **Courage** is not the absence of anxiety; it is, rather, the capacity to advance through life despite discomfort. Many who require counseling will not acknowledge it, or they look for therapy and have difficulty performing any alterations in life. They crave their world, circumstances or others to change, yet they are not amenable to act on anything concerning them self. It is remarkable how much emotional distress a person can experience, merely because they have difficulty embracing the concept of

self-transformation. These individuals struggle with the process of change because it can create stress to step outside of one's comfort zone. New attitudes, different styles of doing things, and adjusting thought patterns or behaviors demand energy and time, as well as endurance. The fear does not deaden the person with courage; they are empowered by it. Asking for help and creating changes in lifestyle demands courage.

4. **Patience** and commitment unlocks the doors of imagination, provides a vision, and supplies the precise ingredients to transform that vision into reality. Those who consider "anything worth having is worth waiting for," will proceed on in the journey to transformation, and are the people who will triumph over misfortune. The counseling process demands such dedication and fortitude. The solution to producing success in counseling is to continue the path of treatment and acknowledge that some concerns may need time to solve because these difficulties evolved and matured over several years.

If people maintain or acquire these qualities in the beginning phases of counseling they will be on the path of progress. Surmounting misfortunes and reaching accomplishment results from the culmination of possessing all four qualities of Desire, Belief, Courage and Patience. People can have the concrete potentiality of gaining success as well as solving any realistic goals valued in life.

How to evaluate successful treatment

People can conclude if their work with a therapist is successful provided that they start to gain insights about thoughts and responses which may have eluded them before they entered treatment. If clients sense they have been satisfied in producing change, learning different behaviors, acquiring something new about their sense of self, possess an improvement in coping abilities, and have fewer symptoms, then the aims have been fulfilled. Reviewing the treatment method is effective in sustaining and building success, thus, clients believe they have gained growth. At the completion of favorable therapy, clients will feel adequately equipped to tackle life's transitions and hurdles, by acquiring a somewhat more flexible stance on how to handle life.

Over time, people should be capable of identifying patterns in the way they function, identify the causes and understand stumbling blocks to comfort and then generate different options. The result is personal growth that empowers innovation and supports people in becoming the person they would like to be in the world. The effect in individual growth empowers people to manage life and experience positive, self-fulfilling relationships.

What are the Benefits of Therapy?

Professor Mick Cooper (2008), of the University of Strathclyde, England, reports that the most significant determinant in beneficial treatment is the client. Psychotherapy develops life skills that stretch beyond the course of treatment. Although medication is proper in some cases, investigations confirm that a combination of medication and treatment is customarily most productive in managing anxiety and depression. The outcomes produced including those for various age groups and across a variety of mental and physical health ailments are equivalent to, or, better than the effects produced by drug treatments, without the potential for adverse side effects that medications often present.

The results of treatment tend to endure longer than psychopharmacological treatments and seldom create serious side effects. One inherent benefit of therapy is that the process provides a safe and protected area to examine problems and therapists have the education to listen and interpret. The healing environment assigns a high importance on the worth of a person and everyone merits a safe and secure environment to verbalize thoughts openly without the risk of judging. The patient and the therapist work collectively to ascertain realistic goals that they want to achieve and producing meaningful options that effect well-being might be a unique experience that can be remarkably empowering, thus building self-confidence. Therapy generates a new perspective on a challenging circumstance that leads towards resolution of the conflict.

The benefits of counseling are:

1. Therapy provides an important although perhaps natural release of psychological distress and suffering.

2. There is promoting of the fundamental inclination to feel emotionally well and in several chronic situations a slowing of the pathological processes associated with the illness.

3. There is a remission of distinct emotional outbursts that acutely disturbed patients possess that may involve the loss of employment, the dissolution of savings, and the disruption of family life.

4. In some cases, there is the improvement of a true growth of ingrained personality difficulties. These people think better of them self and are more equipped to cope with anxiety that relates to their struggles.

5. People who have been in successful therapy have gained mastery over themselves and their circumstances.

6. Psychotherapy may have a meaningful impact in someone who is extremely emotionally confused, slowly, improving both their mental state and their ability function.

In summing-up, people can accomplish progress in counseling to overcome life's hurdles, recover a sense of control thus feeling empowered, regain pleasure in life, and experience a deeper, resilient broader range of emotional composure. The process of therapy is time limited, and attaining success is achieved by investigating the biological elements, psychological determinants and the social conditions that impact the individual problems, and the process then builds on existing strengths.

References

Acharya, M., & Kendra, K. (2003) Food Micro-nutrients & Organic (Natural) Farming, International Journal of Agriculture and Food Science Technology. Vol 4, 379-384.

Ackerman, Diane (1995). A Natural History of Love. Random House Inc.

Aday, J.B. (1995). An analysis of codependency in adult males: A comparison of adult males from chemically dependent families with adult males from nonchemically dependent families. Dissertation Abstracts International: Section B: The Sciences and Engineering.

Ader, R., & Cohen, N. (1975). Behaviorally conditioned immunosuppression. Psychosomatic Medicine, 37, 333–340.

Adolphs, Ralph. (2013). The Biology of Fear. Current Biology, Vol. 23, Issue 2.

Albus, C.(2010). Psychological and social factors in coronary heart disease. Annuals of Med. Oct 42(7):487-94.

Alonso-Blanco, Fernández-de-Las-Peñas C, Morales-Cabezas, Zarco-Moreno P, Ge HY, & Florez-García M. (2011) Multiple active myofascial trigger points reproduce the overall spontaneous pain pattern in women with fibromyalgia and are related to widespread mechanical hypersensitivity. Clinical Journal of Pain. June 405-413.

American Academy of Pain Medicine. AAPM Facts and Figures on Pain. Retrieved on February 21, 2013 from http://www.painmed.org/patientcenter/facts_on_pain.aspx

American Cancer Society: Cancer Prevalence: How Many People have Cancer? Retrieved October 13, 2013 from http://www.cancer.org/cancer/cancerbasics/cancer-prevalence.

American Diabetes Association, Living with Diabetes, Retrieved December 13, 2013 from http://www.diabetes.org/diabetes-basics/type-2/

American Heart Association, What is heart disease? Retrieved September 21, 2013 from http://www.heart.org/HEARTORG/Conditions/Conditions_UCM_001087_SubHomePage.jsp

American Psychological Association (2012). Research Shows Psychotherapy Is Effective But Underutilized. Retrieved September 15, 2013 from http://www.apa.org/news/press/releases/2012/08/psychotherapy-effective.aspx

American Psychiatric Association (2013). Diagnostic and Statistical Manual of Mental Disorders (5th ed.). Arlington, VA: American Psychiatric Publishing. 271–280.

American Psychological Association, division 38. Health Psychology. Retrieved from http://www.health-psych.org/.

American Psychological Association, "Mind/Body Health Heart Disease". Retrieved January 12, 2014 from http://www.apa.org/helpcenter/heart-disease.aspx

American Psychological Association. Self-Therapy: Discipline. Retrieved March 13, 2014 from http://www.helpyourselftherapy.com/topics/discip.html

American Society for Cell Biology. Sleep improves immune function. Retrieved http://medheadlines.com/2008/12/im-mune-system-most-active-during-sleep-2.

Anderson, B.J., & Rubin, R.R. (1996). Practical Psychology for Diabetes Clinicians: How to Deal With Key Behavioral Issues Faced by Patients & Health Care Teams. American Diabetes Association. Alexandria, Va.

Anderson, I., Haddad, P., Scott, J. (2012) Bipolar Disorder. BMJ Clinical Research Ed. 345: e8508 .

Andreasen, N., Black, D. (2006) Introductory Textbook of Psychiatry. (4th ed.). Arlington, VA: American Psychiatric Publishing, Inc.

Antonuccio, D., Danton, W., & DeNelsky, G. (1995). Psychotherapy versus medication for depression: Challenging the conventional wisdom with data. Professional Psychology: Research and Practice, 26, 574–585.

Avicenna, (980-1037). The Cannon of Medicine. https://ia600505.us.archive.org/8/items/AvicennasCanonOfMedicine/9670940-Canon-of-Medicine.pdf Retrieved October 4, 2014

Bartlett, Steven James (2011). Normality Does Not Equal Mental Health: The Need to Look Elsewhere for Standards of Good Psychological Health. New York: Praeger.

Bartoshuk, L. M. (1991). "Sweetness: history, preference, and genetic variability". Food technology 45 (11): 108–13.

Beattie, Melody (1986). Codependent No More: How to Stop Controlling Others and Start Caring for Yourself. Hazelden 2nd Revised edition.

Beck, A., Rush, J., Shaw, B., & Emery, G. (1979). Cognitive therapy of depression. New York: Guilford Press.

Beentjes, T., Goossens, P., Poslawsky, I. (2012) Caregiver burden in bipolar hypomania and mania: a systematic review. Perspectives in Psychiatric Care 48(4): 187–97

Belloc, N., & Breslow, L. (1972). Relationship of physical health status and health practices. Preventive Medicine, 1, 409–421.

Benes, F., Berretta, S. (2001) GABAergic Interneurons: Implications for Understanding Schizophrenia and Bipolar Disorder. Neuropsychopharmacology 25 (1): 1–27.

Benson, P., Roehlkepartain, E. (1993). Beyond Leaf Raking: Learning to Serve/Scrving to Learn. Abingdon Press

Bhupathiraju, S. & Tucker, K. (2011). Coronary Heart Disease Prevention: nutrients, foods, and dietary patterns. International Journal of Clinical Chemistry. August. 1493–1514.

Black, S., Hardy, G., Turpin, G., & Parry, G. (2005). Self-reported attachment styles and therapeutic orientation of therapists and their relationship with reported general alliance quality and problems in therapy. Psychology & Psychotherapy: Theory, Research & Practice, 78, 363-377.

Blum, Deborah. (2011). Love at Goon Park: Harry Harlow and the Science of Affection. Basic Books; Second Edition.

Boeree, George C. (n.d.). The History of Psychology. Retrieved on November 24, 2013 from http://webspace.ship.edu/cgboer/historyofpsych.html

Boehm, S., Schlenk, E., Funnell. M., Powers, H. & Ronis, D. Predictors of adherence to nutrition recommendations in people with non-insulin-dependent diabetes mellitus. Diabetes Education. 23:157-65, 1997

Boylan, Michael. (2008). The Good, the True and the Beautiful: A Quest for Meaning. Continuum 1 Edition.

Boyle, C.M. (1970). Difference between patients' and doctors' interpretation of some common medical terms. British Medical Journal, 2, 286–89.

Bradley, R., Binder, E., Epstein, M., Tang, Y., Nair, H., Liu, W., Gillespie, C., Berg, T., Evces, M., Newport, D., Stowe, Z., Heim, C., Nemeroff, C., Schwartz, A., Cubells, J., & Ressler, K. (2008). Influence of child abuse on adult depression: moderation by the corticotropin-releasing hormone receptor gene. Archives of General Psychiatry. February 190-200.

Bremner, Douglas. (2006). Traumatic stress: effects on the brain. Dialogues Clinical Neuroscience. Vol. 8 445–461.

Brennand, K., Savas, J., Kim, Y., Tran, S. (2014) Phenotypic differences in hiPSC NPCs derived from patients with schizophrenia Molecular Psychiatry http://www.nature.com/mp/journal/vaop/ncurrent/full/mp201422a.html

Bridges, William. (2001). The Way Of Transition: Embracing Life's Most Difficult Moments. Da Capo Press. Reprint Edition.

Brunet-Gouet E, Decety J. (2006). Social brain dysfunctions in schizophrenia: a review of neuroimaging studies. Psychiatry Res 148 (2–3): 75–92.

Bryant P., Trinder J., & Curtis, N. (2004). Sick and tired: Does sleep have a vital role in the immune system? Nature Reviews Immunology Vol. 4 457–67.

Buss, David M. (2000). The evolution of happiness. American Psychologist. 55:5–23.

Buss, David M. (2003) The evolution of desire : strategies of human mating. New York : Basic Books.

Cancer Research Institute. (n.d.). Cancer and the Immune System: Humoral Immune Response. Retrieved October 17, 2013 from http://www.cancerresearch.org/cancer-immunotherapy/resources/cancer-and-the-immune-system

Campbell R. (2009) Campbell's Psychiatric Dictionary. (9th ed.). New York, Oxford

Caponigro, J., Lee, Erica H., Johnson, Sheri L., Kring, Ann M.(2012) Bipolar Disorder: A Guide for the Newly Diagnosed (The New Harbinger Guides for the Newly Diagnosed Series) New Harbinger Publications; 1 edition

Carlson, N., & Heth, C. (2007). Psychology the science of behaviour. 4th ed. Upper Saddle River, New Jersey: Pearson Education, Inc.

Cartagena Protocol on Biosafety. Retrieved on July 23, 2012 from http://www.cbd.int/doc/publications/bs-brochure-02-en.pdf

Cassileth, B., Lusk, E., Strouse, T., Miller, D., Brown, L., Cross, P., & Tenaglia, A. (1984). Psychosocial status in chronic illness. New England Journal of Medicine, 311, 506–11.

Carter-Scott, C., Stewart, Lyn. (2007). Transformational Life Coaching. Florida: Health Communications, Inc.

Caudill, Margaret A. (2008) Managing Pain Before It Manages You. Third Edition. The Guilford Press.

Causes of Diabetes. (n.d.). National Institute of Diabetes and Digestive and Kidney Diseases, Retrieved http://diabetes.niddk.nih.gov/dm/pubs/causes/, on March 12, 2014.

Cedars-Sinai. (2012). Ordinary Heart Cells Become Biological Pacemakers with Injection of a Single Gene. Retrieved October 16, 2013 from https://www.cedars-sinai.edu/About-Us/

News/News-Releases-2012/Ordinary-heart-cells-become-biological-pacemakers-with-injection-of-a-single-gene.aspx,

Centers for Disease Control and Prevention. (n.d.) Heart Disease. Retrieved June 14, 2013 from http://www.cdc.gov/heart-disease/

Centers for Disease Control and Prevention. (n.d.) Immunity Types. Retrieved November 12, 2012 from http://www.cdc.gov/vaccines/vac-gen/immunity-types.htm

Centers for Disease Control and Prevention. (n.d.) Prevention's national health interview survey and behavioral risk factor surveillance system. Retrieved from http://www.cdc.gov/brfss/

Centers for Disease Control and Prevention. (2004). Indicators for chronic disease surveillance. MMWR Recommendations and Reports. 53 (RR-11):1–6.

Centers for Disease Control and Prevention. (2011). Chronic Disease Overview. Retrieved from http://www.cdc.gov/nccdphp/overview.htm.

Center for Disease Control and Prevention (n.d.) An Estimated 1 in 10 U.S. Adults Report Depression. Retrieved on January 25, 2013 from http://www.cdc.gov/features/dsdepression/

EMedicine Health. (n.d.). Chronic Pain Causes, Symptoms, Treatment – Measuring Pain. (n.d.) Retrieved May 21, 2013 from http://www.emedicinehealth.com/chronic_pain/page3_em.htm

Medscape. (n.d.). Chronic Pain Syndrome | E-depression. Retrieved September 25, 2013 from http://emedicine.medscape.com/article/310834-overview

Clark, D., Beck, A., & Alford, B. (1999). Scientific foundations of cognitive theory and therapy of depression. New York: Wiley.

Cloninger, Robert., Arnedo, Javier., Svrakic, Dragan., del Val , Coral., Ph.D., Molecular Genetics of Schizophrenia Consortium; Uncovering the Hidden Risk Architecture of the Schizophrenias: Confirmation in Three Independent Genome-Wide Association Studies The American Journal of Psychiatry 9/2014

Cohen, L., McChargue, D. & Collins, F. (2003). The health psychology handbook: Practical issues for the behavioral medicine specialist. Thousand Oaks, CA: Sage Publications

Cohen, S., & Rodriguez, MS. (1995). Pathways linking affective disturbances and physical disorders. Health Psychology 14:374-80.

Comer, Ronald. (2007). Fundamentals of Abnormal Psychology. Worth Publishers. 5th edition

Cooper, Mick. (2008). Essential Research Findings in Counselling and Psychotherapy: The Facts are Friendly. Sage Publications Ltd.

Cooper, M.G., & Leeser, J.G. (2011). Clinical Social Work practice an integrated approach (4th ed.). Boston, MA: Allyn & Bacon.

Copen, Casey E., Daniels, Kimberly., Vespa, Jonathan., & Mosher, William D. First Marriages in the United States: Data From the 2006–2010 National Survey of Family Growth. Retrieved July 21, 2013 http://www.cdc.gov/nchs/data/nhsr/nhsr049. pdf

Corballis, M. (1991). The Lopsided Ape. New York: Oxford University Press.

Corp, N., Tsaroucha, A., & Kingston, P. (2008). "Human Givens Therapy: The Evidence Base" Mental Health Review Journal 13 (4): 44–52.

Crinnion, W. (2010) Organic foods contain higher levels of certain nutrients, lower levels of pesticides, and may provide health benefits for the consumer. Alternative Medicine Review Apr. 15 (1):4-12

Crocker, J., Hannah, D., & Weber, R. (1983) Person memory and causal attributions. Journal of Personality & Social Psychology. Vol. 44 55–66.

Crowe, S., Wu, L., Economou, C., Turpin, S., Matzaris, M., Hoehn K., Hevene, A., James, D., DuhElia, J., & Watt, M. (2009). Pigment Epithelium-Derived Factor Contributes to Insulin Resistance in Obesity. Cell Metabolism. Vol. 10, Issue 1, 40-47.

Culbertson, F. (1997). Depression and gender. American Psychologist, 52, 25–31.

Darley, J., & Batson, C. (1973). From Jerusalem to Jericho: a study of situational and dispositional variables in helping behavior. Journal of Personality and Social Psychology. 27, 100–108.

Davis, L. (2014). The End of Normal: Identity in a Biocultural Era. University of Michigan Press.

De Mello, M., Lemos, V., Antunes, H., Bittencourt, L., Santos-Silva R., Tufik, S. (2003). Relationship between physical activity and depression and anxiety symptoms: a population study. Journal of Affective Disorders.Jul;149(1-3):241-6

de Boer A, van Buel E., & Ter Horst, G. (2012) Love is more than just a kiss: a neurobiological perspective on love and affection. Neuroscience. June 114-24.

Diabetes Prevention Program Research Group. (2002). Reduction in the incidence of type 2 diabetes with lifestyle intervention or metformin. New England Journal of Medicine. 346 393–403.

Diagnostic and Statistical Manual of Mental Disorders DSM-IV. Cluster C Personality Disorders: Washington: American Psychiatric Association, 4th ed. 1994.

Diener, E., & Larsen, R. (1993). The experience of emotional well-being. Handbook of emotions. Guilford; New York: 1993. pp. 405–415.

Donner, M., VanderCreek, L., Gonsiorek, J. (2008). Balancing Confidentiality: Protecting Privacy and Protecting the Public. Professional Psychology: Research and Practice, 39(3), 369-376.

Dowsett, S., Saul, J., Butow, P., Dunn, S., Boyer, M., Findlow, R., & Dunsmore, J. (2000). Communication styles in the cancer consultation: Preferences for a patient-centered approach. Psycho-Oncology, 9, 147–56.

Dubovsky, S. (1997). Mind-body deceptions. New York: Norton.

Dzivenu, O., Phil, D., O'Donnell-Tormey, J.(2003). Cancer and the Immune System: The Vital Connection. Cancer Research Institute. Retrieved http://www.cancerresearch.org/CRI/media/Content/Cancer%20Immunotherapy/Cancer-and-the-Immune-System-The-Vital-Connection.pdf on March 23, 2013.

Edelman, Gerald. (2001). A Universe Of Consciousness: How Matter Becomes Imagination. Basic Books.

Eliminating Barriers to the treatment of Mental Illness, Bipolar Disorder Fact Sheet. Retrieved Oct. 15, 2014 from http://www.treatmentadvocacycenter.org/resources/briefing-papers-and-fact-sheets/159/463

Evans, R., Staudt – Sexton, V., & Cadwallader, T. (1992). The American Psychological Association: A historical perspective. Washington, D.C.: American Psychological Association.

Everson, S. (1991). Companions to Ancient thought 2: Psychology. New York: Cambridge University Press.

Farmer, K., & Naylor, M. (1996). Sun exposure, sunscreens, and skin cancer prevention: a year-round concern. The Annals of Pharmacotherapy. Jun; 30 (6):662-73.

Fast, J., Preston, A. (2012). Loving Someone with Bipolar Disorder: Understanding and Helping Your Partner (The New Harbinger Loving Someone Series) New Harbinger Publications

Feinberg, A., & Tycko, B. (2004) The history of cancer epigenetics. Nature Reviews Cancer Feb. 4(2):143-53.

Feist, Jess. (2008). Theories of Personality. McGraw Hill Higher Education. 7th edition

Fisher, Helen E. (2000). Brains Do It: Lust, Attraction, and Attachment. Retreived November 16, 2013 on http://www.dana.org/Cerebrum/Default.aspx?id=39351#

Fisher, Helen E. (2004). Why we love : the nature and chemistry of romantic love. New York : H. Holt, 2004.

Foreman, Judy. (2014). A Nation in Pain: Healing our Biggest Health Problem. Oxford University Press, USA; 1 edition.

Forsythe, Paul., Kunze, Wolfgang (2012). Voices from within: gut microbes and the CNS. Cellular and Molecular Life Sciences. Retrieved http://www.indiana.edu/~abcwest/pmwiki/CAFE/Voices%20from%20within-%20gut%20microbes%20and%20the%20CNS.pdf on November, 20 2013.

Frank, Jerome (1988). What is Psychotherapy? An Introduction to the Psychotherapies. Oxford: Oxford University Press. pp. 1–2.

Frankl, Viktor E. (1997). Man's Search For Meaning. Pocket Books Rev Upd edition.

Frances, Allen. (2013) Saving Normal: An Insider's Revolt Against Out-of-Control Psychiatric Diagnosis, DSM-5, Big Pharma, and the Medicalization of Ordinary Life. William Morrow.

Frieden, T., & Mostashari, F. (2008). Health care as if health mattered. Journal of the American Medical Association. 299 (8):950–952.

Gage, H., Hook,V., Brennand, K. Human iPSC Neurons Display Activity-Dependent Neurotransmitter Secretion: Aberrant Catecholamine Levels in Schizophrenia Neurons Stem Cell Reports Retrieved September 26, 2014 from http://www.sciencedirect.com/science/article/pii/S2213671114002458

Gazzaniga, M. (1989). Mind Matters: How Mind and Brain Interact to Create Our Conscious Lives. Boston: Houghton Mifflin.

Geddes, J., Miklowitz, D. (2013) Treatment of bipolar disorder. Lancet 381 (9878):1672–82

Gerulf, Rieger., & Savin-Williams, Ritch C. (2012) The Eyes Have It: Sex and Sexual Orientation Differences in Pupil Dilation Patterns. PLoS ONE, 2012; 7

Gilmore, John (2010). Understanding What Causes Schizophrenia: A Developmental Perspective. The American Journal of Psychiatry, VOL. 167, No. 1

Griffith, Jeremy. (2011). What is Love? Retrieved http://www.worldtransformation.com/what-is-love/ on November 12, 2013.

Gladwell, Hugh (2014). The Ultimate Guide To Immune Disorders: Immune System Treatment For the Weak Immune System (Immune Disorders, Immune Disease). Amazon Digital Services, Inc.

Halperin, E. (2004). Paleo-oncology: the role of ancient remains in the study of cancer. Perspectives in Biology and Medicine. Winter; 47(1):1-14.

Hansell, James., & Damour, Lisa. (2008). Abnormal Psychology. John Wiley & Sons. 2nd edition.

Harris, Michael., & Lustman, Patrick., (1998) Clinical Diabetes. The Psychologist in Diabetes Care. Retrieved http://journal.diabetes.org/clinicaldiabetes/v16n21998/PG91.htm, on March 8, 2014.

Harris, Jennifer L., Schwartz, Marlene B., & Brownell, Kelly D. (2010). Evaluating Fast Food Nutrition and Marketing to Youth. Rudd Center for Food Policy and Obesity. Retrieved http://grist.files.wordpress.com/2010/11/fastfoodfacts_report.pdf on March 11, 2014.

Healy, David (2011) Mania: A Short History of Bipolar Disorder (Johns Hopkins Biographies of Disease) Johns Hopkins University Press; 1 edition

Helliwell, J., Layard, R., & Sachs, J. (2013). World Happiness Report Retrieved http://www.earth.columbia.edu/sitefiles/file/Sachs%20Writing/2012/World%20Happiness%20Report.pdf. on March 21, 2014.

Hemfelt, Robert., Minirith., Frank., Meier, Paul. (1989). Love is a choice: The definition book on letting go of unhealthy relationships. Thomas Nelson Inc. 1st edition.

Hersoug, A., Hogland, P., Monsen, J., & Havik, O. (2001). Quality of working alliance in psychotherapy therapist variables and patient/therapist similarity as predictors. The Journal of Psychotherapy Practice and Research, 10, 205-216.

Høglend, Per. (1999). Psychotherapy Research New Findings and Implications for Training and Practice. The Journal of Psychotherapy Practice and Research 8 257–263.

Hor, K, Taylor M (2010). Suicide and schizophrenia: a systematic review of rates and risk factors. Journal of psychopharmacology (Oxford, England) 24 (4 Suppl): 81–90.

Horwitz, Allan V. (2007). Transforming Normality into Pathology: The DSM and the Outcomes of Stressful Social Arrangements. Journal of Health and Social Behaviour Vol. 48 211–222.

Hu, Frank. (2003). Sedentary lifestyle and risk of obesity and type 2 diabetes.US National Library of Medicine National Institutes of Health. 38(2):103-8. Retrieved http://www.ncbi.nlm.nih.gov/pubmed/12733740, on August 18, 2013

Hunter, D., Foster, M., McArthur, JO., Ojha, R., Petocz, P., & Samman, S. (2011). Evaluation of the micronutrient composition of plant foods produced by organic and conventional agricultural methods. Critical Reviews of Food Science and Nutrition. July, 571-82.

Hur, Taekyun., Roese, Neal J., & Jae-Eun Namkoong. (2009). "Regrets in the East and West: Role of intrapersonal versus interpersonal norms". Asian Journal of Social Psychology12 (2): 151–156.

Ifowodo, Ogaga. (2013). History, Trauma, and Healing in Post-colonial Narratives: Reconstructing Identities (Future of Minority Studies). Palgrave Macmillan.

Inslicht, S., Metzler, T., Garcia, N., Pineles, S., Milad, M., Orr, S., Marmar, C., & Neylan, T. (2013) Sex differences in fear conditioning in posttraumatic stress disorder. Journal of Psychiatric Research. 47 (1):64-71.

Jeffries, F., & Davis P. (2013). What is the role of eye movements in eye movement desensitization and reprocessing (EMDR) for post-traumatic stress disorder (PTSD) a review. Behavioral and Cognitive Psychotherapy. 41 (3) 290-300.

Jones, E., Hyams, K., & Wessely, S. (2003). Review: Screening for vulnerability to psychological disorders in the military: an historical survey. Journal of Medical Screening 10, 40–46.

Judd, L., Akiskal, H., Schettler, P. (2002) The Long-Term Natural History of the Weekly Symptomatic Status of Bipolar I Disorder. Archives of General Psychiatry. 59:530–537.

Kandel, Eric. (2007). In Search of Memory: The Emergence of a New Science of Mind. W. W. Norton & Company. 1 edition.

Kandel, M. & Kandel, E. (May 1994). Flights of Memory. Discover Magazine. 32–38.

Katherine, Anne. (1994). Boundaries Where You End And I Begin: How To Recognize And Set Healthy Boundaries. Hazelden.

Katherine, Anne. (2000). Where to Draw the Line: How to Set Healthy Boundaries Every Day. Fireside, 1 edition.

Kato, N., Kawata, M., & Pitman, R. (2006). PTSD: Brain Mechanisms and Clinical Implications. Springer.

Katon, Wayne J. (2011). Epidemiology and treatment of depression in patients with chronic medical illness, Dialogues Clinical Neuroscience. March pages 7–23

Kelly, Bridget., & Fuster, Valentine. (2010) Institute of Medicine Promoting Cardiovascular Health in the Developing World: A Critical Challenge to Achieve Global Health. Washington, D.C: National Academies Press.

Kessler, R., Berglund, P., Chiu, W., Demler, O., Heeringa, S., Hiripi, E., Jin, R., Pennell, B., Walters, E., Zaslavsky, A., & Zheng, Hui. The US National Comorbidity Survey Replication (NCS-R): design and field procedures. Retrieved http://www.hcp.med.harvard.edu/wmh/publishedpaper_kessler_design.pdf. on December 2013.

Kirsch, Irving. (1999). How expectancies shape experience. American Psychological Association. (pp. 17-39). Washington, DC, US: American Psychological Association, xiv, 431.

Klatsky, A. (2009). Alcohol and Cardiovascular Diseases. Expert Review in Cardiovascular Therapy 7 (5): 499–506

Koehler, D. (1991). Explanation, imagination, and confidence in judgment. Psychological Bulletin. Vol. 110 499–519.

Krantz, David S., & McCeney, Melissa K. (2002). Effects of Psychological and Social Factors on Organic Disease: A Critical Assessment of Research on Coronary Heart Disease. Annual Review of Psychology, Vol. 53. 341-369

Krishnan, K. (2003) Broken Heart: Depression in Cardiovascular Disease. Dialogues in Clinical Neuroscience, 5(2): 167-174, Broken heart: depression in cardiovascular disease

Kuhn R (2004). Eugen Bleuler's concepts of psychopathology. History of Psychiatry 15 (3): 361–6.

Kvan E., Pettersen, K., Sandvik L., & Reikvam A. (2007). High mortality in diabetic patient with acute myocardial infarction: cardiovascular co-morbidities contribute most to the high risk. International Journal of Cardiology 121 184–188.

Lakdawalla, D., Goldman, D., & Shang, B. (2005) The health and cost consequences of obesity among the future elderly. Health Affairs (Millwood). 24 (Suppl 2):W5R30–41.

Lahera, G., Freund, N., Sáiz-Ruiz, J. (2013) Salience and dysregulation of the dopaminergic system. Review Psychiatric 6 (1): 45–51.

Lander, D. & Graham-Pole, J. (2008). Love medicine for the dying and their caregivers: The body of evidence. Journal of Health Psychology, 13, 201–12.

Langley-Evans, S., & Carrington, L. (2006). Diet and the developing immune system. Lupus15 (11) 746–52.

Lancet. (2004). Association of psychosocial risk factors with risk of acute myocardial infarction in 11 119 cases and 13 648 controls from 52 countries (the INTERHEART study): case-control study. Vol.364. Pages 953 – 962.

Lancet. (2010) Type 2 diabetes—time to change our approach. Volume 375, Issue 9733, Retrieved http://www.thelancet.com/journals/lancet/article/PIIS0140-6736%2810%2961011-2/fulltext on August 23 2013.

Latane, B., & Darley, J. 1970. The unresponsive bystander: Why doesn't he help? New York: Appleton-Century-Crofts.

Ledoux, Joseph. (1998). The Emotional Brain: The Mysterious Underpinnings of Emotional Life. Simon & Schuster

Lembcke, Jerry. (2013) PTSD: Diagnosis and Identity in Post-empire America. Lexington Books

Lemaux, Peggy G. (2008). Genetically Engineered Plants and Foods: A Scientist's Analysis of the Issues (Part I). Annual Review of Plant Biology. Vol. 59: 771-812

Levi, J., Segal, L., & Juliana, C. (n.d.). Prevention for a healthier America: Investments in disease prevention yield significant savings, stronger communities. Retrieved http://healthyamericans.org/reports/prevention08/Prevention08.pdf on September 18, 2013.

Levinthal, C. (1988). Messengers of Paradise: Opiates and the Brain. New York: Doubleday.

Lewis, T., Amini, F., & Lannon, R. (2001). A General Theory of Love. Vintage. Reprint edition.

Lindahl, K., Bregman, & H., Malik, N. (2012). Family boundary structures and child adjustment: the indirect role of emotional reactivity. Journal of Family Psychology. Dec; 26 (6): 839-47.

Littman, R. (2009). The plague of Athens: epidemiology and paleopathology. Mount Sinai Journal of Medicine 10, 456-67

Lorenz, R., Bubb, J., Davis, D., Jacobson, A., Jannasch, K., Kramer, J., Lipps, J., & Schlundt, D. Changing behavior: practical lessons from the Diabetes Control and Complications Trial. Diabetes Care 19:648-52, 1996.

Lustman, P., Clouse, R., Alrakawi, A., Rubin, E., & Gelenberg, A. (1997). Treatment of major depression in adults with diabetes: a primary care perspective. Clinical Diabetes 16:122-26.

Lustman, P., Griffith, L., & Clouse R. (1997) Depression in adults with diabetes. Seminars in Clinical Neuropsychiatry 2:15-23.

Lynch, J., & Kilmartin, C. (1999). Overcoming masculine depression. New York: Haworth Press.

Lyubomirsky, S., & Ross, L. (1997). Hedonic consequences of social comparison: A contact of happy and unhappy people. Journal of Personality and Social Psychology 73:1141–1157.

Lyubomirsky, S. (2001) Why are some people happier than others? American Psychologist. 56 239–249.

MacDonald, Cheryl (2014). Schizophrenia and Acute Psychosis, Retrieved on October 14, 2014 from http://healthpsychology. org/schizophrenia-and-acute-psychosis/

Magolda, P., & Kelsey, E. (2008). Students Serving Christ: Understanding the Role of Student Subcultures on a College Campus. Anthropology & Education Quarterly 32 (2): 138–158.

Majde, J., & Krueger, J. (2005). Links between the innate immune system and sleep. The Journal of Allergy and Clinical Immunology 116 (6): 1188–98.

Mancini, F., Longo, M., Kammers, M., & Haggard, P. (2011). Visual distortion of body size modulates pain perception. Psychological Science 22 325-30.

Mandal, Ananya. (n.d.). Cancer Research, News Medical. Retrieved http://www.news-medical.net/health/Cancer-Research.aspx on March 14, 2014.

Mandler, G. (2007). A history of modern experimental psychology: From James and Wundt to cognitive science. Cambridge, MA: MIT Press.

Marazziti, D., & Canale, D. (2004) Hormonal changes when falling in love. Psychoneuroendocrinology. 29 931-6.

Marks, D., Murray, M., Evans, B., & Estacio, E. (2011) Health Psychology. Theory-Research-Practice (3rd Ed.) Sage Publications.

Maslow, Abraham H. (1962). Toward a Psychology of Being. Reprint of 1962 Edition, First Edition. Martino Fine Books

McCloskey, Laura Ann., & Walker, Marla. (2000). Posttraumatic Stress in Children Exposed to Family Violence and Single-Event Trauma. Journal of the American Academy of Child & Adolescent Psychiatry 39 108–115.

McLaren, J., Silins, E., Hutchinson, D., Mattick, R., Hall W (2010). Assessing evidence for a causal link between cannabis and psychosis: a review of cohort studies. International Journal. Of Drug Policy 21 (1): 10–9.

McNabb, W. (1997). Adherence in diabetes: can we define it and can we measure it? Diabetes Care 20 215-218.

McNally K (2009). Eugen Bleuler's "Four A's. History of Psychology 12 (2): 43–59.

McTigue, K., Hess, R., & Ziouras, J. (2006). Obesity in older adults: a systematic review of the evidence for diagnosis and treatment. Obesity (Silver Spring) 14 1485–97.

Means, Patrick. (2005) The Boundaries Book. New York: The Crossroad Publishing Company.

Medzhitov, R. (2007). Recognition of microorganisms and activation of the immune response. Nature 449 819–26.

Melzack, R. (1975). The McGill Pain Questionnaire: Major properties and scoring methods. Pain 1, 277–99.

Mellody, Pia. (2003). Facing Codependence: What It Is, Where It Comes from, How It Sabotages Our Lives. Harper & Row. 1 edition.

Microbiology and Immunology On-Line Textbook: USC School of Medicine. Retrieved http://pathmicro.med.sc.edu/book/immunol-sta.htm on November 13, 2013.

Miller, G., Chen, E., & Cole S. (2009) Health psychology: developing biologically plausible models linking the social world and physical health. Annual Review of Psychology. 60, 501-24.

Miller, Angelyn. (2008). The Enabler: When Helping Hurts the Ones You Love. Arizona: Wheatmark Press.

Mokdad, A., Marks, J., Stroup, D., & Gerberding, J. (2004) Actual causes of death in the United States. Journal of the American Medical Association. Vol. 10 1238–1245.

Moller, Aage. (2011). Pain Its anatomy, physiology and treatment. Create Space Independent Publishing Platform.

Moore, L.A. (2006). Empathy a clinician's perspective. The ASHA Leader. Retrieved http://www.asha.org/Publications/leader/2006/060815/f060815e.htm on September 14, 2013.

Mork, P., Vasseljen, O., & Nilsen, T. (2011) The association between physical exercise, body mass index, and risk of fibromyalgia: Longitudinal data from the Norwegian HUNT study. American Journal of Epidemiology. Retrieved http://aje.oxfordjournals.org/content/early/2011/06/01/aje.kwr087.full on March 31, 2014.

Moss, Michael. (2014) Salt Sugar Fat: How the Food Giants Hooked Us. Random House Trade Paperbacks.

Moyers, B. (1992). Healing and the Mind. New York: Doubleday.

Myers, David. (2011). Psychology. Worth Publishers, 10th edition.

National Academies Press (US), (2001). Health and Behavior: The Interplay of Biological, Behavioral, and Societal Influences. Institute of Medicine (US) Committee on Health and Behavior: Research, Practice, and Policy. Washington D.C.

National Action Alliance for Suicide Prevention (US). 2012 National Strategy for Suicide Prevention: Goals and Objectives for Action: A Report of the U.S. Surgeon General and of the National Action Alliance for Suicide Prevention. Washington (DC): US Department of Health & Human Services (US), http://www.ncbi.nlm.nih.gov/books/NBK109906/ Accessed March 10, 2012.

National Cancer Institute, The National Cancer Act of 1971 Accessed on 3/14/14.

http://legislative.cancer.gov/history/phsa/1971.

National Cancer Institute. , Understanding the immune system, Accessed on January 12, 2014 http://www.cancer.gov/cancertopics/understandingcancer/immunesystem

National Institutes of Mental Health, Depression and Heart Disease, Retrieved http://ftp.nimh.nih.gov/health/publications/depression-and-heart-disease/index.shtml on November 21, 2013.

National Institute of Mental Health. Major Depressive Disorder Among Adults. Retrieved http://www.nimh.nih.gov/statistics/1mdd_adult.shtml on March 12, 2014.

National Institute of Mental Health Bipolar Disorder. Retrieved on October 15, 2014 from http://www.nimh.nih.gov/health/topics/bipolar-disorder/index.shtml.

National Institute of Mental Health. What is Post-traumatic Stress Disorder (PTSD)? Retrieved http://www.nimh.nih.gov/

health/topics/post-traumatic-stress-disorder-ptsd/index.shtml on March 17, 2014.

National Institute of Mental Health. U.S. Department of Health and Human Services. Post-Traumatic Stress Disorder (PTSD). Retrieved http://www.nimh.nih.gov/health/topics/post-traumatic-stress-disorder on January 21, 2013.

Norcross, J., & Goldried, M. (2005). Handbook of Psychotherapy Integration (Clinical Psychology). Oxford University Press, USA

O'Brien, J., Forrest, L., & Austin, A. (2002). Death of a partner: Perspectives of heterosexual and gay men. Journal of Health Psychology, 7, 317–28.

O'Connor, Richard. (2010). Undoing Depression: What Therapy Doesn't Teach You and Medication Can't Give You. Little, Brown and Company

Oppenheimer, Gerald (2005), Becoming the Framingham Study 1947–1950, American Journal of Public Health. 95(4): 602–610.

Oracle Thinkquest Education. (n.d.). A Look into The Heart Function of Heart. Retrieved http://library.thinkquest.org/05aug/01883/functionofheart.htm on August 21, 2013.

Otis, John. (2007). Managing Chronic Pain: A Cognitive-Behavioral Therapy Approach Workbook. Oxford University Press, USA; 1 Workbook edition.

Priebe, Stefan., Wright, Donna. (2006). The provision of psychotherapy – an international comparison. Journal of Public Mental Health Vol. 5 Iss: 3, 12 – 22.

Pancer, Z. Cooper. (2006). The evolution of adaptive immunity. Annual Review of Immunology 24 (1): 497–518.

Parham, Peter. (2009). The Immune System. Garland Science, third edition

Pincott, Jena. (2009). Do Gentlemen Really Prefer Blondes?: Bodies, Behavior, and Brains—The Science Behind Sex, Love, & Attraction. Delta Books.

Pinel, Philippe. (1809). Medico-Philosophical Treatise On Mental Alienation. Retrieved on October 4, 2014. From http://onlinelibrary.wiley.com/doi/10.1002/9780470712238.fmatter/pdf

Pittman, Frank. A Buyer's Guide to Psychotherapy. (1994). Psychology Today. Retrieved http://www.psychologytoday.com/articles/199401/buyers-guide-psychotherapy

Prince, Rob. (2014). Chronic Pain: Finding Hope in the Midst of Suffering. Beacon Hill Press.

Raman, Shanti., Hodes, Deborah. (2012). Cultural issues in child maltreatment. Journal of Paediatrics and Child Health. Vol. 48, 30–37.

Real, T. (1997). I don't want to talk about it: Overcoming the secret legacy of male depression. New York: Scribner.

Rees, C. (2010). Understanding emotional abuse. Archives of Disease in Childhood. 95(1) 59-67.

Reiche, E., Nunes, S., & Morimoto, H. (2004). Stress, depression, the immune system, and cancer. Lancet Oncology 10, 617-25.

Reiss, Steven. (2009) The Normal Personality: A New Way of Thinking about People. Cambridge University Press. 1st edition.

Rey, Roselyne., Wallace, Louise. (1998). The History of Pain. Harvard University Press.

Ribeiz, S., Duran, F., Oliveira, M., Bezerra, D., Castro, C., Steffens, D., Filho, G., Bottino, C. (2013). Structural Brain Changes as Biomarkers and Outcome Predictors in Patients with Late-Life Depression: A Cross-Sectional and Prospective Study. Retrieved http://www.plosone.org/article/info%3A-doi%2F10.1371%2Fjournal.pone.0080049#s3 on March 15, 2014.

Riley, William., Treiber, Frank., & Woods, Gail. (1989) Anger and Hostility in Depression, Journal of Nervous & Mental Disease: Nov. 668-674.

Robertson, D. (2010). The Philosophy of Cognitive–Behavioural Therapy: Stoicism as Rational and Cognitive Psychotherapy. London: Karnac.

Rolls, E. (2013). Limbic systems for emotion and for memory, but no single limbic system. Cortex. Dec 24. pii: S0010-9452(13)00311-0. doi: 10.1016/j.cortex.2013.12.005.

Ropeik, David. (2010). How Risky Is It, Really? Why Our Fears Don't Always Match the Facts. McGraw-Hill. 1 edition.

Roth, Anthon., & Fonagy, Peter. (2005). What Works for Whom? A Critical Review of Psychotherapy Research. Guilford Press.

Rothschild, Babette .(2000). The Body Remembers: The Psychophysiology of Trauma and Trauma Treatment. New York: W.W. Norton & Company.

Rubin, R., Dietrich, K., & Hawk A. (1999). Clinical and economic impact of implementing a comprehensive diabetes management program in managed care. Journal of Clinical Endocrinology. 83(8) 2635–2642.

Rubin, R., & Peyrot, M. (1992). Psychosocial problems and interventions in diabetes. Diabetes Care 15:1640-57.

Sacks, Oliver. (2011). The Mind's Eye. Vintage, reprint edition.

Sadock, Benjamin., & Sadock, Virginia (2000). Codependence. Kaplan & Sadock's Comprehensive Textbook of Psychiatry. Lippincott Williams & Wilkins, 7th ed.

Sagman, D., Tohen, M. (2009) Comorbidity in Bipolar Disorder: The Complexity of Diagnosis and Treatment. Psychiatric Times.

Saltus, Edgar. (1906). Historia Amoris: A History of Love, Ancient and Modern. Retrieved http://www.gutenberg.org/files/32512/32512-h/32512-h.htm on January 12, 2014.

Sarno J. (2006). The divided mind: the epidemic of mind body disorders. New York: Regan Books.

Saunders, K., Guy, M. The course of bipolar disorder. Advances in Psychiatric Treatment Retrieved on October 15, 2014 from http://apt.rcpsych.org/content/16/5/318.full .

Savona, V., & Grech, V. (1999). Concepts in cardiology – a historical perspective. Paediatric Cardiology, 1 22–31.

Schacter, Daniel. (1997). Searching For Memory: The Brain, The Mind, And The Past. Basic Books, reprint edition.

Schacter, Daniel. (2002). The Seven Sins of Memory: How the Mind Forgets and Remembers. Mariner Books, 1st edition.

Schein, Edgar. (2011). Helping: How to Offer, Give, and Receive Help. Berrett-Koehler Publishers. Reprint edition.

Schmitt, A., Malchow, B., Hasan, A., Falkai, P. (2014). The impact of environmental factors in severe psychiatric disorders. Frontiers of Neuroscience 8 (19).

Schimmack U., & Reisenzein R. (2002). Experiencing activation: energetic arousal and tense arousal are not mixtures of valence and activation. Emotion. 12 412-417.

Schizophrenia. World Health Organization. Retrieved August 27 2014. From http://www.who.int/mental_health/management/schizophrenia/en/

Schlosser, Eric. (2001). Fast Food Nation: The Dark Side of the All-American Meal. Mariner Books, Reprint edition.

Schneider, K. (1959) Clinical Psychopathology. New York: Grune and Stratton.

Schnurr, P., Lunney, C., & Sengupta, A. (2004). Risk factors for the development versus maintenance of posttraumatic stress disorder. Journal of Trauma and Stress 17 (2): 85–95.

Schwartz, Bennett. (2010). Memory: Foundations and Applications. Sage Publications, Inc. 1 edition.

Schultz, W., Nola, J., Cialdini, R., Goldstein, N. & Griskevicius, V. (May 2007). The Constructive, Destructive, and Reconstructive Power of Social Norms. Psychological Science. 18 429–434.

Serretti, A., Mandelli L. (2008). The genetics of bipolar disorder: Genome 'hot regions,' genes, new potential candidates and future directions. Molecular Psychiatry 13 (8): 742–771

Siegel, Bernie S. (1998). Love, Medicine and Miracles: Lessons Learned about Self-Healing from a Surgeon's Experience with Exceptional Patients. William Morrow Paperbacks, Reissue edition.

Siegel, Bernie., & Hurn, Cynthia. (2013). The Art of Healing: Uncovering Your Inner Wisdom and Potential for Self-Healing. New World Library, 1 edition.

Seligman, Martin.(1990). Learned optimism. New York: Knopf.

Seligman, Martin. (2003). Positive psychology: Fundamental assumptions. Psychologist. 16 126–127.

Shimoda, Sano M. (2013). Facing the Realities of the Science, the Marketplace, and Transparency. Calgary TELUS Convention Centre. Retrieved http://www.abic.ca/abic2013/PDF/SPEAKER_PRESENTATION/SanoShimoda.pdf. on March 23, 2014.

Shomon, Mary. (2002). Living Well with Autoimmune Disease: What Your Doctor Doesn't Tell You...That You Need to Know. William Morrow Paperbacks, First edition

Shorter, E. (1998) A History of Psychiatry: From the Era of the Asylum to the Age of Prozac. Wiley; 1 edition.

Silverman, D. (2005). What Works in Psychotherapy and How Do We Know? What Evidence-Based Practice Has to Offer. Psychoanalytic Psychology 22 (2): 306–312.

Silverstein, A.M. (2009). A History of Immunology. Academic Press second edition.

Simon, G., Katon, W., Lin, E., Rutter, C., Manning, W., Von Korff, M., Ciechanowski, P., Ludman, E., & Young, B. (2007) Cost-effectiveness of systematic depression treatment among people with diabetes mellitus. Archives of General Psychiatry. 64(1) 65–72.

Simon, May. (2013) Love: A History. Yale University Press. Reprint edition.

Simonds, S. (2001). Depression and women: An integrative treatment approach. New York: Springer Publishing Company.

Singh, Manish. (n.d.). Chronic Pain Syndrome. Retrieved http://emedicine.medscape.com/article/310834-overview#a0101 on January 14, 2014.

Skinner, B.F. (1965). Science and Human Behavior. Free Press. New impression edition.

Skopalová, Jitka. (2010). Social deviations, Labelling, and Normality. Human Affairs (20) 327–337.

Smith Rowland, Robert. (2011). Driving with Plato: The Meaning of Life's Milestones. Simon and Schuster Digital Sales Inc.

Sompayrac, L. (2012). How the Immune System Works. Wiley-Blackwell, 4 edition.

Spoont, M., Arbisi, P., Fu, S., Greer, N., Kehle-Forbes, S., Meis, L., & Rutks, I. (2013). Screening for Post-Traumatic Stress Disorder (PTSD) in Primary Care: A Systematic Review. Washington DC: Department of Veterans Affairs.

Springer, K., Sheridan, J., Kuo, D., & Carnes, M. (2003). The Long-term Health Outcomes of Childhood Abuse An Overview and a Call to Action. Journal of General Internal Medicine. 18(10), 864–870.

Steptoe, A., & Kivimäki, M. (2012). Stress and Cardiovascular disease. National Review of Cardiology 9 (6): 360–70.

Stewart, J., Adler, N., Laraia, B., & Epel, E. (2012). What is eating you? Stress and the drive to eat. Appetite 58(2) 717-21.

Strickland, F. (2001). Boosting the immune system. Chapter 32 Comprehensive Series in Photosciences. U. G. Paolo, Elsevier. Vol. 3: 613-636.

Sullivan, P., Neale M., & Kendler, K. (2000). Genetic epidemiology of major depression: review and meta-analysis. The American Journal of Psychiatry. Oct. 1552-1562.

Sundberg, Norman. (2001). Clinical Psychology: Evolving Theory, Practice, and Research. Englewood Cliffs: Prentice Hall.

Surwitt, R., Schneider M., & Feinglos, M. (1992). Stress and diabetes mellitus. Diabetes Care 15 1413-22.

Tattersall, Robert. (2009). Diabetes: The Biography (Biographies of Disease). Oxford University Press, USA., 1st edition.

Thagard, P. (1989). Explanatory coherence. Behavioral & Brain Sciences. Vol. 12. 435–467.

Thayer, R. E. (1989). The Biopsychology of Mood and Arousal. New York: Oxford University Press

The Abandoned Illness (2012) Schizophrenia Commission. Retrieved 19 August 2014 from http://www.rethink.org/media/514093/TSC_main_report_14_nov.pdf

The British Psychological Society. (2011). What is Health Psychology? A guide for the public. Retrieved http://www.bps.org.uk/networks-and-communities/member-networks/division-health-psychology on January 2014.

The Discovery of Insulin. (n.d.). Nobelprize.org. Retrieved http://www.nobelprize.org/educational/medicine/insulin/discovery-insulin.html on March 15, 2014.

The Mayo Clinic. Bipolar Basics Retrieved on October 11, 2014 from http://www.mayoclinic.org/diseases-conditions/bipolar-disorder/basics/definition/con-20027544

The National Cancer Act of 1971, National Cancer Institute, Retrieved http://legislative.cancer.gov/history/phsa/1971 on March 14, 2014.

The National Institute of Mental Health, What is Schizophrenia, Retrieved on October 4, 2014. From http://www.nimh.nih.gov/health/topics/schizophrenia/index.shtml

The Papyrus Ebers Retrieved October 4, 2014 Retrieve September 13, 2014 from http://oilib.uchicago.edu/books/bryan_the_papyrus_ebers_1930.pdf

The Top Causes of Death in the United States and What You Can Do About Them, Retrieved http://www.healthaliciousness.com/articles/top-causes-of-death.php#Yu-7wv516wcShZJ8J.99, on March 8, 2014.

The Wall Street Journal. New Ways to Treat Pain. Retrieved http://online.wsj.com/article/SB10001424052748704879704575236373207643604.html

Thibaut, John W. (1943). The concept of normality in clinical psychology. Psychological Review Vol. 50 (3): 4–7.

Thomas, Gregory. (2013). Atherosclerosis across 4000 years of human history: the Horus study of four ancient populations. The Lancet, Vol. 381, 1211 – 1222.

Tibaldi, Joseph M. (2012). Evolution of Insulin Development: Focus on Key Parameters. Retrieved http://download.springer.com/static/pdf/901/art%253A10.1007%252Fs12325-012-0034-8.pdf?auth66=1395089296_53cc729d-545f3af8fada496226655e1b&ext=.pdf on March 12, 2014.

Tiffin, Joseph. (1946). The psychology of normal people. D.C. Health & Co. Revised edition.

Tomasi, D., & Volko, N. (2011). Laterality Patterns of Brain Functional Connectivity: Gender Effects. Retrieved http://cercor.oxfordjournals.org/content/early/2011/08/29/cercor.bhr230.full, on March 15, 2014.

Torrey, E. Fuller (2014) Surviving Schizophrenia: A Family Manual. Harper Paperbacks, 6 edition

Understanding the immune system (n.d.). National Cancer Institute. Retrieved http://www.cancer.gov/cancertopics/understandingcancer/immunesystem on January 12, 2014

U.S. National Institutes of Health Bipolar Disorder: NIH Publication No. 95-3679". Retrieved Sept. 18. 2014 from http://web.archive.org/web/20080429204140/http:/www.pueblo.gsa.gov/cic_text/health/bipolar/bipolar.htm

van Os, J., Rutten, B.P. & Poulton, R. (2008) Gene-environment interactions in schizophrenia: review of epidemiological findings and future directions. Schizophrenia Bulletin, 34, 1066-1082

Velasco-Suarez, M., Martinez, J., Oliveros, R., & Weinstein, P. (1992). Archaeological origins of cranial surgery: trephination in Mexico. Neurosurgery. August 313-318.

Vincent, J-D. (1990). The Biology of Emotions. Cambridge, Mass.: Basil Blackwell.

Wachbroit, Robert. (1994). Normality as a Biological Concept. Philosophy of Science. 579–591.

Walker, C., & Reamy, B. (2009). Diets for cardiovascular disease prevention: what is the evidence? American Family Physician 79 (7): 571–8.

Walsh, S., Clayton., Liu, Li., & Hodges, S. (2009). Divergence in Contributing Factors for Suicide Among Men and Women in Kentucky: Recommendations to Raise Public Awareness, Public Health Rep. Nov-Dec; 124(6): 861–867.

Wasser S., Sewall G., & Soules, M., (1993). Psychosocial stress as a cause of infertility. Fertility and Sterility. March pgs. 685-90.

Watt, M.(2009). Link between obesity and diabetes discovered. Retrieved http://monash.edu/news/releases/show/1303 on April 13, 2014.

Wegscheider-Cruse, S., & Cruse, J. (2012). Understanding Code-pendency, Updated and Expanded: The Science Behind It and How to Break the Cycle. HCI. 1 Upd Exp edition.

Weinberg, Robert A. (2013). The Biology of Cancer. Garland Science; 2 edition.

Whitaker, Robert (2010) Mad in America: Bad Science, Bad Medicine, and the Enduring Mistreatment of the Mentally Ill Basic Books; Second Edition.

Whitfield , Charles L. (1991). Co-dependence: Healing the Human Condition. HCI; Copyright 1991 edition.

Whitfield, Charles. (1994). Boundaries and Relationships: Knowing, Protecting and Enjoying the Self. HCI; 1 edition.

Whybrow, P. (1997). A mood apart. New York: Basic Books

Wierzbicki, M. & Pekarik, G. (May 1993). A Meta-Analysis of Psychotherapy Dropout. Professional Psychology: Research and Practice 24 (2): 190–195.

Wilson, John., & Tan, Catherine. (2006). Cross-Cultural Assessment of Psychological Trauma and PTSD (International and Cultural Psychology). Springer.

World Health Organization. (n.d.). The top 10 causes of death. Retrieved http://www.who.int/mediacentre/factsheets/fs310/en/ on October 13 2013.

World Health Organization (2008). The global burden of disease: 2004. Geneva, Switzerland: Retrieved on September 30,

2014 from http://www.who.int/mental_health/resources/schizophrenia/en/

Woolf, S. (2008). The power of prevention and what it requires. Journal of the American Medical Association. 299 (20):2437–2439.

World Health Organization. (2011). Diabetes Fact Sheet Retrieved http://www.who.int/mediacentre/factsheets/fs312/en/ on August 28, 2013.

Wu EQ (2005). The economic burden of schizophrenia in the United States in 2002. Journal of Clinicial Psychiatry 66 (9): 1122–9.

Wunderlich, S., Feldman, C., Kane, S., & Hazhin, T. (2008). Nutritional quality of organic, conventional, and seasonally grown broccoli using vitamin C as a marker. International Journal of Food Science and Nutrition. 59 (1) 34-45.

Yehuda, R., Cai, G., Golier, J., Sarapas, C., & Galea, S. (2009). Gene expression patterns associated with posttraumatic stress disorder following exposure to the World Trade Center attacks. Biological Psychiatry 66 (7): 708–11.

Yuhas, Daisy. (2013). Throughout History, Defining Schizophrenia Has Remained A Challenge. Scientific American Mind.

Zaza, S., Briss, P., & Harris, K. (2005). Task Force on Community Preventive Services (United States). The guide to community preventive services: What works to promote health? New York: Oxford University.

Zeki, S. (2007). The neurobiology of love. Jun 12; 581 (14):2575-9.

16816528R00177

Printed in Great Britain
by Amazon